History *of* Western Political Thought

Volume 1

Radhey Shyam Chaurasia

Published by

ATLANTIC

PUBLISHERS & DISTRIBUTORS (P) LTD

7/22, Ansari Road, Darya Ganj, New Delhi-110002
Phones : +91-11-40775252, 40775214, 23273880, 23275880
Fax : +91-11-23285873
Web : www.atlanticbooks.com
E-mail : orders@atlanticbooks.com

Printed & bound in India by Atlantic Print Services

PREFACE

The study of Political Science is very important in the present epoch of social evolution. The old order seems to be crumbling all over the world and man is faced with a gigantic task of reconstruction. To follow the development of political thought in the historical perspective has a great educative and intellectual value. It trains the mind and develops the faculties of mind to think, to criticise and to construct.

The book is intended to serve as an introduction to the history of political thought. Aim of author has been to place the ideas of political thinkers in the easiest possible language and to achieve this purpose, he has followed easy interpretations. The author has chosen to follow the historical and objective method, he has confined himself to giving an accurate exposition of the views of political philosophers together with fair and reasonable criticism of their views from various stand points.

So far known to author, there is no suitable book on Political Thought in simple language to meet the requirements of M.A. students as well as to meet the needs of the candidates who prepare themselves for the various competitive examinations. This book has been prepared to remove this long felt want.

I shall deem my labour amply rewarded if the merits of the book find due appreciation at the hands of the teachers as well as the students.

Suggestions, if any, for the improvement of the book in the next edition shall be gratefully received.

Radhey Shyam Chaurasia

Contents

Introduction

NATURE AND SUBJECT MATTER OF POLITICAL THOUGHT

Political thought is a very useful and important subject. It is treasure of thought propounded by great thinkers and scholars of different countries which statesmen can still use to run the state affairs on sound lines.

Man is a social animal, he is unable to lead a solitary life and so he had to remain in society but man is not satisfied only by living in a society because of all the living beings that inhabit in this world, he is the only creature whom creator has endowed with rational faculty. His rational faculty impels him to know about himself and the phenomena and surroundings which influence him most. God has endowed man with curiosity and desire to know about his social surroundings and natural environment. From the very beginning man attempted to know something about natural phenomena and so various sciences like Botany, Zoology, Physics and Chemistry etc., came into existence. Natural desire of man to understand himself and the social surroundings in which his life is passed gave rise to social sciences like History, Politics, Economics, Sociology, and Psychology, etc. The desire of man to know something about a creator and universe gave rise to Philosophy, religion and astronomy etc. In this way human being began to study various subjects.

In this way man made all round progress and divided his knowledge into many sciences but the vast progress that man has made is not the work of one race or of one country but various countries in different epochs contributed towards its progress, so a subject had to be studied without dividing in into watertight compartments but knowledge is so vast that none can gain mastery of a single subject, even of a single country. As such we have to study only that material which may be useful for our purpose and study and the present setup of society. As political thought of modern world based on the Western political thought so we have to begin our study of political thought with the western world useful to modern setup.

SUBJECT MATTER OF POLITICAL THOUGHT

Political science in brief may be defined as the study of state and Government or a process in which man attempts to govern himself and his social surroundings. The states and its institutions particularly Government constitute a very important part of social setup. Now, a days with emergence of social welfare state, each and every activity of a man living in society is controlled by the Government and now it is more vital than the physical and biological forces of the world. It is true that the state has been made the subject of human speculation from the dawn of human reflection but now state is all pervading so it is most necessary to study about is most thoroughly. The people of all countries and of all ages have speculated about the state, its nature, function and organisation. They have tried to understand the manner in which the various institutions through which the state achieves its purpose, work and on which these should be organised, if they are to work better. Such speculation gives rise to political thinking which is as old as the recorded history. In this way political thought is as old as the state.

Political thinking does not restrict itself to the state and Government but it has to go beyond them and interest itself in the nature of man and his relation to universe. According to Phyllis Doyle, there are three main subjects that constitute the substance of political thought. *"The nature and function of man: his relation to the rest of universe which involves a consideration of the meaning of life as a whole: emerging from the interaction of these two the problem of the relation of man to his follow man."* The latter is the main concern of political theory in the narrowest sense and involves a discussion on the nature, purpose and function of the state. In Politics man learns to govern himself, to acquire power and to work according to circumstances.

The great thinkers like Plato, Aristotle, St. Thomas, Acquinas, and Marx, Hegel and Green etc. have illustrated the comprehensive scope of political thought. In India in ancient ages Chanakya, Brahaspati etc. and our rishis and munies and in the present age Mahatma Gandhi also provide a good example. So intimate is the relation of the man and goal of his life that there is of no use to try to understand the later without knowing the former. As such ethical, metaphysical and philosophical views of a writer are therefore bound to colour and determine its political philosophy. In spite of all this, it can be said that primary concern of political thought is state and so political thinkers devote more time and attention to the discussion of its nature, origin, and or purpose, functions, organisations etc. than to speculation about the nature of man and his place in the universe.

A FEW PROBLEMS OF POLITICAL THOUGHT

The discussion about nature of the state assumes great importance in the western world, Plato and Aristotle thought that the state is a natural association in the sense of being a natural growth and resulting from the deeply rooted social nature of man. To quote Aristotle, *"it came into existence for the sake of life and continues for the sake of good life."* He goes a step further and says it is contrary to human nature to lead a solitary life and one who leads a solitary life must either be a beast or a God. As such according to Plato and Aristotle in and through the membership of the state, we reach the highest development possible for us.

The Sophists, who were the immediate professors of Plato and Aristotle, refuted their theories and held that state in an artificial continuance designed by man to achieve some gain and which is contrary to natural order of things. The more radical of their thought that the right of life according to nature was live in domination over others so far as one's power permitted. One should obey its laws when one must and ignore them when one can Roman thinkers gave promises to law and Christian thinkers both to God and state. Modern age began with Machiavelli who gave prominence to power.

Hegel calls state as the march of God on earth but Communists consider it as an organisation by which the economically stronger groups exploit the weaker sections. Not only this individualist considers it as a necessary evil and anarchists are of the opinion that human nature reaches its highest development in a stateless society. What to say of anarchists even Karl Marx and Lenin said that there can be no freedom so long the state remains into existence. Mahatma Gandhi also abhorred the omnipotent process of the state and said that man has a soul but state is a soulless machine. It is difficult to reconcile the conflicting whims and to give a definite answer: all that a historian of political thought can do is to chromite the various answers which have been given to this initial question in the course of ages. In spite of all this it can be that pivot on which whole setup depends now is power of the state.

It has been remarked that state is not a mere aggregate to sum total of men, but their unity. But what type of unity it is, opinions differ. Some regard it as the unity of state, some that of an organism. Some find source in the general will of the people and some in self-interest, but all agree to give prominent place to state and Government.

Political organisation is the essence of the state in which a few govern and many obey but who has the right to rule over his fellowmen and why? There are conflicting views about this answer and some support the rule of wise, some of military, some give prominence to wealth or noble birth etc. Similarly there are conflicting views about the end or purpose of the state. Individualists say its purpose is to maintain peace and order and that Government is the best which governs the least, but socialists desire to increase the functions of the state and consider it as an instrument of promoting good life of citizens. On the other hand anarchist recommend its total abolition and at present socialist's views have gained prominence.

In the same way interesting questions and conflicting opinions arise about the organisation and forms of government, closely connected with the government is problem of law and that of rights duties of citizenship and how to reconcile man with society.

These are some of the main problems of political science and different answers to these problems have been given by various thinkers in different ages. Only task of an historian of political thought is to present the views of great thinkers in a detached way and present a balanced and objective view for the convenience of a reader or student which may enhance their knowledge and may help in learning and becoming useful citizen with enlightened outlook.

POLITICAL THOUGHT AND THE ENVIRONMENT

Man is the creature of the circumstances as well as the maker and moulder of the circumstances. Man is a social animal and so social environment makes a deep impact on him. Political thoughts do not arise in vacuum but these are influenced and coloured by the experiences of a man or thinker according to his social surroundings, so it is essential to keep in view the nature of man, his life, his environment, social setup of the age to understand his political thought. Some thinkers become so much involved in their social surroundings and age that their political thoughts do not carry message beyond their age or country but great thinkers like Plato, Aristotle, Marx or Gandhi carry a universal message for mankind at large and such thinkers have moulded the thoughts of mankind and are useful even now with some modifications to suit the present setup.

IMPORTANCE OF WESTERN POLITICAL THOUGHT

It is generally asked that why we should begin our study of the subject with Greek political thought and not with the political thought of ancient Indians, Egyptians, Babylonians, Chinese, Syrians and Persians etc. It cannot be said that these people did not develop their own political thought and that political thought began with Greeks. According to Binoy Kumar Sarkar, *"The Hindu Pericleaes, Caesars, Justinians, Charlemagnes and Fredric Barbarosas could easily challenge comparison with their Western peers on their own terms."* It can be added that in ancient time Indians produced political thinkers like Vidur, Chanakya, Brahaspati and Sukra and law givers like Manu, who can challenge their European counterparts. Similarly Jews and Chinese produced their own political thinkers and law givers as such contention of some writers that these early civilizations were unpolitical cannot be sustained.

Two different reasons are given as to why we begin our study with Greek political thought. First, the ideas developed by other ancient countries did not become part of the European civilization as those of ancient Greeks did. Secondly, the results of their speculation on political problems were not exclusively contained in separate and independent treaties as was case in Greece. To a great extent they formed part of literature which was predominantly religious and ethical and this is particularly true about India where political thought is to be found in *Ramayana, Mahabharat, Buddhist, Jataks* which are predominantly religious and ethical books. What to say of these books in Kautilya's *Arthastra* also, we find mixture of religious and metaphysical thought. In our modern age even Mahatma Gandhi did not embody his reflections on political phenomena in the form of a systematic treaties: the thoughts lie scattered in his speeches and articles and his political thought is also coloured by religious and ethical outlook.

Thus, we have to begin our study with Western or European political thought and study its development from its beginnings in the speculations of the early Greeks. We shall confine our study to leading thinkers and the contribution of each of them to the growth of political ideas.

Political thought does not develop or grow from simple to complex but political problems present themselves in different ways under different circumstances and are discussed in terms of different assumptions. Generally they remain same in essence and answers to them though different in detail, reveal some common elements, at least in the basic point of view from which they are approached, sometimes it happens that an idea which held the field for a long time in one age, disappear completely for a few centuries and is revived again when circumstances favour its revival.

Divisions of the Subject

In outlining the history of human political thought, it is difficult to earmark a definite era or area as being solely responsible for a certain system of ideas or for certain division of period or age but for our convenience, we divide the history of the Western or European political thought into three periods ancient, medieval and modern. Each one of these periods has its characteristic features which distinguish it from the other two. Ancient political thought centered round city state which was regarded as the highest and most perfect form of social or political organisation by Plato and Aristotle. Political thought was primarily ethical in this period, because the city state was primarily an ethical society.

With the eclipse of city states and emergence of the Roman empire, and at a later stage of Christianity, a new form of state organisation arose. Consequently, it gave rise to a new political outlook whose dominant note was universalism; all persons belonged to one universal society with two heads one Roman Emperor and the other the Pope. It created theological problem of determining relationship between the two orders, the state and the Church.

The Renaissance and Reformation changed the social setup and consequently political outlook and gave rise to modern political thought. With the eclipse of Roman empire and emergence of national states, the political thought of modern age is determined by the nature of nation state. Thus thoughts of Hobbes, Locke and Rousseau are quite different from the political thoughts of Socrates, Plato and Aristotle of ancient age or St. Augustine, St. Thomas Aquinas of medieval age. The growth of industrialism created new problems and a different outlook. Now economic factors and national states are the dominating feature of political thought with a tinge of international outlook. Now, each and everything is decided by cash opposing capitalism emerged capitalism and of reconciling two extremes, socialism came into existence. Our first volume deals with Ancient and Medieval political thought second with the thinkers of national state third and fourth with socialism, communism and Gandhism and other thinkers of recent times such as Lenin, Mao, Laski, Bertrand Russel and Graham Wallace and phycologists, Pluralist and pragmatic thinkers etc.

FOUR PERIODS OF POLITICAL THOUGHT

It has been already narrated that the political philosophy can be divided in four periods:

(1) Ancient political philosophy.
(2) Medieval political philosophy.
(3) Modern political philosophy.
(4) Contemporary political philosophy.

According to Gettle, ancient political philosophy is the basic foundation of modern political philosophy. To quote Gettle, *"The problem of present have grown up out of the condition in the past and the political principles that are now being applied are the result of evolution of past political thought."* But it must always he kept in mind as stated before that thought of political philosophers have been influenced due to different social environment and different political outlook of different persons, political thinkers have generally dealt with the following political problems:

(1) The origin of state and its nature.
(2) Relation of political science with the religion and ethics or controversy between the church and state.
(3) The functions of the state.
(4) The organisation of the state and Government.
(5) Sovereignty.
(6) Law and Justice.
(7) Classifications of the Government.
(8) Utility or justification of the state.
(9) Relation of political science with other physical and social science.

A brief description about these has already been given but controversy between religion and the state which was the main theme of political thinkers has still not subsided. India has been declared a secular state but religious sway is still strong among the masses and with bullets, Indira Gandhi Government was unable to curb it and the same Government which used bullets for co-religions had to carve out a separate Punjabi Suba to satisfy the sentiments of religious people. Similarly Bismarck, the iron man of Germany had to bow when he came in conflict with the religious sentiment of German Roman Catholics, what should be the place of religion in a state is one of the unsolved puzzles of political philosophy. In India, Gandhiji remarked those who say that the religion and politics are separate things, know nothing about politics while according to Rafiq Zakaria writer of a book about the Appraisal of Nehru *"Religion to Nehru was a poison."* In Vietnam war, capitalist U.S.A. and Communist Vietnamese both stopped the war to honour the religious sentiments of the people. As such controversy about religion and state is still going on though it has lost its former glamour as it clear due to Arab-Israeli conflict and declaration of Saudi Arabia. So far effect of other science is concerned, from the very beginning state was compared with an organ or body. Later on Political philosophers began to think biologically. With the change of environments. Barker remarked if our fore fathers thought biologically, we think psychologically. Soon psychology gave place to economic and now our thoughts are moulded or are influenced by socio-economic consideration.

SCOPE OF POLITICAL THINKING

Scope of political thinking is very vast and it can be divided in three parts:

(1) Politics or political Act.

(2) Political Science.

(3) Political thought or philosophy.

According to Will Durant, to devise a method of barring incompetence and Knowing from Public office and of selecting the best to rule for the common good is the problem of political philosophy. Politics is practical participation in political affairs or matters but in political science we confine ourselves to theoretical study. Political philosophy speculates about political problems and the idealistic view of the state or as the state ought to be.

Sources of Political Thought

It will not be out of place to cast a cursory glance about the sources of political thought and what factors affect the political thinkers in different circumstances.

(1) Geographical conditions.

(2) Contemporary conditions and social setup or social environments.

(3) Individual circumstances and experiences.

(4) Great philosophers and their works.

1. Geographical conditions. Montesquieu placed much emphasis on Geographical factors and to some extent he was right, as no political thought can be developed by Eskimos in Tundra but with the development of science. Geographical barriers are no longer important as it was before, city states developed in Greece as geographical factors suited for their growth but now same political thought may hold the sway in England, India and U.S.A. etc. in spite of the differences of climate, environment and other Geographical factors. With the development of science and means of communications geographical factors play a minor role. Marx may have been born in Germany and may have written in England but he influenced leaders of Russia, Cuba, India and

China and failed to have his sway in Britain and Germany. Thus, now geographical factors play a minor role.

2. Contemporary conditions. Social environments effect a thinker and perhaps no thinker can remain uninfluenced with his contemporary social surroundings and problems. Aristotle defended slavery because he found it a common feature and was unable to think that how citizens can get leisure to devote their time to solve the political problems and actual participation in states affairs. Similarly contemporary controversy of church and the state effected all political thinkers of medieval period. With the development of individualistic political thought when man was free to think, psychological school of thought came into existence.

With the emergence of omnipotent states which shaped the destiny of individuals and moulded their life, thinkers like Hegel came into existence, who supported the power of state and called it, a march of God on earth. But soon economic forces became all-pervading and so economic surroundings began to colour the thought of political philosophers. Moreover political thinking is influenced by our economic consideration. To a great extent "ism" are influenced by economic considerations. U.S.A., Japan, Germany, etc., being the richest countries of earth are bound to support to capitalism and China being one of the poorest countries is apt to support communism. It is true now-a-days not the public, but ruler or persons in power influence most and if Chiang-Kai-Sheik might have been in power in China, probably he might have supported capitalism, in spite of the poverty of China. Perhaps it is true but it had to be admitted that now economic factors play an overwhelming part and dominant role. In England which contains labour majority even conservative and liberal forces in spite of the dominating personality of Mr. Churchill were unable, to check it in gaining control over the Government. Similarly with the advent of prosperity and plenty, U.S.S.R. had lost its old vitality and force for communism. Thus, economic factors shape our political thinking and setup as recent events of Russia and Europe have shown.

3. Individual experience. Man is the creature of circumstances as such not only social environments but individual circumstances and experiences also colour his thinking. It is said that Plato never lost the image of his teacher Socrates and never supported democracy under which his teacher Socrates was poisoned.

Similarly "fear" which Hobbes experienced haunted all his political thoughts. The poverty which Karl Marx experienced and the inhuman treatment, which he experienced by the governments of different countries never lost touch with the thinking of Marx and perhaps appalling poverty and exilement by the various Government were responsible to give Marx thinking of stateless and classless society. Similarly in spite of the impact of pax Britannia had best administration, personally, Mahatma Gandhi along with his followers had to suffer ruthless suppression and merciless suppression which forced him to say that man has a soul but state is soulless machine and can never be separated from violence. Thus, personal experience colours the thinking of the greatest political philosophers which the world has ever produced.

GREAT POLITICAL THINKERS

Man makes a careful study of the political thinkers and is influenced by them, thus political thinking of old philosophers influences the thinking of coming generation. They follow the footsteps of those who are considered great as Long Fellow remarked:

Lives of Great men, all remind us
We can make our lives sublime.
Departing they leave behind us
footprints on the sands of time.

Thus, great political philosophers mould and influence the thought of coming generation. Karl Marx borrowed freely from Hegel and gave a different interpretation. Aristotle borrowed from Plato though different in many respects. According to Gettle, this source is that it gives a history of political literature rather than of political thought. Political philosophers are often too much removed from practical political life...In any attempt to view political thought in connection with the history, institutions and general intellectual background of its time, this source must, therefore be supplemented by others. Official documents are also important for the history of political thought. As Gettel remarks, *"The official documents of states furnish a most valuable source of political thought. These include written constitution's, treaties, diplomatic, correspondence, state papers and the like."*

IMPORTANCE OF POLITICAL PHILOSOPHY

Study of Political Philosophy is most important. According to Gettel, *"The study of political thought, therefore, has practical value in that, it aids the formation of habits of more thorough and candid* examination of the meaning and tendency of our political understanding." Political philosophy has always held an important part since the creation of earth but now a days due to international circumstance it occupies a most honourable place. Problem before a politician now is to find out a practical applicable policy. In spite of the best efforts neither capitalism nor communism nor Gandhism in true sense has been practically applied. Now, a days when social evolution is taking place with leaps and bounds, political philosophy is doubly important. The task of understanding the deeper implications of the present situation and of planning future can be assisted by a careful study of political thought of the ages. Study of Political thought in the historical perspective trains the mind to think, to criticize and to construct and leads to mature thinking and enables a politician to solve contemporary in a better way.

Chapter 1

Greek Political Thought Before Plato

Western Political thought in a systematic way was developed in Greek city states many thousand years ago. As such Western Political thought begins with Greek thinkers. As such according to Barker, *"Political thought begins with the Greeks. Its origin connected with the calm and clear rationalisation of Greek mind."* It is not true because the recent researches of historians and of a chailogists show conclusively that the people of ancient India, Egypt, Babylonia. Persia and China had not only developed many political institutions but had also speculated on political problems. According to Maxey, "Egypt" has the story of civilization lasting more than three thousand years, similarly according to same writer *"The great thinkers of China did not neglect political thought, nor were political ideas alien to the Chinese people."* Similarly he writes political motivation was an unconquerable element in Hebrew psychology. Same author further observes "It cannot be said that Hindu political ideas have had any great influence upon Western political thought, but the extent of their influence upon the past and present, and possibly upon the future, political life of India, no Western mind is wholly competent to measure." Thus, this statement that political thought begins with Greek is wrong; but at the same time it had to be admitted, that no book containing the systematic political thinking which we find in Plato and Aristotle is available now. For understanding and appreciating the present day political thought it is not at all necessary to acquaint ourselves with the ancient political thought of other countries as of Greece. According to Mayer, *"It is not possible to make any progress in our political thought. As without Greek Political thought the categories of*

European thought and approach to their understanding of life have been permanently moulded by the Greeks from the very beginning."

Greek Political thought developed due to existence of numerous independent city states. To quote a famous writer, for the development of political thought the emergence of Greek city state is of cardinal importance. The heavy routine of near eastern empire, the bureaucracy of Egypt and Mesopotamia, the reckless irresponsibility of own age tyrants of the Old Testament give place to something new. The free play of speculative intelligence, the brilliant formulation of vocabulary of thought in a language of the subtlest shades of meaning, the purposive coherence of Greek ideals — all these things mark the greatest step forward that political speculation has ever made. To be brief, the Greek city state furnished the data for the first systematic thought of the ancients upon civic relations. Indian, Chinese, Persians and Helrem thinking is based on religious outlook. *Vedas, Gita,* confined its teachings, *Zooronteras Zendarvestar* and *Bible* etc. are basically religious books while Greek Political thought avoids religious background and confines itself to state and Political activities.

THE SCOPE OF GREEK POLITICAL THOUGHT

Greek thinkers approached the subject in the scientific spirit examining the facts without any mental presuppositions and formulating generalisations to explain them and devoted their attention mainly to the nature of the state and to man as a political animal, Greek thinkers came to conclusion that man is political animal which is their main contribution to political thought. Being a political animal, man can realise himself only in and thought membership of state and as such state naturally became the centre of Greek political thinkings.

Greek thinkers discussed about the origin of the state and its end or purpose. They named the various forms of Government as Monarchy, Aristocracy, democracy, oligarchy and tyranny etc. They were profoundly impressed by the fact that forms of government are subject to change, and tried to find out the reasons of change, as well as the laws governing them. They discussed about liberty, education and fundamental questions of political obligations and revolution etc. They also examined carefully the various grounds on which different social classes based their claims to political authority and also tried to find out the ways by which government can be stable, these topics are of permanent interest and of considerable value to a student of political thought.

A thinker is influenced by his environments, so thoughts of Greek thinkers were influenced by the nature of city state which constituted the background of their thinking and furnished date for it. As such a cursory glance about the city state is indispensable and useful.

THE CITY STATE

The conquering Aryan nomads conquered the region of Aegean about 1500 B.C. and as military masters, the Aryan raiders settled down upon this per-Hellenic (Probably systematic) Social order. Each conquering hand fell heir to a more or less insulated section of territory and succeeded in erecting an independent city state. The rivalry or kinsmen did not encourage in voluntary unification and separation became the very keynote of their behaviour. Greek city state was a community, a true commonwealth or republic.

A modern city like Calcutta, Bombay, Delhi or Madras or New York is a huge congregation of man living in a given area brought together mainly due to economic needs. In such cities persons living in the same building do not know one another, but in a Greek city state citizens used to share a common life or purpose. As per Barker, *"It was the place of a common life"* and the home of union of classes. Life within common walls drew men together in a natural intimacy. If it did not abolish prestige of wealth and birth and culture. It established a tradition of easy intercourse between all classes. Like a college they walked talked, played and met together in Assembly for deliberations to discuss or settle their matters.

Greek City State and Slaves

Aryan conquerors after the completion of conquest, become free citizens, while the conquered aboriginal population was reduced to the status of serfdom, or slavery, no slave, no freedom, no resident alien could take part in public assemblies, cast a vote, hold an office, appear in a court of law or enjoy any of the privileges of membership in the body politic.

Slave labour gave the citizens the leisure which he needed for the performance of civic functions. Slavery was an essential feature of Greek civilization and the basis of the political life of the state. Aristotle explicitly justifies slavery as a necessary institution and Plato nowhere condemn it. Greek philosophers generally exhibited a pronounced contempt for manual labour which was performed by slaves. But this did not mean that nobody worked there as a manual labourer. In Athens there were 40 thousand citizens and 80 thousand slaves but some slaves used to work in silver mines and others were owned by wealthy persons. The average artisan and farmer had no slaves and depended on his own labour for livelihood, but adequate payment enabled them to devote their leisure time for political matters and for participation in civic duties. As such all Greek citizens participated in civic affairs.

The States of Athens and Sparta

These were the two most powerful and prominent states which influenced the political thought of Plato and Aristotle etc. Plato was a full-fledged Athenian. The citizens were generally allotted one plot of land outside the city and one building within the city. The city states were even smaller than the district of U.P. and Plato imagined population of 5040 citizens enough for the ideal city state. If we include women, dependents, children and alien even city population comes about 20 or 25 thousand in all. Thus, city states were very small in size and population. The city states included and absorbed the entire collective activities of the citizen. City states played the same role in the life of citizens, which society plays in the life of modern man. Thus, Aristotle said man is a political animal as we now today say that man is a social animal. This city was small in size, possessed a corporate or communal character, the combination of urban and rural elements and above all it was self-sufficing. As such Aristotle defined the state, as a union of families and villages having for its end or purpose a happy and self-sufficing life. Individual and state were so much identified that the idea of individual state would have appeared meaningless to the ancient Greek. Athens was a closed communion in which only citizens were allowed to participate, so according to H.G. Wells patriotism of these privileged people (citizens) took an intense and narrow form. A man's love for his country was reinforced by his love for his native town, his religion, and his home, of these were all one. Gods of Greeks were little more than human beings of heroic world, so their political ideas were undefined by religious heads and priestly class was small and inconsequential. Economically in Greek society particularly in Athens, there was no landed aristocracy. Diligent artisan, clever tradesmen and even slaves made fortunes and so it was involved in every class of economic forces.

The active management of Athenian state was in hands of citizens. Every adult male citizen was *ipsofacto* a member of general assembly of citizens which possessed supreme authority. In addition to it, a citizen may also be called upon for service in courts. In addition to it, in Athens there were the archons, a board of magistrates, in generals (minister) and a council of five hundred whose function was reconsidering, proposing and supervising body elected by the citizens.

Sparta. Sparta was an agricultural state with a monarchical form of government dominated by military junta. By a most rigid system of athletics, military exercise diet and education. The Spartan boy was trained for warfare and government. Girls were trained for motherhood and only strong children were allowed to survive. Perioikai had civil but no political rights and helots or agriculturists possessed no rights at all. There was a popular assembly though nominally it was supreme but it delegated most of its powers to five officers. Senate was judicial body.

Athenian thinkers charmed by the martial organization, repressive discipline, standardised education social regimentative and concentrated authority of the Spartan state, considered these qualities essential for polity.

Athenians defeated Persians at the battle of Marathan in 490 B.C. and its imperial age began under the leadership of Thermistocles and reached to its climax under the Pericles. Athens became the leader of maritime states and Sparta of the land states. But a clash took place between these two states which lasted about eighty years in which Athens was defeated and it gave setback to Greek city states.

CHARACTERISTICS OF GREEK POLITICAL THOUGHT

On the marrow of her political splendor, as melancholy anticlimax, came the everlasting political philosophies of Athens which produced immortal thinkers like Socrates, Plato and Aristotle etc., and Historians like Herodotus and poets like Homer. To a Greek thinkers state was an enraged and sublimated family, fusing the individual the community into a harmonious and perfect whole.

Citizens duty bound to conform his behaviour with patterns prescribed states as its part. To them law was commonsense and right reason in the form of specific rules of human action. They approached political thought with a moral point of view. Political science in their hands became an ethics of whole society. Republic of Plato is as much a treatise on politics as an ethics and its subtitle is concerning justice. For Aristotle Ethics was an introduction to politics. In the words of Barker, *"Political Science is a triology. It is a theory of the state; but it is also theory of morals and theory of love. It contains two subjects which have since been removed from its scope and treated as separate spheres."* Greek political thought was connected with municipal or parochial character of the city state. There was conflict among the states as well as between rich and poor within the states deals with philosophy but deals with practical political problems, but it differed from medieval thought. In a nutshell differences of ancient and medieval political thinking may be given as below:

(1) Greek thinking was secular while medieval thinking was religious and they thought about body and soul *i.e.* about worldly affairs to be guided by the state and spiritual affairs by the church.

(2) Greek thinkers believed man is the measure of all things and as such were individualistic but medieval thinkers gave prominence to state and the church and man was bound to obey both king and the Pope.

(3) According to Socrates, Plato and Aristotle etc. state is the means of good life and highest development but medieval thinkers were of the opinion that state come into existence due to sin of man and they considered state based on violence and for punishment of sin. It is true Epicurians, Sophists and Cynics did not give high place to state but they also did not support church while medieval thinkers gave prominence to church in their political thinking.

(4) Keynote of Greek thinkers was city state but of medieval thinkers was universalism and of world empire based on Christian outlook.

(5) Greek thinking was intellectual and rationalistic while medieval thinking was based on faith and superstition and maxims and gospel based on *Bible.*

(6) Greek thinkers were egoistic and discarded equality and brotherhood of man but medieval thinkers believed in the fatherhood of God, equality and opposed slavery but supported

universalism, equality and brotherhood. Greek thinking was practical while medieval thinking is speculative.

MODERN THINKING

Like Greek thinking modern thinking is intellectual, secular and rationalistic but now state or politics is considered separate from ethics. Modern thinking centres round national states as Greek thinking round city states but now universalism is also going to gain centred prominence with the emergence of world organisations like League of Nations and U.N.O., Universalism is also gaining ground. In modern age, biological, Psychological, sociological, humanistic, pragmatistic and economical school of thoughts have emerged which were unknown to Greek thinkers and were not prominent in medieval age. New ideas are developing in modern age and contemporary political literature is so vast that it is studied separately. No synthesis of capitalism, socialism, communism and Islamic republican ideas may emerge.

POLITICAL THOUGHT OF SOPHISTS

The 5th century B.C. was a period of great economic and political disturbances in Greece. The country faced with the great Persian war, in which Greeks were victorious. That the Greek of the 5th century had formed already a timely curiosity about the queer loves and anthropological which filled his world is amply proved by the fund of anthropological love embodied by Herodotus in his history. An active and violent link between rival institutions *i.e.,* between Persian absolutism and Greek autonomy and between Spartan oligarchy and Athenian democracy presented a scene which provided much food for speculation to the keen intellect of the Greeks. They discussed the monarch tends to degenerate into a tyrant, while democracy makes all men equal before law. But democracy follows mob rule and government by the best person is certainly preferable. Perhaps rule by the best man, is best of all. This period was characterized by great intellectual activity and freedom of thought. Political philosophy became one of the favourite subjects of study. This naturally gave rise to a class of teachers who discussed and lectured on political and taught the eloquence, disputation etc. They were called Sophists. According to Barlner, the Sophists were half teachers and half thinkers — (and) combined also something of philosopher.

Their Philosophy

Sophists have no systematic philosophy. They taught what well to do students who were willing to pay for. The Sophists represented a transitional period in the growth of Greek philosophy rather than any particular system of thought. Their teaching of philosophy was characterized by common method of approach and common point of view rather than by any community of thought. As they taught everything and so this led them to systematize different subjects of knowledge. Positive side of their thought was humanism. The twisting of knowledge towards man as its centre. To the sophists abstract nations about universal truth and justice meant nothing. They believed that knowledge is the creation of senses and other human faculties and so it is a strictly human enterprise — To them *"Man is the measure of all things."* In other words, they propounded that *"the proper study of mankind is man."* An individual himself was to be the judge of whether his action was good or bad. This resulted in upsetting old ethical and legal code of conduct and pointed conclusively to individualism.

The Sophist did not believe in the natural origin of laws, the state and other associations. The laws were not natural but conventional as evidenced by the fact that there was an endless variety of laws. If laws were natural, they would have been characterized by uniformity rather than by variety. To the sophists the laws were often based on political expediency, were divorced from morality, and, therefore obedience to them was a question of personal interest. They believed in the selfishness of human nature, and, therefore, held that power *i.e.,* political authority was based on force. Even rebellion was defended in the name of a higher law, against the standing convention and the existing laws of society. In Antigone of Sophocles an artist exploited the conflict between or duty to human law and a duty to the God. Antigone defended herself in the name of law of God when she was charged with having broken a law by performing funeral rites of her brother. She replied *"Justice enacted not these human laws,"* Euripides denied the validity of social distinction based on birth and even opposed slavery and side like freeman. He hears an upright soul and says honest man is nature's nobleman. Thus, sophists according to Maxey were not a body of philosophers united by devotion to common principles but were sharp fellows who made a good living by acting as private tutors in rhetoric's, argumentation, eloquence and other subjects.

IMPORTANT SOPHISTS AND THEIR TEACHING

Word 'sophist' has been formed from sophists which means to be wise and learned. The fundamental idea of sophists was harmony of a life shared in common by all its members. Solon commanded his legislation as producing a harmony or a balance between the rich and the poor. Anaimander tried to picture a system of opposite properties which are divided off from an underlying neutral substance. Harmony or proportion or if one prefers 'justice' is an ultimate principle. The Pythagorean philosophy specially 'regarded harmony or proportion as a basic principle in music, in medicine, in physics and in politics. In English, justice is still regarded as square number.

Alcidamas was of opinion, *"God made all men free, nature has made no man a slave."* Sophist Antiphon denied that there was "naturally" any difference between a Greek and a Barbarian. Antiphon in his book 'On Truth' wrote law is merely conventional and hence contrary to nature. The advantageous way is to hold the law in public but when one is not observed to consult one's own advantage. For Antiphon 'nature' is simply egoism or self-interest. Legal justice is of no use to those who follow it.

Thrasymachus said that justice is only interest of stronger, since in every state the ruling class makes those laws which it deems most conductive to its own advantage. Nature is not a rule of right but a rule of strength. Callicles observes Natural justice is the right of the strong man. Similarly ambassador Melos says, "of the Gods, we believe and of men we know, that by necessary law of their own nature, they rule whenever they can."

It seems that two views developed among sophists, one view was that nature is non moral and human beings are motivated by self-assertion or egoism, the desire for pleasure or power. If interpreted moderately it comes near to utilitarian theory but it may also be taken that it supported anti-social theories. Other view was that nature as a law of justice and inherent in human beings and in the world is intelligent and beneficent consequently moral and in the last resort religious.

Their Importance

Knowledge before the sophists was unsystematic and indefinite. Led by necessity of teaching, the sophists systematized knowledge and thus rendered an inestimable service to humanity. On account of this, systematization of human speculation in future could be more definite and accurate. It was again Sophists, who made political science a practical study. Plato borrowed many of his ideas from the sophists and Glucon in Book II of the republic developed idea of nature with egoism in a kind of social contract of not to do injuries so that they may escape form the injuries of others, a kind of enlightened self-interest.

The Sophists represented a sceptical time and their scepticism and subjectism led later on to the idealising a man, like Plato and others. General teachings of sophists and their individualism gave birth to the philosophy of Socrates. Their main contribution was that they look upon the individual reason being the sole criterion of truth, Epicurians philosophy was based on lust for pleasure based on sophist philosophy, Aristotle was also influenced by their teaching. View that Law of God or conscience is higher than man made laws was supported by Tilak and Gandhi, who opposed unjust laws which were against their conscience. During British rule in India sophists gave political shape to political ideas, their contribution was that they accepted Reason as measure of truth.

POLITICAL THOUGHT OF SOCRATES AND ITS IMPORTANCE

Socrates was a great thinker and teacher of Plato. He sacrificed his life in obedience of wrong legal punishment.

Life

Socrates was born in Athens about 469 B.C. He was the son of a sculptor and midwife, thus he belonged to working class. He was given customary education at Athens and he entered into the profession of sculptor which was a skilled trade of artistic calling. He also served in army in several companies and also served as member of various Government bodies in minor capacities.

As a sculptor, he did not succeed and so he began to teach like sophists. But unlike sophists, he did not charge any fee and teach systematically. He adopted a unique mode of teaching, wandering about in the city with his friends and disciples on whose bounty he probably depended for his livelihood, he would encounter someone, who could be drawn into discussion. In streets of Athens, men were ready to discuss anything at any time, so it was not difficult for Socrates to find man for discussion. Socrates would then start grilling his opponents with questions and continued question and discussions until his opponent was exhausted. This method infuriated the opponents thus publicly. Socrates was handsome, eccentric and a striking figure and in spite of shrewish reputation of his wife. Antippe, he created sensation and created public interest in himself. In old age, he became member of council and committee of council and opposed and criticized unconstitutional immoral and illegal acts of ruling elite class. He was firm believer in obedience of laws. Socrates was accused of irreligious acts and was imprisoned. His friends tried to bring him out of prison but he refused and accepted death sentence in obedience of laws in 399 B.C. Thus, he sacrificed himself in obedience of laws and set an example before mankind that obedience to laws is a sacred duty of citizens.

Methods

His methods were inductive and utterly irrelevant. He based his reasoning of facts but with the front of his tantalizing, he nipped many a promising blossom of political omniscience, though he influenced Plato, Isocrates and Xenophan etc.

Socrates used to say, *"I am following the occupation of my mother in as much as I bring about the birth of new ideas."* Barker remarks, *"A steady discharge of civic duties, and a steady refusal to go outside the bonds of civic law,"* are thus, two features, which mark his life as a true citizen of Athens. According to same writer, there was definite method and the rules for the relevant answering of question.

Man, he taught must be guided by knowledge, true knowledge, which penetrated the surface of things disregards the motives and interests of passing periods and personalities and arrives at truth that is universal and eternal. Like other Greek thinkers, he believed that man is a political animal but he opposed the setup of the Athenian Government, which was based on equality and believed that all citizens are not equally qualified to participate in governmental activities and offices. He opposed idea of equality and supported that only virtuous and wise persons should be entrusted with the administration of Government. This was too much for the Government which was based on equality to suffer, and he was prosecuted and condemned to death for irreligious ideals.

In the words of Barker, "yet he always and never more than in his death, was a loyal son of Athens. He had served in her army, he had been member of her council, her laws were to him only less sacred than the commands of God, and not to be disobeyed except for righteousness' sake nor would be leave the prison where he lay doomed forever when escape was easy, lest the laws should rebuke his life." As per Maxey, *"his death by the cup of hemlock, which subsequent ages have made a symbol of fallacy of trying to exterminate ideas by killing the man who advocated them."*

Socrates and Sophist Thinking

Socrates was heir to Sophists. He supported their contention that *"conceptions of right must be subjected to the scrutiny of individual and not rest upon religion or traditional custom."* According to Will Durant, he was rich in crafty dodges and argumentative tricks, slyly changed the scope or meaning of terms, drowned the problem of loose analogies, quibbled like a schoolboy, and beat the wind bravely by studies. But he was not a sophist as he refuted their theories and aimed in reforming moral nature of man. He was more a prophet than a philosopher. To Socrates, "knowledge was virtue" but his knowledge was intimately related with character. "Know thyself" was his motto. Against the ideas of equality, he was in favour of wisdom and not of birth or equality. He was for creating a professional class of moral and political leaders representing an aristocracy of intellect. There was in Socrates an anti-democratic touch due to which he considered democracy an impossible form of Government and favoured aristocracy of talents.

Briefly point of differences can be stated as below:

(1) Sophists used anti-thesis between nature and convention to deny the validity of social laws and customs but Socrates held that these must be observed. He taught virtue is knowledge and vice is ignorance.

(2) Ionians confined themselves to mechanical explanation of things; they tried to find out how things are made but Socrates enquired into their purpose or final cause. In short Ionian's method was mechanical but method of Socrates was teleological which was further developed by Plato and Aristotle.

(3) Sophists maintained that goodness was special art, which could be mastered by attainment of a special knowledge but

Socrates believed goodness was general capacity and thus unique. Goodness according to him was the knowledge of nature of things of ultimate reality.

(4) He taught without taking fees and showed a greater independence of spirit than the Sophists.

Socrates on Law and State

Whereas the sophists did not believe in any abstract notions of right and justice. Socrates believed that out of the general mass of laws, conventions and customs, a general code of ethics could be prepared to guide mankind. He entertained a great respect for laws and could conceive no natural justice outside laws. Laws was to him sovereign both for ruler and ruled. It was "the written agreement of the citizens, defining what should be done and what should not be done."

Socrates on Democracy

Socrates was opposed to equality and favoured that only wise persons should rule. He preferred rule by aristocracy of talents and did not support contention that everyone is fit to rule and any man can fill any office.

He objected to the use of lot for the selection of office bearers because it treated as equal those who had knowledge and those who lacked it totally. He was of opinion that only wise and learned persons should rule. This notion was developed by Plato through his famous theory of philosopher king who rules by the aid of trained intelligence. The supporters of enlightened despotism thus find support in the political ideas of Socrates and his notions may be termed as anti-democratic. His contention was that political is an art, and as an artist should be well-versed in his art, so a political or ruler should also possess the expert knowledge of ruling over the man and he should utilize his knowledge for the welfare of public and humankind.

Other Ideas

Socrates believed that virtue is knowledge and ignorance is vice. He followed the motto "Know thyself."

I know Dharma but it does not have inclination towards it, I know Adharma but I cannot get salvation through it. So Socrates placed emphasis on "Know thyself." He said, "a man who desires to lead good life should know aim of his life."

I taught by his example for the sake of conscience, a man may rise up against Ceasar but that in other matters, he must render up to Ceasar, the things that are Ceasar's even at the cost of his life.

Significance of his Death

Though Socrates, believed in a close inter-relationship between ethics and politics, but his life showed that there may be conflict between them and so he suffered for his impiety. The way in which he died constituted his greatest contribution because it taught:

(1) He believed that individual reason was the final tribunal of appeal and not only man is measure of all things but each man is the only measure of himself and he should follow his own conscience.

(2) Though a citizen is free to follow his own conscience but it was his duty to submit to the laws of the state and its judicial decisions. He should suffer punishment imposed by the state for breaking its laws. Gandhiji went a step further and said a man should follow his conscience and should oppose unjust laws and should suffer punishment cheerfully for breaking these laws. According to Adams, 'Socrates like Hobbes asserted the uncompromising authority and irresponsibility of the ruling power.'

His Influence

Socrates drove home the importance of clear and rational thinking. He introduced inductive reasoning and definition His teachings are based for the education of knowledge, According to Aristotle, gist of Socrates' teaching is virtue and knowledge are one. Sin is a mistake. His ideas; and the way he suffered death made him immortal in the history of political ideas. He proved by his death that ideas cannot be killed by killing a person. He was executed in 399 for atheism and for his irreligious ideas.

His ideas were carried forward by his disciples and heir Plato and Aristotle etc. According to Sabine, "*some considerable measure of political principles developed in the Republic really be traced to Socrates and were learned directly from him by Plato.... the inclination to find salvation in an adequately educated ruler, is certainly that virtue, political virtue, not excluded form knowledge.*" As stated before

Gandhiji was akin to Socrates in following conscience against the unjust laws and accepting punishment cheerfully but he believed in democracy and egalitarian ideas and worked for the down trodden masses, so he succeeded while Socrates failed. Socrates is considered as a great political thinker as his thinking was clear and rational. According to Aristotle, Socrates introduced inductive, reasoning and definition. Thus, Socrates was a great political thinker, who guided great thinkers like Plato and others.

Chapter 2

Plato (348 B.C. to 322 B.C.)

PLATO'S LIFE AND HIS PHILOSOPHY

Plato is considered as one of the greatest political thinkers which world has ever produced, so his ideas are to be studied carefully.

The 4th and 5th centuries B.C. represent the classical period of Greek political philosophy, of galaxy of talents which has immortalised ancient Greece, Plato and Aristotle are most eminent. Plato was born in an aristocratic family and lived at a time when golden age of Athenian democracy was over. He remained and studied with Socrates for about eight years and on the latters death travelled for more than a decade to Megara, Cyrene, Egypy and Southern Italy. He then founded his own Academy and taught and wrote Academy in the grove of the here Academy. Plato's father was Aristotle who belonged to the family last Athenian King Codras. Unlike, Socrates, Plato was aristocrat, claiming descent from the half mythical Solen vocation but devoted himself to goddess of learning and fame. Plato came under the influence of Socrates in his early manhood and was 28 years of age when his master was forced to die. Instead of entering into active politics, he launched his carrier as a teacher, writer, publicist and philosopher. He taught in his academy until his death 322 B.C. at the age of eighty. He was called in as a consultant and expert advisor to rulers and by other persons and legislators in whole Greece. He even succeeded in persuading Dionysins II ruler of Scily to give him free hand in governing that kingdom but his plan did not succeed and had to save his life by fleeing from that place, James Urick holds the view that Plato probably visited India also and learnt something of the higher Vedant of which there are many traces in his general philosophy. He is said to have visited Persia also. Politic instability made a deep impression on him it led him to make a search of those eternal principles of human conduct which along can bring happiness to the individual and stability to the state.

Ultimate aim of Plato's teaching was essentially practical. According to Barker, *"he sought to impart knowledge which should issue into action and to teach a philosophy which should be a way and inspiration to life. His philosophy is the conversation of a soul ...... and the service of mankind."* According to Will Durant, *"The difficulty in understanding Plato lies precisely in his intoxicating mixture of philosophy and Poetry of science and Art we cannot tell in which character of dialogue the author appeals."*

THE SOURCES OF PLATO

Plato based his teaching on Socrates motto that knowledge is virtue. Plato came across with sophists, thinking with Socrates, Cynics and Cyrenics, etc. But he was influenced mostly by Socrates. Socrates's study can by divided as educational method based on dialogues and study method. He has divided into two parts. One based on sense organs and other based on truth and reason. He was of opinion that knowledge gained by senses is short lived but followed both dialogue method and based his knowledge on reason and truth.

THE METHOD OF PLATO

In his work, Plato followed dialectic method which is most suitable for proving that truth is best discovered by co-operation. To push home his point, Plato used analogies. To support plea of trained skill he drew analogy with the pilot or doctor and to prove that women should function as guardian, he drew analogy with watch dogs but there is differences between art of a pilotship and of a politician and similarly analogy of women with watch dogs is farfetched as a law or rule which applies to animals may not apply to human beings. An argument form analogy is not proof. However sound and valid an analogy may be. Finally, Plato is an utopian. Probably first utopian of Western world. He is interested not in describing the state as his perfect ideal state which can only exist in imagination. His books 'The Republic,' 'Statesman' and 'Laws' are conversation of persons in search of the perfect ideal of the state.

HIS WORKS

"The Republic", according to Jowett is the greatest of all the works of Plato. He finished Republic about 386 B.C. It deals with Metaphysical, ethics, education and political philosophy. "The politics or statesman" was finished about 380 B.C. and 'the laws' was published after the death of Plato *i.e.,* after 322 B.C.

Besides these three dialogues, he produced, other dialogues such as the Apology, the "MEMO" the Gorigias, the Gritias and the Crito etc. The apology of Socrates represents a splendid defence of the right of individual conscience. Both, the Memo and Pythagoras deal with the important question of whether or not virtue is communicable *i.e.,* teachable. The Gorigias represents an attack on sophists. Plato exposes sophists teaching as mere sham. The Crito indicates obedience to laws if they do not clash against conscience. *"law is the creator of social setup and possesses absolute claim upon the citizen."*

According to Prof. Earnest Barker, Plato has described mainly following four points:

(1) Symptoms of virtuous man and about his personality.

(2) Symptoms of ideal state.

(3) Need of knowledge for virtuous man.

(4) Qualities of an ideal state and ideal man.

Writing about the Republic Prof. Sabine states, *"In origin Republic was a critical study of the city state as it actually was, with all the concrete defects the Plato saw in it, though for special reasons he chooses to cast his theory in the form of the ideal city. The ideal was to reveal those eternal Principles of nature which existing cities tried to defy."*

'The Republic' of Plato is based on ideal and contains bold sweep of speculative construction but in laws. Plato has a realistic approach. 'The Republic' is timeless because of the generality of his principles but it cannot be said about other books. But so far influence is concerned 'Statesman' and 'The Laws' produced an everlasting influence as his successor Aristotle was influenced by 'the Statesman and Laws.' Through Aristotle these books made profound influence over western world. "The laws" signify by its title the step in the transition of his philosophy from the field of ideal to actual realisation Statesman tells how to govern people, "The laws" emphasis importance of laws.

Place of Plato in the History of Political Thought

As per P.B. Shelly, "*He (Plato) is the first and the last man to maintain that a state ought to be governed not by the wealthiest or the most ambitious or the most cunning but by wisest.*" Writing about "The Republic" Sabine remarks "*The true romance of the Republic is the romance of free intelligence, unbound by customs, untrammelled by human stupidity and self — will, able to direct the forces even of custom and stupidity themselves along the road to a rational life." According to Rousseau, "The Republic is the best treatise on education."* According to Maxey "*as an analyst of social and political institutions and a seeker of the idea he was the forerunner and inspirer of most of the antimaterialistic philosophies,.... something of Plato is to be seen in all Utopias.* He adds, "thought specially (of) favouring education and eugenics as the most practicable modes of bettering human society reaches back to Plato. Milton, Locke, Rousseau, Goethe and other great apostles of social idealism have drawn heavily upon him ....Virtually all socialistic and communistic thoughts have its roots in Plato, Plato also influenced, Sir Thomas More, who wrote Utopia'. Rousseau agreed with Plato that state is a moral association and by participation in common life man realises his moral personality. He also supported Plato's contention that state is an educational institution. In Germany Plato influenced Hegel and in England it influenced idealist thinkers like Green and Bosanquet etc. According to a writer "*Generations of British students have learnt from Plato (and Aristotle) that by nature man is a member of political community, that the state is partnership in virtue, that law is expression of passionless reason, and that righteousness consist in the performance by each mean of his allotted duties. The Republic of Plato is still a source of inspiration to many because the generality of his principles is almost timeless.*" Prof. Gaggi points out that "*the ideal state of Plato and that of Russian communists have many elements in common thus communism of Russia and even of China goes back to the days of Plato.*" According to Prof. Bhandari, "*Plato was the first systematic thinker of the west. He was the father of Political radicalism. His emphasis on justice and functional specialisation his feminism, his engenies are features of everlasting interest in the political philosophy.*" It may be added his theory of philosopher king, communism views have great sensation and interest. He is one of the greatest philosopher of Greece know to history. Plato was one of the greatest philosopher of western world and Western philosophy in a systematic manner begins with him.

Republic of Plato is a very important book as it aimed at the representation of human beings in a state perfected by justice and governed by thinker of good. The true romance of the Republic is romance of free intelligence. Unbound by custom, untrammelled by human stupidity and self will, able to direct the forces even of custom and stupidity themselves along the road to rational life as stated by writer Sabine. It is said that the fundamental issue of Republic is the discovery and presentation of justice.

According to Barker "The Republic and Laws" are the communist treatises, Plato is the first communist Catlin or he is fascist thinker. The Republic didn't spring in life, self together in Plato's search, it had its prelude and its presentation of practical thoughts.

According to Rousseau, Platonic *Republic* "must be considered as a brilliant exercise of philosophic imagination. The *Republic* is not a work of Politics but the finest treatise on education that was ever written."

Similarly writer Sabine states, "so striking is the part played in Plato's ideal state by education that some have considered this to be the chief topic of the Republic."

Others are of the opinion that Plato's *Republic* is an exposition and evaluation of Socratic principles. He had old thinking that Republic culminated in the conception of justice.

Briefly it can be stated that Republic is the crowning achievement of Plato's art and philosophy.

Plato wrote *Republic* when he was about forty years old and it is greatest of all Plato's dialogues. It represents the aim of Plato's philosophy, and it can be considered as the centre of his other dialogues. In its sweep, comprehension, perfection and universality of thoughts, to show Greek philosophy at its best. The *Republic* comes to us with double title. Firstly its title organisation of the state, that it is fundamentally political treatise. Secondly, concerning justice, it implies that its fundamental problem is the nature of justice or moral goodness, and as such it may be called ethical, treatise. Actually it deals not only with politics and ethics but also with educational metaphysical and sociological problems also; and in addition, it is the first work to deal with the philosophy of history. As such according to Sabine, *"The Republic, is a book which defies classification, it gives a picture not of any existing state of Greece but of an ideal state in which the apparent weakness and short comings of the existing states were to be avoided."* The Platonic ideal was not a creature of imagination but an ideal perfected speculation and logic, experience and test, comparison and criticism.

There are many reasons for its diversified contents:

(1) During the days of Plato, there was no rigid division of the field of knowledge into watertight compartments as it is now so one question led to another and process continued.

(2) There was unity in Greek city life. There was no rivalry between family, church, state, religion or civic duties. Religion of the citizen was a state religion and religious duties of citizen were has civic duties.

(3) Method of dialogue adopted by Plato gave him much freedom to move from one subject to another.

The *Republic* can be divided into five divisions:

(1) Book I and part of Book II are introductory and deal with representative views about human life and about the nature of justice and of morality.

(2) Books II, III, IV concern themselves with the construction of the first state and the first system of education. Plato is of opinion that the best form of human society which would reflect the three elements of human nature *i.e.* reason, spirit and appetite, justice is traceable to a society so constituted.

(3) Books V, VI, VII are given mainly to the construction of the second *i.e.* ideal state based on the rule of philosophy and principles of communism. Plato enlightens us on his idea of good.

(4) Books VIII, IX deal with persons of the states and individuals.

(5) Book X forms a rather detached part of the dialogue and discuss the relation of philosophy of art and the capabilities and destinies of the human soul. The real importance of the *Republic* lies in Books II to VI and Book VIII.

Plato's Emphasis on Virtue

Plato starts with ethical question, what is good man and how can he be made good? As a man cannot be good apart from the state, so second question arises; what is good state and how is it made good? In this way ethical philosophy leads to political philosophy. But Plato applies here Socrates principles that virtue is knowledge and the goodness of the state presupposes knowledge of the good on the part of those who administer its affairs. This leads us to third question about the absolute knowledge which the rulers of state must possess and how state can lead its citizen towards the ultimate good? Reply of this question leads us to the theory of education. Finally, harmony between the ultimate end or purpose of the state leads to its educational methods and its social structure. In this way, he enquires about the proper social and economic organization of the state. Thus, republic becomes a treatise on ethics, politics, education, sociology and metaphysics. In this way Plato attempts to deal with the complete philosophy of man, of man not only in action but also as a thinker.

According to Sabine, *"fundamental idea of the Republic come to Plato in the form of his master's doctrine that virtue is knowledge."*

Plato's theory is divisible into two main parts or thesis:

First that government ought the be an art depending on exact knowledge and second that society is a mutual satisfaction of needs by persons whose capacities supplement each other.

The *Republic* is Plate's masterpiece. It is growing glory of Plato's art and Plato's ideas. In origin, the *Republic* was a critical study of the city state as it actually was with all the concrete defects that Plato saw in it, though for special reasons, he chose to cast his theory in the form of an ideal city. This ideal was to reveal those eternal principles of nature which existing cities tried to defy.

Justice

Plato considered justice as the supreme virtue and in this book, he tried to draw a picture of an ideal state in which justice would reign supreme. He thought that he individual represents almost the same features and qualities as a society, on a smaller scale, Reason, spirit and appetite are common and ideal state is an imitation of the best and noblest life. According to Barker *it is a single treatise of an ethics, political order, treating man as a member of the state and state as moral community*. It has been remarked *"Republic culminates in conception of justice."*

Education

Plato may be called an ideal rather than idealist because he believed that his ideal state was not impossible of realisation if any place be found suitable for the habitation of philosophers and the growth of philosophy. Plato held virtue was teachable. So the *Republic,* has been regarded as one of the greatest treatises on education by Rousseau. It deals in detail about the system method subjects and mode of teaching with a purpose. In his *Republic* Plato deals firstly with justice principles of right action and what is good? Secondly, as virtue is teachable so that educational system would best promote virtue? Thirdly, it deals about the ideal man or citizen and his ideal qualities, Lastly, it deals with the question of best type of Government in which the qualities mentioned above would find their fullest possible development and expression.

Evaluation

According to Prof. Maxey *"To the thrill of intellectual exploration is added the thrill of search for ideal ..... the standard of the ideal ..... become structures unreality but will be better structures than men have ever made."*

In this book "The *Republic*", Plato refutes the ideas and theories of the sophists and discards all other views and gives free play to his imagination without any fear or favour or caring for nay tradition or custom, so Prof. Sabine remarks, the true romance of the Republic is the romance of free intelligence unbound by custom, untrammelled by human stupidity and self-will able to direct the forces even of custom and stupidity themselves along the road to a rational life. To quote him further few books that claim to be treatise on politics are so closely reasoned or so will be coordinated as the republic. None perhaps contains a line of thought so bold, so original, so provocative. It is this quality which has made it a book for all time, from which later ages have drawn the most varied inspiration .... The *Republic* is eternally the voice of a scholar, the profession of faith of the intellectual, who sees in knowledge and enlightenment the forces upon which social progress must rely. The *Republic* is perhaps greater than Rousseau's social contract and can be ranked with *Das Capital* of Karl Marx. Most idealist thinker borrowed something or other from Plato.

In Plato's, *Republic* justice is the central theme. According to Thrasmoehus, in Plato's. *Republic* justice is the interest of stronger. But others are of the opinion that according to Plato justice is the order of state and the state is the visible embodiment of justice under the conditions of human society. Plato says each individual should be put to the use for which Nature has intended him to work.

Thus, theory of state in Republic culminates in the conception of justice. Thus, Plato speculate upon justice as a single idea operating the mind of individual and state.

Perhaps no philosopher can think in vacuum, he is affected by his social surroundings as well by his predecessors particularly a disciple is always influenced by his teacher. Thinking of disciple is moulded by his teacher and it makes deep impression on him although when a man grows old, he makes his own contribution and sometime he discards his own ideas. Same is case with Plato when he wrote Republic, he was deeply influenced by the teachings of his teacher Socrates and developed Socratic ideal that virtue is knowledge but when he grew old, he developed his own ideas in his books 'The Statesman' and 'The Laws' because he realised by his long personal experience that imaginary or idealistic ideas do not work in this realistic world and an ideal human being perfect in wisdom and justice cannot be available easily in this world. Similarly it is difficult to find an ideal state in this imperfect world. Thus, influence of Socrates was performed on Plato when he wrote "The Statesman and laws," he never departed from the Socratic principles that virtue is knowledge and virtue is teachable. As such Socrates made an everlasting influence on him, moreover he is at his best in his books the Republic" than in other works where influence of Socrates is profound we already discussed about Socratic ideas and about "The Republic" in previous pages, only a cursory glance about the development of ideas of Socrates by Plato can be started here.

Many thinkers are of opinion the Plato's *Republic* (ideal state) was a repercussion of Socrate's death; Sophists taught man is the measure of all things and state comes in existence on account of the selfish motive of man but Socrates refuted the ideas of sophists and stared 'virtue is knowledge'. In *Republic* Plato developed this ideal. Against the teachings of sophists that the state is unnatural and is based on selfish motives. Socrates began to preach man is a social animal and state is the natural result of man's nature and as such state is natural and is based on the basic natural instinct of man. He is of opinion that basis of law may be considered justice or virtue then these will be based on true reason. Socrates opposes democracy and desires for political education.

Indebtness to Socrates

Republic borrowed the idea from Socrates that 'virtue is teachable' and develops the ideas of 'justice' discovering all the previous ideas of sophists thinkers and comes to conclusion that proper duty allotted to each man is justice.

Plato supports this idea of Socrates that origin of state lies in social instincts of man. State is natural and wise persons should rule over the masses for their welfare by their quality of virtue.

Plato also opposes, democracy because his master Socrates opposed it and it put Socrates to death. Hate of democracy remained in the mind of Plato throughout his life and image of Socrates; death never faded from his mind which is depicted by his opposition to democracy.

Plato like Socrates believes in inequality of man, because he finds that virtue is not available in human beings in equal quality. Moreover temperance, courage, justice and reason are not available in all persons in equal quality, moreover he thinks that neither the persons who give prominence to appetite nor the persons, who possess courage can rule properly. For performing the duties of administration wisdom is necessary and so wise persons possess a right of ruling over others as mind ruled over the limbs and other organs.

Philosopher King

He is of opinion that only wise persons can achieve virtue, so wisest person should have a right to rule with the help of otherwise persons. Thus, he develops the theory of philosopher king who rules with the help of trained bureaucracy. He is of opinion that generally problems before ruler or ruling class comes of general nature and require commonsense rather than knowledge of law, so widest person *i.e.* philosopher king should be allowed to rule. It reaches to highest climax in the hands of Plato in his theory of philosopher king.

Education

Similarly for teaching virtue and for moulding man according to the ideal of state, Socrates desired state education. Plato also supported idea of state education to teach citizen his ideal duties particularly to guardian class so that by acquiring knowledge they may be able to perform their duties of proper administration properly.

Plato's Communism

He was aware of the weakness of man and feared the guardian class may drift from the path of duty and virtue on account of selfish motives of economic gain and love of family, so he maintained that guardian class should neither possess property nor family but should have communism of wives and commonness. Thus, to safeguard virtue, Plato did not allow the basic interest of guardian class to have a fair and free play. Thus, the idea that 'virtue is knowledge' reaches the highest perfection in the mind of Plato on which he bases his book "The Republic" and for this, he is generally indebted to Socrates.

Influence of Socrates

According to Sabine, *"the fundamental idea of the Republic came to Plato in form of his master's doctrine that 'virtue is knowledge."* Form this it follows that the man who knows the philosopher or scholar or scientist ought to have decisive power in government and that it is his knowledge alone which entitles him to it,....... (because) he knows what tasks the good state requires....... (and) education will supply the citizens fitted to perform...... (thus) "the Socratic principle that virtue is knowledge proved to have a larger applicability than appeared on the face." In short Plato developed his ideas on the basis of Socratic principles and he is highly debated to him but it is genius of Plato who brought these ideas of highest climax. "Thus, most of the ideas which Plato propagated and perfected show an element of Socrates ideals." Justice is very important theme of Republic and he is of the opinion that the state is the visible embodiment of justice under the conditions of human society. As such theory of the state in *Republic* culminates in the conception of justice.

The 'Republic' is a book which mainly deals with the justice and conception of justice, leads to ideal state as such Prof. Nettleship has remarked, *"Republic is a dramatised philosophy of human life."*

The sub-title of the *Republic* shows the extraordinary importance which Plato attached to justice. Plato saw injustice as conceived by himself, the only ray of hopes of saving Greek city states, particularly Athens. Nothing pained Plato's mind in contemporary affairs more than the amateurish meddlesomeness and political selfishness which was prevailing in Athens during those days. Persons and classes doing different work must confine themselves to their own specific duties to the state and their selfishness must give place to full devotion to the state which is only possible if justice as conceived by Plato reigns supreme in the state.

The main theme of the *Republic* is sustained search after the location and nature of justice. He ponders over the various theories of justice of his predecessors and then gives his own theory. He considers the theory of Cephalus and his son Polemarchus based on traditionalism or proverbial morality which states *"Justice is giving to every man what is due to him."* Plato rejects this theory on the basis that it is not universal application. To restore arms to a person who has gone mad, is not justice even though weapons are theoretical due to him. As such, he examines another theory of Thrasymachus based on radicalism which states *"Justice is the interest of stronger."* But according to this theory 'might is right' a law of jungle may prevail which may be harmful to the society. According to Gulcon's pragmatic theory of justice, it is a product of convention and is bases on utility. It is born of fear of the weak. Glucon regards it as the necessity of the weaker and bases it on the instinct of fear. According to Prof. Nettleship *"it is a mean or compromise between the best of all, which is to be injustice and not be punished or worst of all which is to suffer injustice without the power of realisation."*

The fundamental postulate which emerges, forces Plato to proceed with the construction the state is that it arises out of the needs of mankind. Every individual has several wants particularly of food, clothing and shelter etc. but he cannot satisfy them only by his unaided efforts. This forces men to organize themselves in society for the satisfaction of common wants. Society is organized on the principle of mutual exchange of Services which itself is bases on division of labour. Thus, according to Plato, the bond which united first, men in a state is the bond of mutual economic dependence or the principal of reciprocity.

COMPARISON OF STATE WITH INDIVIDUAL AND CONCEPTION OF JUSTICE

Plato is of opinion that the state is the individual writ 'large'. As such he divides the persons of the state in Appetite *i.e.,* farmers or labourers who supply our basic needs, courage *i.e.* soldiers who defend the state and wisdom guardian class who is entitled to rule. He is of opinion that the state will be temperate of self-controlling, if there is harmony among the different groups or classes born of devotion to the same end in all. And justice is nothing but the principal that each man should pursue that one function for which he is best fitted by nature. As such Plato defines justice with the help of ideal state from which justice is inseparable. Justice resides in the state and is to be identified with complete virtue which consists wisdom, courage, temperance *i.e.,* self-control and justice. As such justice is the quality which is at once a part of human virtue and the bond which makes man social. It is an identical quality which makes man good and which makes him social. Thus, he supports the contention that a man just in manner in which a city was just or Socratic idea that "justice is doing one's own business and not being a busy body. To quote Barker, *Justice according to Plato consists in the will to concentrate on one's own sphere of duty, and not to meddle with the sphere of others, and its habitation, therefore is in the heart of every citizen who does his duty in his appointed place."* Thus, justice is the condition of every other virtue of the state and grows with specialization of functions. The justice of the state is citizen's sense of duty. According to Sabine, *"Justice is the bond which holds society together, a harmonious union of individuals, each of whom has found his life work in accordance with his natural fitness and his training."* It is both a public and private virtue because the highest good both of the state or of its members thereby is conserved. Thus, justice is the regulative virtue which produces general harmony in character and general good order in the conduct of very individual. Prof. Sabine is of opinion that justice is the proper inter-relation of the three functions whether of the classes in the state or of the faculties in an individual. Platonic justice divides the citizens in three rather in classes akin to Hindu society and fourth of slaves which he did not mention. Similarly he propounds the theory of Gita of Satwik, Rajas and Tamas and places emphasis on Swadharma that is of doing his own duty similar to Lord Krishna who says it is better to die in doing his own duty than to follow other one's duty and advises Arjun to fight as it is duty of Kshatryas to fight. According to Maxey, *"To each according to what nature has fitted him to be and to have is...... Plato's definition of justice." It seems that Plato has two parts of justice, individual justice and social justice.* To quote Prof. Barker, *"Social justice thus may be defined as the principle of the society, consisting of different types of men. ...... who have combined under the impulse of their need for one another, and by their combination in one society, and their concentration on their separate function have made a whole which is perfect because it is the product and the image of the whole of the human mind. Thus, justice is an indispensable quality of moral life and according to him state is the reality and justice is only an idea."*

According to Plato complete justice postulates an ideal state and is identified with it, justice like the ideal state, therefore, demands division of society in three classes representing reason, spirit and appetite, one man, one work, on the basis of functional specialization, a state controlled scheme of education, emancipation of women and their equality with men and the rule by wisest person *i.e.,* of philosopher king with the help of trained bureaucracy and their safeguard from selfish motives and emancipation from domestic and economic worries by a system of communism far guardian class. Plato says, "*God has put gold into those who are capable to rule, silver into auxiliaries, iron and copper into peasants and the producing class.*" Thus he gives justice or duty according to class. Plato holds that only a few persons are wise, possess virtue and quality to rule. As a virtuous man is entitled to rule, so wisest and most virtuous should rule with the help of trained wise persons. He is of opinion, only wise and virtuous can remove ills of states, so states cannot get rid of their troubles unless these are ruled by the persons, who possesses quality and wisdom to rule, as such philosopher should be kings, *i.e.,* ruler, because only these philosophers are best fitted to rule and can remove the ills of the states. Thus, according to Plato, rule by the wisest person *i.e.,* philosopher king with the help trained and expert bureaucracy is the best rule. If state is ruled by such a ruler and justice prevails in that city, all the evils will be removed.

Criticism of the Plato's Justice

(1) Plato's conception of justice is idealistic and moral and not legal.

(2) It is against the spirit of individualism and makes a man as integral part of an organic whole.

(3) It makes too much demand on a citizen's devotion to the state.

(4) It did not embody conception of right, but of duty only.

(5) It does not take into account clash of individuals and clash of classes.

(6) It does not provide for the proper development of individuality and consequently of society as it provides one man one work.

(7) It gives monopoly of power to guardian class and is against democratic ideals.

(8) It provides philosopher King, who may easily become a despot.

(9) System of communism of Plato ignores the essentials of human psychology and human nature.

(10) Plato's conception of justice is static, It allots a person, a particular position in life and condemns him for his whole life while a person may get better development by change of his work or profession.

(11) In reality, Plato's conception of justice is not properly the principle of virtue in which reality has been ignored.

(12) Plato is not quite clear about his conception of capacity of ability. Whether it is to be based on birth or wealth or on any other conception. If it is to be based on wisdom, then what will be the criterion of wisdom. How a man is to be given particular duty or special work. Human knowledge is fallible. It is not possible that a wrong work or duty may be allotted to a particular person and he may grudge this and this may create a problem to be solved and may also give rise to many connected problems.

(13) Division of Plato in different classes may give rise to class consciousness and consequently to class wars.

(14) Division of different classes may be akin to Indian caste system which has proved to be harmful to society.

(15) One man one work hinders the full development of the individual.

(16) Plato's conception of justice is idealistic and it does not take into account the real situation. In human society there are no three natural divisions. His teacher Socrates, himself, was a stone cutter and according to opinion of that time, he was a man unfit to remain in the world. How should such a man be allowed to preach? According to Platonic justice, he should have done his duty by doing his work of stone cutting, if a man like Socrates can change his duties then why others should be condemned to do one work for their whole lives?

(17) Historically, ordinary persons became rulers, while according to Platonic justice, they should have never thought of changing

their duty. Similarly if tradition is to be believed a foolish shepherd became Kalidas and a stable boy became Shakespeare. Iltutmish and Balban, who were slaves became rulers, Stalin son of shoemaker and Khrushchev as coalminer became rulers. As historically and in democratic setup his conception has proved wrong.

If these genius would have been guided by Platonic justice, man would have remained without their masterpieces as such Plato's conception of division of work cannot be sustained.

(18) Plato has placed much emphasis on state and no emphasis on the individual.

(19) According to George Grote, Plato has confined life of guardian class, so much so that they cannot enjoy life or happiness.

(20) According to Xthenophon it is profoundly undemocratic and gives appetite class only animal existence.

(21) It has also been remarked *"Plato identifies with justice, the principle of class rule and class privileges."* These ideas are against liberty equality fraternity and democracy and cannot he accepted in democratic setup.

PLATO'S IDEAL STATE

According to Plato the state is individual writ large. Plato seeks a superman, who will create a state as good as it ought to be. As such the Platonic state can be an aristocracy, a government of virtue and intelligence exercised by one or few.

According to Plato, any state however, small is in fact divided between poor and the rich and they are at war with one another. He offers democracy and is of the opinion that "In a democracy even the horse and asses have a way of marching along with all the rights and dignities of free man all things are ready to burst for liberty."

According to Plato philosopher should be king and king should be philosopher. Thus, he favours Govt. by most intelligent person. As such he believes in rule of wisest person and in aristocracy. But he does not believe that state should control every sphere of life. He states the truth is that the state in which the rulers are reluctant to govern is always the best and state in which they are most eager the wisest.

In this world every individual has several wants and in order to satisfy his wants, he needs help and co-operation of his fellow beings.

The bond of mutual economic dependence first unites men in state. Food, cloth, shelter are necessary for a human being. Tiller of soil needs help of weaver of iron Smith and mason and carpenter etc. As such, he requires help of other persons for fulfilment of his wants. As the life grows complex, so division of labour becomes more complex and very man specializes himself in his own field. To protect the goods created or manufactured by various persons, military class is necessary and to keep all persons to perform their duties consciously and efficiently ruling class is necessary.

Organic Conception

He compares the various groups of persons with the full human body and thus he introduces an organic conception of state. He compares farmers and labourers *i.e.,* producing class with appetite, military class with limbs *i.e.,* with courage and ruling class with mind *i.e.,* with reason and wisdom, Members of the ruling class show a higher capacity for virtue so they are qualified to build political authority because of their superiority in virtue. Thus, according to Foster, *"Plato maintains that the necessary and sufficient qualification for the function of government is superiority of virtue."* All persons do not possess an equal capacity so people should work for those who possess it. In human body, mind, rules over all the parts, similarly wise and virtuous persons should rule over the whole state as a few persons possess capacity to rule, so Plato's ideal state can only be aristocracy of talents *i.e.,* of Philosopher King assisted by intellectual and experienced persons.

States as Individual Writ Large

According to Plato, state is individual writs large and he compares the appetite with the producer class, spirit with the warrior and mind with ruler, so virtuous and wiseman rules over the state. His ideas are as similar to Hindu ideas of caste in which Shudra is considered as feet, Baniya as appetite, Kshatryas as arms and Brahmans as brain.

Plato builds his ideal state in three ways *i.e.* state regulated by education, communism of property and wises among the guardian class the state and rule by philosopher King represent season, and therefore virtue in action. Plato's scheme of education was calculated to ensure a constant supply of philosopher guardians and to help every individual to discover his true vocation in life and to excel in it. The communism of family members to keep them out of economic and worldly temptations and ambition and to force them to concentrate on their duty to the welfare of state, he did not allow them either the property of family like rishis of India. His ideal state is ruled by philosopher King, state regulated education and for guardian class communism of wives and property, functional specialization, equality of men and women and censorship of art etc.

The Rule of Philosopher Kings

Plato is of opinion that due to superiority of wisdom, a philosopher King will be able to remove the defects of the state and he will rule in an ideal way, he says:

"Until philosophers are kings, or the kings and princes of this world have the spirit and power of philosophy cities will never have rest from their evils nor the human race."

Philosopher King

This conception of philosopher King is unique contribution of Plato to Political science. Philosopher King or Kings are the sole ruler of the state. Their rule is absolute because they are not bound or limited by written laws and they are neither responsible nor responsive to public opinion. Thus, they rule like enlightened despots and masses have no voice in the determination of policy of any king or share in their rule. Thus, he goes against the Greek ideal of citizenship according to which citizens are allowed to take part in the affairs of the state.

Before pointing out the defects on this conception, it is necessary to give the arguments in support of this utopian conception of Plato. Firstly, it is said that the philosopher King is not absolute because it is his paramount duty to see that the state it adheres to basic principles. It has been further argued that such a man would exhibit complete self-control and be free from hatred, spitefulness and meanness and as such it will be truly a human rule. But these arguments can be advanced by those persons who have studied only imaginary books in which picture of such persons have been painted. History bears witness that no ruler on earth has been of this type. Of course world had produced saints but they have abhorred themselves from actual rule because according to Marx, Gandhiji and other thinkers, state is based on violence and exploitation. How a ruler who rules actually can keep himself free from it? Plato forget that duty of judge is to do duty and the judges who were duty bound to do justice forced Socrates to die because he opposed their ideas or rule. What is the guarantee that philosopher king will not crush his opposition ruthlessly. Power corrupts a person and absolute power corrupts absolutely and if a philosopher King is a person, howsoever wise and learning he or she may be, they are she bound to be power drunk, if he is a man of flesh and blood. Philosopher King as pointed by Plato can be a God or at least a saint but not a ruler. It is true that conception of Plato of philosopher King was the result as demanded by force of logic *i.e.,* to identify of virtue with knowledge, the distinction between real or scientific knowledge on the one side and conception or opinion on the other, and the supremacy of the first over the second is once taken for granted, whole structure of the Republic with its philosopher King or Kings at its head, who rule with the help of trained bureaucracy of intelligence becomes clear. Such a ruler or ruling class does not need public opinion or law as guidance because supreme virtue is knowledge. Thus this conception becomes clear because it is the result of logical conclusion. It is not exception, that the wisdom which arises from knowledge of the idea of the good to abdicate its claim before written law which belongs to convention or tradition. Thus according to Foster, *"The philosopher King is not a mere addition or assertion: he is the logical result of whole method on which Plato's construction of state has proceeded."* To quote same writer again, *"The fundamental truth lying behind the conception of philosopher Kings is the most profound original concept in the entire political theory of Plato."*

Merits and Demerits

Now question arises "Has the ideal of absolute rule by a trained intelligence, no element of truth or value in it? It is difficult to give a wholly negative answer to this question; it embodies a great and fundamental truth of universal application. It is difficult to deny that Government is a difficult art and it requires specific education and training, democracy itself would itself would be complete failure unless it is guided by the people skilled or trained reason. Democracy in England according to Ramsay Muir, Lord Dewart and Allen is carried on by the trained bureaucracy and according to Finer in U.S.A., it is guided by judicial oligarchy." It is true that they take into account public opinion also but it can also be run without caring for public opinion as in some countries by military dictatorship or by only a ruling elite class. Thus, we have to say that it was the great merit of Plato to have realised that unless political power and reason are mixed together, unless statesmanship is combined with most profound wisdom, and those persons who lack in wisdom, are excluded from political power, states will never have rest from evil. Society should be governed by real knowledge but defect lies in stating the naked truth. Modern democracies make a show periodical elections to give public illusion that bureau or oligarchy of judges or politicians govern on their behalf while bureaucracy rules with the help of coercive powers of the state.

It may be feared or perhaps rightly, that philosopher Kings may rule for their own benefit. To safeguard this, philosopher Kings as well as the guardian's life is one of renunciation and surrender. If they have political power, it is at the cost of their personal interests, like the desire for wealth and bodily pleasures and family life, because they are not allowed to keep property or wives and children etc. This is a great safeguard against their selfish motives. If philosopher Kings have been given political power, they have been denied wealth or bodily pleasure. Thus, economic power and luxurious life have been denied to them. Conception of class war arises because those who have political power possess economic power also and enjoy bodily pleasures also. While poor and labourer classes are denied even bread to carry on their body and soul together. If a particular class of person enjoy all power and deny even existence to other persons, cities cannot have rest from evil. It goes to the credit of Plato that he separated political power from economic power and bodily luxury and in such a society, conception class war may not arise because other classes have been given economics power and family life to console themselves. Thus, Plato showed a great wisdom in proposing the rule of philosopher King. But Aristotle being aware that such persons are rare on earth so he based his government on best science or constitution or law. Plato during his old age also realised human weaknesses and came to conclusion if best person cannot be found then second best government can be that based on law, which is Aristotle's best and Plato's second best government. Thus, Plato based his superman *i.e.,* on philosopher King, without realising whether such a person is available in this world or not.

Indian still born Ram Rajya Christians city of God and Muslims rule of first three caliph in which state was ruled by an ideal person but such persons are rare on this earth, therefore, Plato's dream cannot be realised or is at least very difficult to be realised so history does not bear witness to such a rule of philosopher Kings perfect in all respects. Similarly to deny property and family life to guardian class and civic right to producer class are unjustified.

Defects

(1) To find out a philosopher King is difficult and as such it is not a feasible or practical proposition.

(2) Power corrupts a person and absolute power corrupts absolutely and man of flesh and blood is but a man and perfection cannot be found in him, so it is doubtful that philosopher King or Kings would not be corrupted by lust of power.

(3) History provides ample examples in which what to say of kings even religious philosophers or saints were unable to tolerate the opposite opinion and killed their opponents mercilessly. What is the guarantee that absolute philosopher Kings will not do the same and will tolerate free expression of views and also opposite opinions and acts which he did not like.

(4) Plato's ideal state is based, not merely on analogy but almost an identification between the individual and the state. Such an ideal puts hindrance on the growth of human personality as individual possess his own separate existence.

(5) His ideal state is based on communism of property and wives and on the absolute rule of philosopher King, unfettered by law, is too collectivistic and idealistic.

(6) Aristotle did not agree with Plato's communism of property and wives as creative of organic unity and harmony in the state. Spiritual medicines cure the spiritual ills. Unity of state can be best achieved not by abolishing family life and property but by organising and training individuals of various types and capacities according to the Constitution of the state. Every individual should be allowed certain minimum possession and liberty of action to express his thought and render service for the well-being of society. Organic unity of state can be also achieved by proper utilization of individual differences, in furtherance of social needs for common good.

(7) Aristotle criticised Plato's communism based on many conception of human psychology. It was impracticable and harmful in its consequences.

(8) Communism of views may give rise to constant faction as there may be difference of opinion in selecting the proper pain for meeting with one another as beauty provokes more than wealth. This instead of producing unity, it may give rise to reaction even among the guardian class, History is full of examples where wars book place for beauty also and not only for meeting but even for seeing only. From the very beginning wars have been caused due to beauty such as Helen, Draupadi and Padmini etc.

(9) Aristotle expresses dis-satisfaction regarding vagueness of Plato's reference to the non-guardian classes. Plato neither provides education nor does he give any share in the participating of the Government. According to Harald Laski, no class should be permanently excluded from power because it gives rise to discontent and consequently to revolution or discontent and instability to state.

(10) Plato himself says that a state consists of two classes *i.e.,* rich and poor and it gives rise to faction but will not Plato's division of population into the guardian and non-guardian divide the state into two mutually hostile parts in an artificial division, and will not if give rise to calls conflict or class war? It is a problem which is now a menace to whole world and there is no solution to this problem in Plato's ideal state.

(11) Thus, Aristotle criticises ideal state of Plato on the conception of the unity of the state. Communism of property and wives and comparative neglect of the non-guardian class in the ideal state of Plato and proposes best state on the basis of super science, best constitution and best law.

(12) Plato's functional representation hinders the growth of individual.

(13) Plato in his ideal state fails to denounce slavery.

(14) He ignores appetite class and reduces them to the status of hewers of wood and drawers of water and thus condemns them to perpetual subjection.

(15) Ideal state of Plato lacks law or constitution.

(16) Only philosophers can be king is not possible in this realistic world. Historically kings have been either generals or conquerors or based on heredity.

(17) Lastly, in search of ideal state Plato finds the utopian ideal but losses practical state.

According to Maxey defects *"did not impair clarity of vision"* and Foster says it is most profound original contribution of Plato. In short in spite of defects it is of abiding interest and most fascinating conception of Plato.

(18) Now everybody claims himself intelligent, so problem of selection is very difficult.

(19) His ideas favour falling elite class.

(20) Man is guided by self-interest, so probably Plato's thinking himself philosopher enticed to rule propounded these ideas.

(21) His conception of philosopher King leads to despotic and autocratic rule, in which common men are excluded from power.

(22) Plato did not care for producing class and common man while no progress is possible without the miracle in production and no government can be stable without the support and sympathy of common men. These are the citizens of the state who make it great.

PLATO'S COMMUNISM

Plato propounded theory of communism. He proposed communism of wives and no property for ruling elite class.

According to Foster, "In respect of wives and children, Plato is definitely propounding a system of communism in the sense of common ownership. But it is to a very small extent that Plato recommends common ownership of property." As such it has been remarked that virtually all the socialistic and communistic thoughts have its roots in Plato.

Plato suggests communism for guardian and ruling class as he thinks both the community of property and the community of families tend them to make truly ruling class.

Plato's communism differs from modern communism but it may be stated that the socialistic and communistic ideals originate with Plato.

Plato was of the opinion that the ruling elite class should not have any property of their own beyond what is absolutely necessary. According to Sabine, "so firmly was Plato concerned of the previous effects of wealth upon Govt. that he saw no way to abolish evil except by abolishing wealth itself, so for soldiers and rulers are concerned. To cure the greed of rulers there is no way short of denying them the right to call anything their own."

Plato's ideal state represents a new social order in which the guardian class and warrior class live in a state of special regimentation. Representing the elements of reason and spirit, they are made to renounce the appetite. For this purpose Plato advocates system of communism of property and wives which was not wholly without local Greek support, institutional and ideological. There was a minor touch of communism in Sparta as shown by the common messing out of private lands. Wives were lent by husbands to others for the purpose of the state. In 'Grete', there was public tilling of public lands. In 5th century B.C. in Athens, communistic theories appear showing a distinct tendency to idealise the ancient nature people, who hold things in common. Euripides in his 'Protestilaus' advocated communism of wives. Plato's communism of wives and property had psychological as well as practical basis. He brings out communism of wives in two waves *i.e.,* emancipation of woman and reform of marriage.

Ideas that lead Plato to Communism

Plato put state before the individual and divided the community on the basis of functional usefulness. As man was to do the duty for which he best fitted. He had to merge himself in the state and render the greatest possible service to the state. The Plato's state was raison d'tere. Plato was a thorough collectivist, who ignored the individuality of the citizen some writers consider him fascist and others as communist. Individual must not have other interests than those of state. Hence, he was not to be allowed to collect and keep property as owner. He feared a desire to collect and own property, would lead to selfish personal ambitions and would bring about a clash between an individual's personal state and with those of the rulers of the state. To get rid of this clash and to bring about perfect harmony in the state, Plato emphasized on communism of property and of wives for guardian class only. The theoretical basis of the conception of communism was furnished by the conception of the state as an organism and of justice as the duty of performing strictly and thoroughly one's own work which has been called 'Swadharma' in *Gita.* Plato's communism was *"a material and economic corollary of the spiritual method of Plato regenerate the state."*

He introduced communism to safeguard the general public from selfish motives of the guardian class now termed as ruling elite class.

He was of the opinion that none of them should have any property of his own beyond, what is absolutely necessary. He was convinced that nothing is more disastrous for the purity and efficiency of administration than that of political and economic power in the same hands. If economic class possesses the power of the state then he utilizes the other classes for his own advantage and for grinding his own axe.

According to Sabine, "*so firmly was Plato convinced of the pernicious effects of wealth upon government that he saw no way to abolish the evil except by abolishing wealth itself, so far as soldiers and rulers are concerned. To cure the greed of rulers there is no way short of denying them the right to call anything their own.*"

Plato's Opposition to Family

Family and property are so interrelated that if either goes, the other cannot survive. Plato is opposed to family because he thinks with its narrow life, hoarded wealth and secluded women, it is against the unity of the state and the free development of all its members. Love of wife and children is not only a serious rival to the loyalty of the state but generally it gains an upper hand. Now a days India is rampant with bribery and corruption because everybody in government office or in power desires to hoard as much money and enjoy all amenities of life – for himself and for his family members as he can, without coming in the clutches of law. Thus, to avoid family affection or wealth gaining upper hand than the loyalty of state, he brings idea of communism into existence for the guardian class which in now called ruling elite class of bureaucrats in alliance with politicians and capitalists.

Secondly, family life prevents men and women form developing their individuality or personality fully, particularly women confined to homes have no other function except of learning and rearing of children and cooking etc. This state did not get benefit of half of the population *i.e.,* of woman who, due to domestic duties are unable to do state work. Thirdly, home education home education is a poor substitute for a state controlled education, Fourthly, according to one writer Plato desired this because he considers woman a bond servant .... and his ruling class demanded women, who were the equal of their men's and for such a purpose he propounds abolition of marriage so it is "a tremendous assertion of the rights of woman. It raised her to the level of man, and postulated hear rational nature." In this way Plato is one of the first feminist thinker.

His Plea Against Family

Plato sought to abolish family for eugenic reasons also. He saw that even in animals rearing and bearing of children is maintained in such a way so that best breed may survive but in human beings no regard is paid for producing best children. As such, he proposes care should be taken to see that the best among men and women are united at the proper age; only in this way human race can show improvement. It is said Hitler also proposed such temporary unions to produce best race. Children will be provided education by the state, so that they may get best education. To avoid mine and thine, children produced by these temporary unions will not be aware of their parents but children born in a season will be the common sons and daughters of the persons who assembled together for this purpose. Thus neither parents will know their children nor children will know about their parents. In this way perfect unity will be realised. Thus, Plato's communism has therefore a strictly political purpose. The order of ideas is exactly reverse of that which has animated modern socialist utopians, he does not mean government to equalize wealth, but he equalizes wealth in order to remove a disturbing influence in government. Plato is of opinion that not only unity of state can be gained but it leads to the improvement of race, emancipated woman for the service of the state and puts them on a equal level with men.

To Plato family system and family feeling were the causes of personal ambition and restricted feeling and inimical to the loyalty and unity of the state. Plato was convinced that not only proper system of education but proper environment and habitation were necessary to produce and maintain, honest, best and uncorrupted guardians. For this communism of wives and property was necessity. According to Prof. Sudarsurely, *this communism of wives is a novel thing; there is hardly any parallel to it in the literature the world.* To quote some writer again "There can be no gain saying the fact that selfishness and corruption in a society cannot cease and the unity of the state cannot be restored so long as the members of guardian class continue to have private economic interest which might compete with those of the subject." Democracy has not been the success because the union of political and economic power is in the hands of a few individuals. Prof. Bhandari calls Plato as "first engenist" proposer of reforming the race. According to Prof. Sabine *"He (Plato) was appalled at the casualness of human mating.... the improvement of the race demands.... selective type of union."* *To Plato.... domestic duties of woman seemed "to deny the state the services of half of arts; potential guardians."* As such proposal according to him was necessary. Thus he supports communism of wives and property for guardian class but rule of philosopher King *i.e.,* of one man and racial theory leads him to fascism. His opposition to democracy and equality leads him to fascism.

Aristotle's Criticism of Plato's Communism

Plato's conception of communism has been severely criticised by his more practical disciple Aristotle, to whom it leads to excessive unification and destroys the richness and variety of life. According to him not the dead uniformity but unity in diversity is the right thing. Common property would destroy the sentiment of benevolent and charity. Aristotle is of opinion that true unity should be brought about by proper education and environment and not by communism of and wives' property. Plato's communism divides society in two classes *i.e.,* guardian class which is governed by communism and other class which is free from communism. Communism of wives may lead to unholy acts against near relatives and it may lead to disharmony as well as to incestuous love and rivalry to possess beautiful counterparts. State regulation and proper selection of proper mates in not an easy task. Common children are bound to be neglected a due to neglect, these may be converted into scoundrels rather than best guardians or citizens. Such experience of Muslim rulers of Turkish Sultans and to some extent of Sparta has failed and now Russian and Eastern. European experience has also failed. Aristotle opposes communism of property on economic, moral, political and psychological basis. On economic grounds Aristotle opposes communism of property because common ownership property tends to common neglect. Secondly, man puts hard labour what he regards his own business and his own property. It is the magic of private property that turns sand into gold, thirdly common may promote conflicts among the co-owners and co-workers. Fourthly those who may think that they have put hard labour may resent unfair distribution and instead of like mindedness, it may give place to factions. It is said disputes arise for private property's ownership but these arise due to wickedness of man, similarly disputes in communism of property may arise due to its very nature. Experiment of communism in Russian and eastern European countries and of fascism in Italy and Germany etc., has failed. Morally Aristotle says, it is only providing property which gives ethical conception to man of generosity, liberality, hospitality, self-confidence, self-support, and righteousness. Secondly, private property is essential for the good of life and full development of personality. Thirdly, by acquiring personal property, man feels self-satisfaction as he comes to know that he has acquired something due to his own efforts. Private property is a mirror in which an individual finds himself reflected. Fourthly, a citizen two possesses nothing cannot develop civic sense and cannot contribute anything to state. Fifthly, an unpropertied man becomes only a tool in the hands of ruling class and hunger may force him to lose his own thinking and may force him to work as a lifeless machine for the benefit of his owner. He is either reduced to slavery or to become a bonded labourer.

Psychologically Aristotle says that man possesses possessive instinct and gets satisfaction by calling a thing of his own. A feeling of joy will be destroyed if a man does not possess anything of his own *i.e.,* even utensils clothes, wife and children of his own.

Politically Aristotle is of opinion that this permanent division in two parts gives rise to a class war and this action may destroy the harmony of state. Thus, right to property has been in all states including China and Russia.

Aristotle's Criticism of Community of Wives

Aristotle agrees with Plato that unity of state is essential but he says unity of state is different in nature than unity of the family and it is wrong to convert state into a large family because unity of state lies in diversity. Secondly, Aristotle is of opinion that communism of wives is not a way to achieve the unity of the state. Community of wives means that every man's wife will be the wife of every other man. This will create faction, fight, discord, disharmony and jealousy. Thirdly, Aristotle dreads that there will be no fatherly or brotherly love among children and so he says it is better to be a real cousin than to be a platonic son. Fourthly, orphans cannot be substitutes of citizen's sons. So common sons cannot be good citizens. Fifthly, personal affection of relationship and sense of personal, possession is lost in Plato's scheme, which may prove harmful. Sixthly, according to Aristotle love of possession of property and family is deeply rooted in human nature and these are difficult to be discarded, so these instincts should be used properly. Seventhly, family and private property possess wisdom of ages so these should not be abolished due to him. Lastly, Aristotle points out that home is eternal school of natural affection and the child learns a thing between the mother's kiss and father's caress. Lessons learned at home may prove useful to society. Lastly, it is an impracticable idea as family is first school of children. As such nowhere in the world conception of communism of wives has been followed, so his idea of community of wives seems unrealistic.

General Criticism about Plato's Communism

(1) According to Barker, by abolishing family and private property, Plato *"destroys the instrument by which an individual can know himself as an individual."* It may also be pointed out that the demand of Plato that an individual shall not identify himself with any lower association like the family is rather too high for human nature, an impracticable idea.

(2) According to Sabine, *"It is possible, he (Aristotle) pointed out, to unify a state the point where it ceases to be a state."* Thus, communism's conception brought Plato to a height where state does not remain a state but becomes a large family.

(3) By abolishing family and property, Plato sacrifices the individual at the altar of the state and destroys its individuality and liberty and conscience or at least he demands a sacrifice too high for a common man unrealistic.

(4) Universally man needs a certain minimum of personal and private property through which alone man can develop and express his individuality. Private property enables a man to self-reliance and to have recourse to it in old age and sickness.

(5) Private property has the sanction of time etc. and utility and its abolition represent or reaction to primitivism and as such private property has been recognised as fundamental right in all constitutions of the world including China, Russia is now

resorting to free market economy and allowing full rights to private property.

(6) It goes against human freedom and equality, kills diversity and brings excessive centralization and makes human being as dead person.

(7) It is only half communism, *i.e.,* only for guardian class.

(8) It may bring indolence as it represses instinct of acquisition.

(9) Communism of wives ignores the fundamental sex instincts as well as paternal instinct and is unrealizable.

(10) Private family is an institution of civilization and its abolition may prove disastrous to healthy influences of heredity and family environment.

(11) Emancipation of woman by Plato is not really an emancipation but condemnation to them to the masculine life and public duty and even an object of common possession.

(12) Breeding for public on a system of mating reduces women to the position of stud animals, without giving them right to lead a family life.

(13) Parentless children may be poor specimen of humanity and retard progress of the state.

(14) Forced mating may be curse because human beings are not merely animals who may like forced mating against their will. Mating without love is too mechanical and unrealizable.

(15) Lastly, ideal is very difficult to be realised and it has not been realised anywhere.

Similarities between Plato and Modern Communism

(1) Both are against private property and think it is a curse for humanity as it gives prominence to selfish motives and sacrifices public good on the altar of private property.

(2) Both desire ideal society organised on the basis of common social service and not on birth or wealth.

(3) Both are utopian dreams as is depicted by its failure in Russia and other eastern European countries.

(4) Both bring practically despotism one man of party in the name of proletarian dictatorship and the other of philosopher class and philosopher King.

(5) Both sacrifice individual for the sake of society.

Dissimilarities or Differences between Plato's and Modern Communism

(1) Modern communism abolishes private property for all as an ideal but Plato's communism for guardian class only.

(2) Modern communism replaces individualistic means of production by collective production while Plato allows producer class no communism at all.

(3) Plato's communism affects articles of consumption because he provides common mess but modern communism recognizes private property in goods of consumption but not in goods of production.

(4) Plato's communism is political because it aims at the unity of state while modern communism is mainly economic because its aim is equitable distribution of wealth.

(5) Plato's communism is based on the basis of city states but modern communism is universal and international in character.

(6) Plato's communism has spiritual basis or significance but modern communism is materialistic.

(7) Plato's communism praises philosopher class or ruling class and leads to aristocracy or enlightened despotism but modern communism praises appetite class of Plato *i.e.,* workers and in a intransitory period desires their dictatorship but ultimately desires classless and stateless society.

(8) According to Plato ills can be removed by philosopher King, but according to modern communism by stateless and classless society.

(9) According to Barker, Plato's communism is ascetic in character, and it is surrender, imposed on the best and only on the best.

(10) Plato has put emphasis on soul and not on body because guardian class is denied bodily pressure.

(11) Plato have cared to make his conception of communism successful but he forgets to care for humanity and social moral as Barker says "He abolishes and establishes institutions for the state of a problematic goods, and in the name of unity, he destroys a school of morals, in which duty is earned more easily because it is tingled with affection and coloured by personal feelings."

(12) Prof. Maxey tauntingly calls Plato *"Reddest of reds."*

(13) Modern communism does not support idea of the communism of wives.

(14) Plato pleads communism strengthen the state while ultimately aim of state is to ultimately abolish it.

Conclusion

In spite of dissimilarities Prof. Jazi points out many similarities.

Both regard property as the sole source of all evil, both would eliminate wealth and poverty, both favour a collective education of children exempted form paternal care. Both regard art and literature as a means of state education; both would control all science and ideology in the interest of the state, both have a rigid central dogma, a kind of state religion to which all individual and actual activities may be subordinated as such his ideas possess germ of totalitarian states like communism and of fascism.

Importance

(1) Plato's communism is only a means to the unity of state.
(2) It did not give any undue importance to working class.
(3) It proposes unselfish or ascetic guardian class.
(4) It favours superiority of knowledge for the welfare of all.

Though communalism of Plato is not perhaps his original conception but he is the person who brought this conception on forefront. Government of many countries and even of India are thinking to open protection homes for unwanted children and unmarried mothers.

In U.S.S.R. and eastern European countries even limited communism has not succeeded and Turkish Sultans tried to produce Memluk soldiers nursed, educated and trained persons by the state but Memluk proved troublesome and useless persons, historically these efforts failed but idea of Plato has survived due to visionary persons thoughts it is an utopian dream because it is against human nature, and unrealisable in modern setup. Probably Marx's vision of communism is more realistic in modern setup than of Plato but he gave this ideas on ancient days, so his ideas about communism are still studied.

PLATO ON EDUCATION

To achieve the harmony in the state and to make individual fit to perform unselfishly the function which his situation in life demands, a proper intellectual and material environment. Plato supports state regulated by system of education "to cure a mental" melody by mental medicine. He regarded education as "a social process by which the units of a society become instinct with social consciousness and learn to fun fill all social demands. He was of the opinion that spirit of devotion and that excellence in the performance of public duty which was demanded of every citizen. Public education was, a direct result of Platonic justice, to him, education did not mean the storing up of external knowledge but the bringing of the soul into proper environment for its development. The eye must be turned to the light. To him, education whose object is to create right surrounding and environment is a lifelong process. He believed in the perfectibility and plasticity of human nature. According to him, function of education is not to put ideas or knowledge into the soul. It is rather to dropout the best things that are latent in it by directing it to the right objects.

Plato is of opinion that the function of the state is very positive. He believed that the state could promote right action virtue and justice and can prevent crime providing man's sand in corpore Sano, which could be done by a proper system of education, intellectual and physical. Thus in his opinion, education was the most important function of the state and the most important departments. As such Russian said, his book mainly deals with education.

Plato gives more importance to education than any other Greek thinker. His motto was First among human things, I reckon education. Plato preferred educational system of Sparta than his own city state Athens. Education system of Sparta was under the direct control of state and placed emphasis on education, so Plato recommended both those things in his system of education. Platonic system of education discovered the difference in the system of education between men and women. His education culminated in the realisation of idea of good. Purpose of education was to promote justice and to enable a man to fulfil his duty. Aim of his education was to make a man or a woman socially and economically useful and fit.

System

Platonic syllabus of education was systematic and progressive. During infancy and childhood the soul is affected thought fancy and imagination, so he did not place emphasis on imparting of knowledge as cultivating certain type of attitude towards things and men. During adolescent period education means the development of understanding through science and philosophy. In youth education should be both intellectual and physical, so he places emphasis on music for soul and gymnastic for the body. In adult stage, education was to be general and vocational and should be helpful for individual to discover his or her true vocation in life. During later stage education becomes more a way of truth, a vision of the absolute. Because of the vital importance of education, Plato devotes a great attention to it. The details of the elementary and higher education cover a large part of his book, "The Republic" and many reforms or innovations are suggested by him. As such Rousseau was perfectly right in describing the *"Republic" as greatest work on education ever written before.*

As to Plato, education is the positive means by which the rulers mould the characters of the individual and generate in them unselfish devotion to duty, so it should be controlled by the state and must be compulsory to the guardian class. According to Barker *"this is a running criticism upon the democratic custom of leaving every man to purchase for his children such education as the fancies or market affords."* As such he favours sate controlled education than education imparted by private institutions.

Educational Curriculum

Plato provides state controlled compulsory education to both boys and girls.

He proposes elementary education Up to the age 17 or 18. Up to this age he provides education of music, gymnastic and in elements of science. From 17 to 20, he proposes exclusive training in gymnastic. Similarly the study of poetry and literary master pieces etc. are intended to give a proper temper to element of spirit. It is meant to habituate the young soul, which is still the stage of feeling, to feel as it should feel about such problems as it has to solve, and in the strength of a feeling ingrained by habit to do as it ought to do without knowing the why and wherefore of its action. He favours narrative literature and poetry of epic mould. He desires to preserve their moral message and desires that these should conform to the policy of state and should be simple.

According to Barker "*Art combined and confined by the state to a moral purpose, will lose its appeal to the emotions, and failing to touch the hearer or the reader as art, it will fail to touch him as ethics.*"

Barker is right as we see in India that names of worthless poets and writers have been glorified by the Indian. Government because they praise it but these glorified persons have failed to get any response from the general public and from foreign countries and adorn only government liberties or adorn themselves with government titles which they get due to favour of some person in power.

Higher Training

Plato's earlier education is meant to be the training of the youth in civic virtue, the higher education is to be provided to train the selected few to become the guardians or rulers of the state. It extends from twenty to thirty years and thirty to thirty five. In the first, young persons are to be helped to choose their true vocations in life and get trained in them. This course's aim should be to make them wise. There was to be a systematic scientific course including study of Mathematics and astronomy of the time. Dialectical power must be developed. Military training should also be provided. At the age of 30, a second elimination test would follow and those who they are successful would be the perfect guardians and will be provided for five years training in Mathematics. Astronomy and logic etc. Special attention is to pay to dialect. The highest to these ideas is idea of the good akin to absolute Brahmin of Vedanta. He is of opinion that the philosophers, who are to rule the state are the persons, who possess real wisdom or knowledge, so they are the only fit persons to rule the state. To produce wisest rulers through proper education and training is according to Sabine, most original as well as the most characteristic, proposal of Plato in the *Republic.*

Book I and II of the *Republic,* deal with Platonic education which is a compromise between Sparta organisation and Athenian individualism. It anticipates many modern theories. It was aimed to provide harmonious development of the individual and the state. It is not burdensome and aims at the progressive education arousing the latent talents of the individual. It provides not only for body but also for soul by putting emphasis on practical as well as on theoretical aspect. Plato's system of education allows initial opportunity of education to all though it did not provide equal opportunity to all. Education of Plato is a lifelong process as even after retirement, individual is to concentrate on realisation of the ideas of the good.

Plato sponsored his education to associate governing body with the broadest knowledge and culture and to provide philosopher statesmen or rulers to the state. Plato cared to provide proper education to guardian class, Aristotle also cared for education for the ruling class only. Guardian class must be trained properly so that this class may unite among themselves philosophy, spirit, swiftness and strength etc. Only wise, virtuous and perfect ruling classes could create a perfect state and so he desired to provide for them proper education.

Special Qualities

(1) Plato has divided education according to age and prescribed subjects according to the suitability of the students. He prescribed exercise and music and importance to Mathematics and logic for higher education.

(2) He has given importance to all the three qualities in his education as well as to mental and physical development.

(3) He placed emphasis in his education for the development of full personality of an individual.

(4) He has given due importance for the developing of virtue in his system of education.

(5) He provides equal opportunity of education to woman and provides them some type of education as for men.

(6) He tries to give education to provide ideal rulers and citizens for the ideal state.

(7) He provides a process for lifelong education and changes it, according to age.

(8) He favours professional or useful education not only theoretical knowledge.

Criticism

(1) Plato has not provided education to all. To quote Sabine, "*In view of importance of which education has in the state, it is extraordinary that Plato never discusses the training of artisans and does not even make clear, how, if at all, they are to be included in the plan of elementary instruction.*"

(2) It is beneficial to upper classes only.

(3) Plato does not pay heed to individuality and duty, philosophical background man may lose initiative.

(4) He makes his education, tool of the state policy and sacrifices the individual at the altar of the state.

(5) Plato places emphasis on Mathematics rather than on science and social subjects.

(6) His education is more philosophical and less practical.

(7) In Plato's education there is no place for individual liberty.

(8) According to Barker *"There is certain difference between the ideal of action and that contemplational, sometime goal of life seems to be the vision of area of good, sometimes it seems to be the betterment of humanity and the turning away from the vision of social service."*

(9) According to Prof. Jowett *"Plato gives undue importance to basic and there is undue control of soul on the body."*

(10) Plato did not realise that education should be relative to the character of the individual and does not give importance to diversity of intellectual development which alone can tone up the character and status of the society.

(11) Long education up to 35 years makes a person thinker rather than a man of innovation and self-confidence.

(12) His system aims to produce citizens of particular type only.

(13) In his educational system he did not give importance to law, literature, medicine and agriculture etc.

(14) His educational system is long, difficult and expensive.

Evaluation

According to a writer *"Plato's Republic is a university, a church and a family."* Another scholar says *"A modern reader cannot fail to be astonished at the amount of space devoted to education as the meticulous are with which the effect of different studies is discussed or at the way in which Plato frankly assumes that state is the first and foremost an educational institution."* In short educational system of Plato is more to be praised than practiced as it is difficult to be realized and is theoretical and philosophical and lacks suitability in modern age but it gives some ideas which may be useful even now.

Plato in addition to *Republic* wrote "The Statesman" and "The Law." In these books he changed his outlook. It has been said Plato's *Republic* overshadows laws, yet the later has a practical value denied too former. The state of Plato's later theory is to he held together by the golden chord of law and this implies that the ethical principle of organization is different from that of the *Republic.* But Catlin is of the opinion that the *Republic* and the *Laws* are communist tracts. Plato is the first communist. But this view has not been accepted. In his book *The Law,* Plato concludes law is the expression of reason and since reason is sovereign, law should take the form of a sovereign command.

Plato's "The Politics or the *Statesman*"

If Republic can be said as a treatise on ethics and education, his 'Statesman' can be considered treatise on politics. He did not abandon his idealism in the statesman but here his idealism has given place to some kind of realism or practical idealism. As such he is more logical and exact in this book. He discusses that what a man ought to be and do, if he is to rule. What is the part played by politics and political science in fostering education? He came to conclusion that politics should aim at educating people in virtue and justice.

Change

In statesman, Plato has changed attitude towards law as reflected in his classification of states in this book. In his classification, he confines himself to actual states and prefers law abiding states than to lawless states. He also shows distinction between the theories of government and the theories of politician. He also declares that an ideal ruler is not merely a politician or a mere administrator. He must be ideal philosopher also and according to him, duty of such a ruler is not only to administer the state but to make men adopt the ideal standards of good and justice and that a ruler and state is good or bad whether this achieved or is not achieved, If ruler is learned and philosopher, laws are useless and he should not be fettered by laws but as such individuals are rare, law, which contains practical wisdom and experience of the past age, is essential. Thus, he gives importance to laws in this book.

Classification of Governments

Plato gives six kinds of governments according to number of rulers *i.e.,* ruled by one, few or many an whether these are law abiding or lawless.

Government directed by law	*Government not directed by law*
1. Rule of one - Monarchy	1. Rule of one - Tyranny
2. Rule of few - Aristocracy	2. Rule of few - Oligarchy
3. Rule of many - Moderate democracy	3. Rule of many - Extreme Democracy

In the above mentioned classification, Plato is of view that the rule of one *i.e.,* monarchy is the best form from the point of view of the good of the people in a law governed state, but monarchy may perverse in tyranny which is the worst form of government. The rule by a small number of ablest men who devote themselves to the service of the state is aristocracy and its perverted form in which they rule for their own benefit, is oligarchy. The rule of many *i.e.,* democracy is the worst form of in a state directed by law because it reflects the rule of an average man who is incapable of political speculation. But on account of its inefficient and defects inherent; democracy is the best form of government in a state which is not governed by law. As such Plato comes to conclusion that Democracy is worst of law abiding stated but the best of lawless forms. As such democracy is higher than oligarchy and this reflects complete abandonment of the attitude towards democracy adopted in the Republic. To quote Barker *"Seeing the virtue of law, as the fruit of experience and invention of wisdom. Plato can now see the value of democracy which is based on the rule of law."* Thus he supports democracy supported by Rule of Law.

The Laws

The Central theme of *Republic* is that the world would not cease from evils unless philosopher. Thus, in the union of wisdom and power in the same individual or group of individuals that Plato seeks the panacea for all the ills of the state. But failure of this experiment in Sicley, forces him to give up his ideal. According to Barker has still believed that *"It is not impossible nor do we speak of thing that are impossible, even though by ourselves they are admitted to be difficult."* However, he now drifts to sub ideal state in *The Laws.*

Plato's approach is more realistic in the laws, than his approach in the *Republic* and in this book, he attempts to discover a legal system, to help, guide and restrain the imperfect governmental machinery. Experience has forced Plato to be more realistic and modify his views about many things such as communism of property and wives. In the laws, he admits that private property and family are indispensable for human beings though even now he does not give them full support. He allows both private property and marriages under strict supervision of the state. His educational system is also far less strict than the system proposed in 'The Republic'. The only real restriction on marriage is with a view to prevent the perpetuation of really bad types of humanity. Similarly in case of women, he places emphasis on domestic duties though he allows them same education as to men and to take part in political affairs of the state. He is, however, in favour of establishing censorship over the intellectual and moral and artistic interest of the citizens. Thus, he comes to conclusion "*Law is the expression of reason and since the reason is sovereign, law should take the form of a sovereign command.*"

Political Power and Wealth

Plato allows wealth to share with intellect and philosophy, the monopoly of power in his book "The Law." He prefers landed property than commercial wealth to share the monopoly of power. Thus he shows preference to agriculture in this conception of city states but he tries to limit the landed property through the state. Thus, he prefers Chinese setup giving preference to farmers than Russian setup giving preference to bureaucracy and workers. He divides population into four classes on the basis of wealth in land. At the lowest ladder, people were to be allowed a definite area of land, produce of which may enable the owners to maintain bare necessities of life as was done in Russia to private owners of land who did not form co-operatives. The other three classes are allowed to have double, triple and four times respectively, the landed property assigned to the lowest class. But nobody was to be allowed property more than allowed to his class and surplus land is to be confiscated by the state as governments of India is attempting now. He believes that vast difference in holdings may destroy the harmony of the state and give rise to conflict between the rich and the poor, and may result in the corruption and inefficiency of the state. In Republic, Plato proposes complete abolition of property for the guardian class but he here makes a retreat though not complete, and provides land with proper safeguards against concentrations of property.

Administrative Machinery with Proper Checks

In the 'Laws', Plato suggested many useful checks on the abuses of different forms of governments. He allowed every citizen to have his share in the government of his state, according to his ability to do so. He outlined his scheme of machinery of government with following necessary main checks.

State's, supreme authority was to be vested in the like board of 37 whose members were to be between the ages of fifty and seventy. He gave preference to old age as it bring experience and stability with it. These members were to be chosen by elections and were to be guardians of law. This board is to function as supervisory body. He preferred old and experienced persons like Panchayats in India. There was to be an administrative council of 360, appointed to execute the orders of board of 37. These men were to be chosen by election and vote, based on possession of land. He liked jury system in which every citizen of either sex would take part. Finally, there was to be council of ten to ensure the proper and smooth working of whole constitution to watch the correct execution of laws and to prevent unconstitutional laws being proposed. The council of ten was to be assisted and advised by a council of twenty priests famous for virtue and by a council of twenty young men to counter act the conservatism of the older men. Thus, he favoured mixed and balanced form of government with proper checks.

In the laws there is no insistence on exclusive right of reason to rule ever appetite. He put emphasis on the free concord of appetite with reason. As per Sabine, this is brought about through the virtue of self-control of temperance which may be defined as law abiding disposition or a spirit of respect towards the institutions of the state and a readiness to subordinate oneself to its lawful powers. Thus in such ideal state of 'the laws', Plato proceeds from harmony between the different individuals. According to Barker, *"its unity springs out of sympathy. Issuing it does in sympathy, self control brings into a different atmosphere from that of the Republican atmosphere less here but human; less clear but also cold."* In his book "The Laws", he makes an attempt to trace the development of human civilization mark its stages, not the causes of progress and decay and by analysis of whole derive the laws of political stability, which the wise statesman will observe in order to direct and control the changes that beset human society. In 'Law', Plato does not provide for collective farming but insists on private possession and common use. Thus, he becomes practical.

The Republic and *The Laws*

Plato in his book "The Republic" offers a sound analysis of the most general principle underlying human society. In 'The Republic', his most original idea is of the philosopher King ruling without any restriction of laws, which he developed on the basis of Socratic doctrine of the identity of virtue and knowledge which led him to reject the democratic ideal of citizenship which was the very essence of the city state. In the 'Laws' Plato tried to make good his omission of law by resorting law to its proper place. Such a task required complete change of his psychology of the human mind and of his theory of knowledge. In the 'laws', he suggested a really careful analysis of actual institutions and laws and the attachment of such studies of history. He also suggested the principle of balance .... of a mutual adjustment of claims and interests as the proper means for forming a constitutional state ..... It was from these beginnings in the laws that Aristotle started, without abandoning the general principles stated in 'the Republic'...... he adopted almost in every case the hints thrown out in the laws, enriching them with more pains taking and more extensive examination of the imperial and theoretical knowledge.

Difference

Political thought of Plato as represented in the *Republic* and in the *Laws* is quite different. The fight of imagination which charms us in the 'Republic' gives way to realistic approach in the 'Laws'. It may be said "The Republic" is based on ideal but "The Laws" is based on experience and imagination modified by realistic approach. In 'The Republic' Plato starts with the assumption that government is purely a matter of scientific knowledge and it leads to confusion that the philosopher King as the enlightened despot, whose rule is best and highest. This leads Plato to ignore the necessity of consent, public and law because ideal ruler did not stand in need of these things.

Influence of Plato

Hegel's glorification of the state and monarchy and Fascist theory of the government and Roman Church with its emphasis on the infallibility of Pope, hierarchical organization and theory of education to clergy comes perhaps nearer to Plato's political thought. His thinking about communism did not exercise much influence but Prof. Maxey calls *'Plato Reddest of reds'* and Prof. Jazzi compares modern communism with the conception of Plato's communism in the 'Republic'. There are differences between modern communism and the communism of Plato but perhaps "The Republic" is the book which gives clear conception of communism and in a way of fascism also. As such according to Prof. Maxey, *"Virtually all socialistic and communistic thought has its roots in Plato, were he alive today he would be 'the reddest of reds."* He adds "It (Russian's communism) departs from Plato in too many important aspects .... Notwithstanding this, there is enough of Plato in Soviet system to evoke profound reflection of the deathless might of vital political ideas. Thus there are germs of communistic and socialistic thought in the thinking of Plato and so it can be said that his political thought affected communistic and socialistic theories in a modified way and his views on human inequality, opposition to democracy, liberty and support to powerful ruler asking to art to Fascist ideas. But the *Republic* had little influence of the thought of Aristotle, who is sharply critical of the concept of philosopher King who rules unfettered by laws. He criticised the communism of wives as well as communism of property most vehemently. "The Laws" exercised a far greater influence on Aristotle as well as on subsequent thinkers because it was more realistic and conformed to the Greek ideal of constitutional rule and participation by the citizens in the deliberative functions of the state. In 'The Laws' Plato put emphasis on law and the conception of mixed constitution for securing the stability the state.

The Laws exercised a profound influence of Aristotle and on other thinkers. He placed emphasis on sovereignty of law and brought about the conception of rulers as guardians of law and its servants. By saying that a man outside lawful state can either be God or beast, he echoes the conception of Plato as expressed in 'The Laws'. Aristotle is indebted to 'The Laws' for his theory of mixed constitution. Ideal state as depicted by Aristotle resembles to Sub Ideal state of Plato as stated in the laws. On account of this some scholars are of opinion that Plato's second best is Aristotle's best state. Professor Barker stated a large number of points in which similarity between the Laws of Plato and Politics of Aristotle has been shown.

The *Republic* influenced St. Augustine and affected the cononical theory of property and the organization of medieval church. Church put Pope above all akin to the conception of Plato's philosopher King and gave powers to clergy and considered others lower like Plato due to lack of knowledge of good. It also influenced Utopians like Sir Thomas More, political philosophers like Rousseau and thinkers like Green and Bosanquet etc. and other socialistic and communistic and to some extent Hegel and fascist thinkers, but the laws being a greater practical book influenced Aristotle and there majority of thinkers, who had scientific and realistic approach. Thus, thought influence of 'The Republic' is great but influence of the laws is probably far greater than the Republic.

Plato was a great thinker, his books *Republic, Statesman* and the *Law* are most famous books. He pleaded for rule of wise *i.e.*, of philosopher King. He preached of communism for ruling class and communism of wives for them and stated that women are entitled for sharing in all offices of the state. Thus, Plato propounded ideas of everlasting values. As such Plato is considered as one of the greatest political thinkers known to history.

During the days of Plato, Greek democracy has degenerated into mob rule where selfish man ran riot and can create disorder. Reins of Government passed to multitude and justice became the interest of stronger. Personal ambitions and factions prevailed in public life. Law and conventions gave place to licence and unfettered liberty. This mobocracy and execution of his teacher Socrates, affected adversely on the minds of Plato. Being an Aristocrat by birth, in democracy, he saw the ills of ruin of Athens. He confused democracy with rule and social dissolution. He believes that democracy means equality to equal and unequal alike. He believes that democrat is given to vain concepts. He mistakes modesty for silliness, temperance for unmanliness, equality for insolence and anarchy due to licence for liberty. He condemns liberty too much and says even horse and asses ..... are ready to burst with liberty. Plato forget that God or nature has created even a slave or produce class as a human being and to condemn them as beast is against the laws of God or creation. It is possible that man may differ in virtue, knowledge or capacity but to treat human being as a beast is a crime, against the humanity and God. Being born as an aristocrat he fails to realise the virtues of democracy. According to Prof. Jazzi *"this (Plato's) scheme would have been capable of realization only under the protection and violence of armed force .... of tyrant. How can such a person bestow-praise on democracy.* He says next to ideal state will be the establishment of private property, which will be divided by guardian class reducing others to slavery. The chief concern of guardian class will be war, as was the case in Sparta or during Rajput age in India. Such a state, he calls timocracy. Next will be oligarchy in which wealth-accumulates and men decay. In oligarchy wealth remains concentrated with a few men, who become richer on the cost of poor persons, who are reduced to abject poverty. But this breeds discontented and oligarchies are overthrown and democracy comes into existence as was the case with French revolution.

Everybody hails democracy as it as an age of fraternity equality and of liberty. He believes that people are not capable of self-rule, so freedom perverts into laxity and lawlessness, while equality makes good and competent equal to bad and incompetent persons. In democracy only way to rise and to gain power is to flatter and beguile the people. For this hypocritic class of politicians having a special talent of flattery and of deceiving people by false promises comes into existence. These clever politicians become the supreme in the state and exploit the people, while pretending to serve them. A person who is greatest trickster become the special darling of the people. He promises everything to everybody befools the public promising by remission of land revenue to farmers, higher wages to labours, land to landless, wealth to poor, peace, prosperity and honey to all. Thus, by befooling and cheating he comes to highest ladder and tries to brush aside opposition. Thus, Plato condemns democracy from the core of his heart and fails to realise virtue of self-rule, liberty and equality and fraternity. But this is true for others also Lenis came to power by promising land to farmers, employment to unemployed, peace to soldiers and bread and butter to all. To some extent same is true about Hitler.

The Hellenic and Universal in Plato

A thinker is affected by his social environment and some is true about Plato also to a great extent. He has based his ideas and institutions of contemporary Greek conditions. The superstructure of the platonic state is in general sympathy with

Lycurgean institution. He adopts the educational system of Sparta as his ideal. Similarly following the example of Sparta, he sacrifices the individual at the altar of the state and gives special statues to ruling class only. Similarly his ideas of men of silver and gold, recommencing military training for the youth including women, hatred of trade and usury, equality of sexes, exposure of weak children etc., are Spartan in original, even his conception of communism of wives is of Greek origin as during these days, wives were lent for state purposes. His constitution given in 'The Laws' is based on Athenian model. His condemnation of democracy is based as he saw mob rule in Athens in the name of democracy and execution of his teacher Socrates. He fails to be impartial and being an aristocrat by birth and thinker by profession, he glorifies both aristocracy and philosophy and condemns democracy. He even did not condemn slavery which clearly shows how much Hellenic he was in his conceptions.

Universalism

In spite of all this, his emphasis on education, his emphasis on emancipation and equality of women, his preamble to laws, his emancipation and distinction between civil and criminal laws, his constitutionalism and idea of mixed constitution has something to universal nature. He not only influences medieval institutions and thinkers but Utopian, Socialistic and Communistic an Idealistic thinkers were also influenced by his ideas. The profoundness of his philosophy, his idealism as well as practical realism and his grasp of fundamentals of life give him of high place for all times and places in spite of his Hellenic ideas.

Functional Specialization and Division in Classes

The Socratic conception that knowledge was virtue led Plato to specialisation of functions. His idea is based on the reciprocal needs of human beings and the necessity of division of labour because no man is sufficient in himself. He allots everybody, one special work or duty and expects that every individual and class should stick to it. He divides the population in the classes of appetite *i.e.,* producer, and armed soldier and reason *i.e.,* guardian class because he believes that harmony can be achieved if everybody sticks to his allotted duty. Theoretically it seem right but practically it makes a person's life stationary and forgets that division of classes may give rise to class wars. He condemns appetite class to permanent subjection which cannot be defended. Though he states that every city is divided into rich and poor class and natural corollary of it should have been to place the conception of classless society as Marx and Gandhi did. But instead of doing this, he divided the society into three classes which may further complicate the issue. He forgets that the common good of a state may flow by the co-operation by which people may make their mental and physical contribution for general welfare and not be perpetual subjection of one class, as such his view was lopsided.

His Ideas about Women

Perhaps Plato was the first effeminate, who gave equal rights to woman. He considers them fit to rule like men, a conception which is unique as except India and England, Israel, Ceylon and Philippine and France etc., no country has elected women as their Prime Minister or President. Plato was realistic and right on his conceptions. Some persons have said "The fact, that sex is not an isolated thing in a women's nature, and in which alone she differs from man; it colours her whole being or as Lord Byron states love for a man is side issue, but it is whole existence for a women and Plato condemns them to state duty or communism which is unnatural but they forget that women are as good rulers as men as recent events in England, Ceylon, Israel, France and in Philippines etc. women are still ruling." Moreover, on the laws Plato also provides with a tinge of domestic duties as his ideas as such his ideas about women are appreciable.

Plato was teacher of Aristotle and Sabine is of the opinion that Aristotle's ideals and principles stand upon the ground which he had clearly occupied because of his association with Plato. But both differ in all respects because according to Maxey, Plato was first Utopian and Aristotle first practical scientist. Aristotle opposes Plato's idealism and communism.

Aristotle defends possession of private property and even allows slavery as private property because he thinks that from hour of birth some are marked out for subjection, others for rule, Thus Plato and Aristotle differ with one another, so study of their differences require very careful study.

Both were great political thinkers but Plato was idealist while Aristotle was pragmatic and practical.

Plato and Aristotle are tow political thinkers who have put great influence in shaping the political thought or not only of Greece but of the whole mankind. Prof. Maxey calls *"Plato as first Utopian and Aristotle as first political scientist."* Similarly it has been remarked that virtually all the Socialistic, Communistic, Fascistic and Idealistic, thoughts can be traced to Plato and all Realistic, Individualist, Utilitarian and pragmatic thoughts can be traced back to Aristotle. There was fundamental difference in the social surroundings of these two, Plato was aristocratic by birth, thinker by nature and idealist by his conception, mystic, ascetic and Athenian, while Aristotle was as middle class professional man, a husband and a father and a practical administrator and tutor to Alexander, the Great. To quote Sinclair "we shall not then be surprised to find the political thought of Aristotle marked by such man. Platonic features as the value of family life, the pursuit of health and happiness, to use Jefferson's phrase importance and value of property, respect for public opinion and for the tastes and preferences of the man in the street above all his sense of possible, his conviction that one of aim at least of politics is, 'marking the best you have'. Circumstances make the man and social environment influence the thought of man. No one can think in vacuum. As the temperament and surroundings of these two thinkers differed, so their political thought was bound to differ. Aristotle gained his substance of political thought from Plato but due to different temperaments and background they differed because thoughts reflects image of man, as impact which fell upon the mind of a particular thinker. The Kalidas's Meghdoot carries message of Yaksha to his beloved, to Surdas's Gopies, it expresses the comparison of rain with theaters of Gopies. To Tulsidas's Ram Chandra clouds increase pangs of separation and to Shelley, these give another expression and thought. Thus, same thing gives different thoughts to different poets because reason follows the passion and temperamentally and psychologically each and every individual differs and this difference becomes vast when their socialistic and economic grounds differ. As such there is not much difference between Plato and Aristotle as he took thoughts from Plato but due to their temperamental and other differences their conceptions differed widely and Aristotle vehemently criticized many conceptions of Plato, some of which have been already mentioned and others may be given as below:

(1) Plato believed ultimate good is to be found in the ideal *i.e.* philosophy in universal forms. Aristotle based his thought on contrary assumptions that reality is not to be found in Idealistic or perfect ideas. He placed his emphasis on experience and observance which is called philosophy of individual experience *i.e.,* that one followed inductive and the other followed deductive method, based on observation, comparison and conclusion etc.

(2) Plato is imaginary, Aristotle is reactionary. Plato is eloquent and Aristotle is exact. From general concepts, Plato draws logical conclusion 'Aristotle slowly works from various facts but not final'. Plato paints a picture of ideal commonwealth. Aristotle provides the materials requisite out of which according to circumstances, model state can be constructed.

(3) Plato wants complete assimilation of individual in the state but Aristotle allows private rights to individual.

(4) Plato's outlook was literary but Aristotle's outlook scientific that is why Prof. Maxey has called 'Aristotle as a first scientist.'

(5) Plato was lover of Mathematics and he wrote *"Let no one devoid of interest in Mathematics enter here"* and mathematics deals with number and figures which are straight and fixed, so Plato thought of real world as consisting of eternal immutable and fixed archetypal essence of things. Aristotle was lover of biology which deals with the facts of growth or development. As such Plato's universe is static but Aristotle's dynamic.

(6) Plato was a master artist in the use of words but Aristotle is careless for style but places emphasis on meaning. Plato is poetical, Aristotle is philosophical.

(7) According to Prof. Borule, *"where Plato is set on constructing a planned state in the light of assumed principles and will often brush aside practical objections, Aristotle is constructing and testing his hypothesis by the facts."*

Some writers are of opinion that a thinking man is either a Platonist or Aristotelian. It means that two philosophers are quite opposite to one another. It is because of the fact that Aristotle criticised Plato very harshly and devoted Book II of the politics to criticise, Plato's 'Republic' and 'Laws'.

Aristotle complains that ideas of Plato are brilliant but too radical and imaginary to be realised in realistic world. To quote Aristotle, "Let us remember that we should not disregard the experience of ages; in the multitude of years, these things. If they were good, would certainly not have been unknown; for almost everything has been found out at although sometimes they are put together; in other cases men do not use knowledge which they have. Prof. Sabine remarks that *"Aristotle is the soberer, if less original genius."* Plato was imaginative and synthetic in his philosophy. Whereas Aristotle is master of facts and analytic. Plato liked metaphors and analogies in his philosophy whereas Aristotle was highly logical. Plato was deductive and when he borrowed the facts of induction, he incorporated them in his philosophy and made them organic part. But Aristotle utilized inductive method for illustration. In style Aristotle preferred rational explanation to metaphors of Plato.

Plato based his philosophy on ideas and ignored historical facts and imagined schemes of Government without much reference to actualities. Opposite to it, Aristotle put emphasis on facts, their collection and examination. He possessed thorough knowledge of political institutions of past and present and attached great importance to them. This is the reason that Plato's ideal state is based on myth, and reason could not find favour with him. Aristotle liked definite and scientific knowledge, so he favoured Plato's sub ideal state of laws. His biologist view can be treated back to his descent from a family of medicos and scientific interest to his early life at Sagire, where scientific culture of Macedon prevailed. Thus, Aristotle parted company with Plato where he noticed experienced is unreal.

Aristotle's Criticism of Philosopher King

Aristotle clearly distinguishes between the theoretical and practical exercise of reason which was not known to Plato. Due to this reason, Aristotle rejected the most profoundly original doctrine of Plato that states should be ruled by philosopher Kings. He divided science into theoretical, practical and productive classes. He considered Mathematics, Physics and Chemistry in theoretical sciences which comprehend the world of nature, Ethics and Politics in practical sciences, which study the working of mind and building, sculpture and painting in productive sciences. As per Aristotle "the prime qualification of a Statesman is not knowledge but practical wisdom which is acquired by ruling experience with the work handling men and their affairs" and not by study of Mathematics of Dialectics as supposed by

Plato. Politics or statecraft will enable a statesman to govern men in proper way, not theoretical knowledge. As such Foster remarks *"Aristotle's own treatise on Politics is work of just such practical reason. It is handbook for statesmen containing the wisdom as distilled as it were from the collective political experience of the Greek states."*

Aristotle's Criticism of Plato

Aristotle's criticism about Plato may be discussed hare briefly. Aristotle argues that the unity of state as emphasised by Plato would destroy that differentiation of function which is the law of nature. He says that such a unified state would destroy the self-sufficiency of the state as "The nature of state is the be plurality, and leading to greater unity, from being a state, it becomes a family, from being a family, an individual. As such attainment of greater unity would be the destruction of the state. He says "A unity based on the removal of all destruction in individual is fatal to the state just as identity in musical tones is fatal to musical harmony." He believes in the maxim that unity lies in diversity. He believes Plato's system of state would create perpetual disunity and discord; because of two diverse and antagonistic elements of educated guardians and uncultivated masses.

Aristotle is not fair in criticism of Plato, As Plato never sought to reduce the state to the unity of an individual. He provides three clearly distinguished classes and recognized the diversity of functions as such Plato's state is as diverse as of Aristotle.

Aristotle's criticism of uniformity applies only to upper classes of Plato and not to majority class for which Plato allowed diverse functions and interests.

Aristotle's Opposition to Plato's Communism

Aristotle criticised Plato's conception of communism very harshly. Plato and Aristotle both consider unity of state as desirable but they differ in its form and its method of achievement. Plato in order to achieve unity of the state desired to abolish family and private property but Aristotle desired to create unity in the state by educating the people in the spirit of the constitution. Aristotle puts emphasis on moderation, individual liberty and private property which are essential for development of individual's personality and for the benefit of the people.

Aristotle believes that common ownership of property leads to common neglect as every body's business is nobody's business. People pay most attention to their own property. In a system of common property those who work hard and get little will have a grievance against those who work little and get much. There will be no incentive for hard work because it is love of private property which turns sand into gold. Disputes in private property arise due to wickedness of men, but in communism these may arise also due to its very nature, as those who travel together and have a common purse come to quarrel, same may happen in case of common property.

Aristotle believes perhaps rightly, that sense of private property is a source of great pleasure as it is a form of self love. Private property can be used for charity, benevolence and for the benefit of humanity etc. It gives a man feeling of independence. If men are deprived of property, they will have no attachment which the people and hence will lose all interest. Property is essential to enable to perform their duties well. According to Aristotle personal attachment alone can develop sociable character. He advocates that property should be owned privately but must be shared on common and in this way, he secures the advantages of individualism and communism. Communism will upset the natural inequality of capacity and industry of individuals, Moreover, human selfishness cannot be eradicated in this way because it is inherent in the nature of man. It can be minimised only by properly educating the people to common use of their private possession. Denial of certain minimum of property will check the fullest development of individuality and will result in the impoverishment of the whole state thereby. Private ownership brings economic and moral advantage and common use following from private spirit produces that unanimity which is desired most; but he is against the accumulation of wealth beyond the need of good life. He wants to improve the institution of private property by proper custom and registration etc.

To Aristotle, Plato's communism of wives and children is unnatural and foolish. Plato believed that unity of state is best achieved when all the citizens say 'mine' and 'thine' for the same things *i.e.,* when all of them regard all children as their own and none of them has a separate private home. In this way a man will feel an equally high affection for all the children in the state. But

Aristotle is of opinion that this communism will not result in greater love for all common children but no love to any, because the sense of personal possession and exclusive relationship is the only basis of affection. If it is extending, it may be reduced to merely friendship. The children will be neglected because every body's business is nobody's business. He believes that it is far better to be real cousin than a Platonic son. In Platonic plan each man will have a thousand son and every child a thousand fathers. Public creche can be a poor substitute for the home and mother.

Community of wives means that every man's wife be the wife of every other man. Practically this may bring discord harmony and may give rise to jealousy Moreover, all the guardians cannot be in actual possession of one wife. Unknown relationship may result in unholy acts between blood relatives and even may create suspicion among them. Cousins are better than sons of Platonic conception.

It is to be noted here that perhaps Aristotle misunderstood Plato because Plato never contemplated nationalisation or socialisation of women of guardian class so that wife of very man may be the wife of every other man. Perhaps his aim was abolition of permanent marriage and provision for temporary mating between properly selected pairs. Such marriages have been described in ancient Indian literature as Niyogya or as Mutah in Arabic literature. Here it may be noted provision of divorce has nullified the permanent marriages. But persons generally did not resort to divorce proceedings, proves that human nature is more akin to Aristotle's permanent marriages than Plato's temporary marriages and even modern communism did not believe in communism of wives.

Plato thought family and property as source of evil and therefore sought to abolish them. But Aristotle found them deeply rooted in human instinct and saw much good in them. He rooted in human instinct and saw much good in them. He abhorred the idea of throwing the baby along with bath water. He clanged to the experience of ages and thought that Plato was too radical and speculative in his political philosophy to be a good guide in practical life. To Aristotle, the home and family is the great school of wisdom. The lessons learnt by the affection of parents in the family later extend to wider life of the society. Family is the natural unit of human life and private property a necessary part of social economy and this quality made him the philosopher of medieval world.

Criticism of Ideal State of Plato

Aristotle vehemently criticized the Plato's ideal state and says at times experience is better guide than expert knowledge. Plato believed in wisdom of few but Aristotle believed in collective wisdom and would like to give equal share to all citizens. Plato favoured philosopher King *i.e.,* enlightened ruler but Aristotle favoured constitutional rule because he feels that philosopher guardians can never be always altruistic as was supported by Plato.

Aristotle also criticised Plato for the neglect of overwhelming population of non-guardian class for which Plato did not provide education. Aristotle feared it may result in class conflict and mutual jealousy. But it may be noted here that Aristotle himself did not grant rights of citizenship to lower class in his ideal state by stating. *"From the hour of their birth some are marked out for subjection, others for rule"*, as such criticism of Aristotle did not carry much weight.

His Criticism of *The Laws*

Aristotle also criticised 'The Laws' of Plato on many grounds. He opposed the increase of warriors from 1000 to 5000 as it will make Plato's sub ideal state too large. He says that Plato should have defined the limit of population and amount of property. He objects that if other property can be four fold, why it did not apply to land also. He is of opinion that Plato's system of double election will transfer the power of election into the hands of clique. Plato mixed oligarchy and democracy and did not mix tyranny and democracy which are worst institutions. Plato believed in the ideal state of Republic and grudgingly accepted law to be supreme in his second best state as a concession to human frailty, but Aristotle believed that law is the product human progress by stating "The Law is reason unaffected by desire." He also pointed out to the neglect of foreign relations in the state.

Evaluation

Criticism of Aristotle is neither fair nor always accurate. His criticism of Plato's ideal state is unfair because it was Plato's ideal and not to be followed in practice. Ideal state is to serve as a measuring rod to judge their nature. Secondly Plato did not destroy differentiation as Aristotle thought but clearly emphasized for three classes in the ideal state. Moreover, his communism was meant for only guardian classes. Moreover, what Aristotle criticises, he adopts them later on as he says at places that great majority of men are natural dunces and sluggards, infanticide is to be replaced by abortion, offices should be resumed for the best equipped and so on. According to Sabine *"in his construction of the ideal state almost every subject discussed is suggested by the laws and there are many parallelisms (even, verbal) in small points."* As such now we may discuss influence of Plato on Aristotle.

To quote Prof. Suda, *"There is no doubt that Aristotle never misses an opportunity to criticise his master, and is more conscious of his difference than of points of agreement with him. These differences should not be allowed to minimise or conceal the great extent of what is common to them"*; and these differences should not bind us to see the indebtedness of Aristotle to Plato. It is true that keen intellect of Aristotle did not allow him to be blind follower of Plato and *accept his all teachings*. *But he made Plato's teachings as the main basis of his own thinking and developed them along the lives determined by his earlier biological studies and scientific temperament.* As per Will Durant, Aristotle says, *"Dear is Plato, but still dearer is truth."* To quote Foster, *"Aristotle is the greatest of off Platonist, that he is permeated by Platonism to a degree in which perhaps no great philosopher besides him has been permeated by the thought of other."*

According to Wayper, *"In spite of Aristotle's criticism, usually niggling thought occasionally trenchant of Plato, the difference between them is more formal than real."* C.E.M. Joad holds the same view, and he says Aristotle has a habit of starting and starting avowedly from positions which are anti-thesis of those of Plato and ending in conclusions which are scarcely if all distinguishable from these of his predecessor. Dunning states *"He (Aristotle) differs from his master Plato, much more in the form and method than in the substance of his thought."* Most of the thought which seems characteristically Aristotelian, are to be found in Plato. But Platonic expression of them is generally in the form of a suggestion or allusion or illustration, while in Aristotle they appear as definite clear cut dogmas, bearing an unmistakable relation to the general system of scientific doctrine. This contrast is rooted in the respective intellectual peculiarities of the two philosophers and in environment and in economic and social setup.

Similar Points

Aristotle's similarity with Plato has some background. He remained Plato's disciple for 20 years in his Academy and he was the head of Academy after Plato's death but Spensippus became its director and he could not succeed. According to Sabine, *"Every page of his (Aristotle's) later philosophical writings bears witness of this connection."* Both Plato and Aristotle were product of Hellenic civilization and commonly inherited the legacies of Homer to Socrates. As per Foster *"Both of them looked with alarm on the instability of Greek political life and on the moral anarchy which they believed to be its cause and both accordingly believed that the remedy lay in education for a better or living. Both believed that good life could only be lived in a city state of moderate size, could not be attained by all men but be those who sufficient schooling to do so. Both therefore wished to limit citizenship so as to make this possible and both thought it right manual labourer should be slaves or non-citizens."* Ideas of Plato and Aristotle were identical in setting up an ethical purpose as the chief end of the state and believed that real aim of the state should be moral improvement of its citizens and it ought to be an association of men living together to achieve the best possible life. They believed that the state alone is self-sufficing in the sense that it alone provides all the conditions within, which the highest type of moral development can take place. Both believed that man is social animal and state is necessary.

There are many similar points between Plato and Aristotle. Both are conservative and confine their ideal to the state as the basis of their political thought. Both are influenced by Athenian and Spartian outlook and champion the cause of oligarchy. Both oppose Democracy. Plato hated lower class and Aristotle defended slavery. Both are of the view that education should begin when a child is conceived. Both place emphasis on check of population by birth control and destruction of unhealthy children. Both are metaphysical in so for as they say that nature has made some men of gold, silver and copper. Both regard state as a moral and spiritual entity as they believe that "Good" is the ultimate end of the state although in case of Plato it is absolute and in case of Aristotle it is relative. Both are of opinion that Ethics and politics constitute a single and invisible science and their thought possesses ethical character. Both believe that the life which is worthy of man is a life of virtue and that it is made possible for an individual in and through membership of the state. Aristotle and Plato both oppose sophist and hold that state came into being for the sake of life and continues for the sake of good life. Both aim for the unity of the state but their methods differ. They equate state and society and give no right to individual against the state. Both plead against trade and industry and usury. In taking all knowledge to be his province Aristotle follows Plato and is a true child of the Academy. Both possessed encyclopedic knowledge and were giant philosophers.

Differences

There are minor differences between the two, because Plato was firm to his ideal to the end; but Aristotle was after ideals which he borrowed from Plato but modified as and when he tested them according to practical experience. This is the reason, that Plato is known as idealist and Aristotle as realist. According to Barker, Aristotle gives equal importance to women as Plato did and attacks Plato's ideal state but not his sub ideal state. This is the reason that Aristotle's ideal state is considered as Plato's second best state.

Plato and Aristotle, both give equal importance to education. In reality *"Aristotle was genuine Platonist in so far as he believes that the greatest need of the times was the proper education of the rulers."* As per Plato, education is the instrument through which the ideal of state can be realised. According to Aristotle thought it is not the medium but still it occupies a prominent place in his best average state; as he discusses very much about the place and importance of education in the best practicable state, though due to his death, it was not carried to its logical conclusion.

Aristotle borrows considerably from the Laws of Plato in constructing his ideal state. Plato stated in his laws that when men are without laws, they did not differ at all from the most savage beast. Aristotle states *"Men when perfected is the best of animals but when separated from law and justice, he is worst of all."* This is almost true copying. Plato come to conclusion that it is not possible to procure philosopher guardian so he supports law in state. Similarly Aristotle borrowed the origin of state from Plato as stated in *The Laws* that first, there were isolated families then villages and then came the state. The requirements of his ideal state, like the specifications regarding population in character, size, nature and situation are derived from *Laws*. As such though his ideal state differs from the ideal state of Plato as depicted in Republic but identical, a good deal with Plato's sub ideal state of law *i.e.* Aristotle's best is, Plato's second best. His remarks while introducing the best state are inspired by Plato's discussion on the physical, economic and social factors which govern the nature of state. Aristotle was influenced by 'Laws' of Plato and stated in any good state, law must be made sovereign and not any person whatsoever.

Plato condemns excess as dangerous and Aristotle is one of the exponents of the golden mean. Both state that man is a political animal and can only develop himself in the state. Aristotle's classification of the state is similar to that of Plato because the names of the classified states are the same even though the methods are different. For both individual and the state are complementary and not contradictory. Both possess aristocratic temper and Plato supports philosopher guardians and Aristotle limited citizenship and believed some are marked out for fabrication and others for rule and opposed democracy.

According to G. Grote "*the organisation of government proposed by Aristotle in the last two books on his politics, as representing his own ideas of something like perfection is incidentally profounded upon the Republic of Plato from whom he differs in the important circumstances of not admitting either community of property or community of wives and children. Each of these philosophers recognized one separate class of inhabitants relieved form all private toil and all money, getting employment and constituting exclusively the citizens of the commonwealth; the remaining inhabitants are not a part of commonwealth, they are only appendages to its indispensable indeed but still appendages in the same manner as slaves are kept.*" Grote feels that Aristotle's best state where he deviates from the *Republic* largely copies Plato's *Laws*.

Aristotle's best state is compromise between three things: a romantic Platonic aristocracy: a sound balanced feudalism; and some democratic ideas but feudalism was the best of it. With the democrats Aristotle requires that all citizens should have the right to participate in the government. But really it is not so radical as it seems because Aristotle at once explains that not only slaves but all members of producing class are excluded from participation in state affairs and citizenship. Thus he supports Plato that the working classes must not rule and the ruling class must not produce. As such he repeats his contention that *"the first principle of all action is leisure."*

Aristotle dominated the thought of Plato to a large extent. Somewhat grudgingly Aristotle followed Plato, his teacher as closely as his temperament permitted. As such he endorsed and systematised Plato's rationalistic theory of slaves, though in some minor points, he slightly mitigates Plato's theory of slavery and duly censors his teacher, Plato for being too harsh.

The only difference between Plato and Aristotle worthy of note is that Plato's approach is idealistic and that of Aristotle is practical. Aristotle believed that the prime qualification of statesman is not knowledge but practical wisdom, which is acquired by long acquaintance with the work of handing men and their affairs as such while Plato's *Republic* places best ideal state. Aristotle's politics places the wisdom distilled from the collective political experience of the Greek state. But view of laws and politics are to a great extent similar.

Evaluation

Under these circumstances it is remarked that Aristotle made a profession of Platonic philosophy and only systematized Platonism.

As per Zeller Aristotle *"can inspire us in the same way as Plato does.* "His work is direct and more professional than Plato's work. It may be said that *"in fundamental of his political philosophy, Aristotle was a faithful disciple of Plato." To sum up in the language of C.E.M. Joad. "in the end he (Aristotle) is found to have done little more than to dot the i's and cross the 't' s of the proposition, already reached by Plato.* "Lastly, we agree with Sabine that *Aristotle's theory of political ideals stands upon ground which he had clearly occupied because of his association with Plato."*

But both differ as Plato was idealist and Aristotle was pragmatic and practical thinker. Careful study of both is necessary as Plato is utopian and socialist and communistic thinker and believer in rule of Philosopher King and Aristotle is pragmatic and practical and defender of Private property and of aristocratic rule.

Chapter 3

Aristotle (384 B.C. to 322 B.C.)

If Plato wrote *Republic, Statesman* and the *Law*, Aristotle wrote lot of books but his book "Politics" is of everlasting value to scholars and students of Politics.

Life History

Aristotle was born at Sagira in Thrace in 384 B.C. and died in 322 B.C. He was not an Athenian but studied in Plato's Academy for about 17 years. He served as Alexander's tutor and then kept his school in the Lyccum for about twelve years. He was pupil of Plato and Tutor of Alexander.

Aristotle's father was a physician to the King of Macedon and Stagira where Aristotle was born, is situated on the Macedonian coast on the fringe of the Greek world. The culture of Macedonia was different from that of Greece proper and the Macedonians were not considered as true Hellenas as they were governed by Kings and did not live in city states which were republics. Culture of Macedonia was predominantly scientific while in city state politics dominated activities. Disposition of Aristotle to view things from the stand point of a biologist can be attributed to his descent to the family of medicos. Aristotle did not adopt his father's profession as the fame of the Plato's Academy caught his fascination and desire to get the best education attract him to Athens. Due to family background biology attracted him and this led Aristotle to develop the scientific methods.

Plato's Influence

For the age of 18, he joined Plato's Academy and remained there at about 20 years *i.e.,* up to the death of Plato in 348 B.C. Here he came in contact with Plato and other greatest scholars of Hellenic culture, who made a lasting influence over his mind. He had to leave the Academy after Plato's death because he did not succeed as its head and this honour was bestowed to Specussippfus. After clearing at Athens, Aristotle went to Asia Minor and visited the convent of Hermes and the Kings and also observed decadent despotism of Persia. He observed weaknesses of Persian rule and this observation enabled his pupil Alexander to defeat Persians. At Mytilene, he studied maritime and in 343, he became tutor to Alexander the great at Macedonia. In 335-4 he established his own school which became famous as Lyceum and he remained there for twelve years doing research work and teaching. In 322, after the death of Alexander he had to leave Athens as charge of impiety and nearness to Alexander and hostility to Athens was brough against him. Unlike Socrates, Aristotle Thought discretion as better part of valour and went to Chalcis and died after months in 322 B.C.

According to Foster, *Greatness of Aristotle is exhibited not in life but in his writings.*

EXPERIENCE AND KNOWLEDGE OF ARISTOTLE

During 62 years of life, Aristotle, saw ruin of Greek city states, rise of Alexander the great and other upheavels, so political fatalism appears in his writings which was due to historical events of contemporary world. The spirit which he expresses (at least) in his political works, is that of classical age of Greece which passed before he was born and he is a theorist of city states like Plato before him. But unlike Plato Aristotle was not pure theorist but he put emphasis on facts contrary to Plato. As such Plato is father of idealism while Aristotle is father of realism. According to Dunning: *He gave politics character of an independent science.*

His Method

Political studies became empirical or inductive in his hands because. The loved facts and limited his theory on careful and systematic observation of facts. It is said, he studied 200 constitutions before writing his Politics. Some writers are of opinion that the chief title of Aristotle's fame as a political philosopher rests on his employment of comparative method and it is one of his chief contributions of political science.

In addition to comparative method, he is also famous for laying stress on the importance of measuring their significance or value.

Thus he not only introduced comparative or historical method but also biological method which led him to organic view of state and to regard politics and ethics as one science.

Aristotle possessed great regard for tradition and as such he is reformer and nor a revolutionary in politics. In short, it can be said that Aristotle's method was determined by his empirical or inductive habit of mind, historic temper, respect for tradition and a general readiness to accept the verdict public opinion and so he differed with Plato in all these aspects. He championed the case of moderation. These fundamental differences forced many writers to remark that a man can be either Platonist or Aristotelian in his method of study idealist or pragmatic. As such Aristotle is regarded first known Political scientist.

Books

Aristotle wrote lot of books on theology, metaphysics, ethics, economics aesthetics, Physics and Politics etc.

Politics

Scholars hold opposite opinions about the worth of his book politics. According to Dr. Zeller, *it is the richest treasure that has come down to us from antiquity, the greatest contribution to political philosophy that we possess."* Similarly Prof. Boule, *declares that of all the books on the subject, (Aristotle's books) "the Politics" is the most influential and most profound. It is the book which must be mastered before all others*. But Dr. Taylor holds that no work of Aristotle is quite so commonplace place in the handling of so vast a subject.

Evaluation

The divergent opinions are due to character Politics to which arises from the fact that it is full of cross and references and there are abrupt changes. According to Barker "it is a collection of different essays rather than a single treatise." Some scholars are of the opinion that the *Politics* represents the rough notes prepared by Aristotle himself.

The *Politics* is available to us historically arranged in eight books whose order differs in different editions. It is probably an unfinished work in the form of knowledge and represents thought at work and not the finished product of thought as depicted by constant digressions. It is probably a justification of existing institutions like the slavery, the state and family etc. calculated to suggest the remedies for the ills of body politic of the city state. It covers a wide range of ethics, jurisprudence, law, justices, state, revolution and Political Science etc. It is spread over eight parts, but it can be divided into three parts. Book I, II and III give us Aristotle's view of the nature of the state, its origin and its international organization, Book II gives his examination of states and his Book III gives classification of states with a view to finding out the ideal state. As such it gives two constructions, independent of each other. Book IV, V, VI hanging together represent the first construction, explains the nature and classification of constitutions and also deal with political upheavals *i.e.,* with changes in states due to revolutions. In Book VII and VIII, Aristotle portrays ideal *i.e.,* the best book. Thus, it is a handbook for moralists and legislators, politicians and scientists. It deals with educational system also.

Critical Appreciation

To quote Jaegour "The Politics" represents two stages in the development of political thought of Aristotle, one part deals with the ideal state and study of earlier theories together with a criticism of Plato comprising book II, III, VII, and VIII. Book IV, V and VI deal with actual constitutions, their distinction and divisions, oligarchy, democracy and their sub-divisions, causes of decay and best ways of preserving them. They are more practical and less idealistic. Approach is entirely empirical and ethical considerations recede in background and even sometimes his approach is Machiavellian. Thus, his new and more general science of politics is 'an empirical study of its elements' both political and social, of actual constitutions, their combination and his object is both practical and speculative. He wrote *Magna Moralia,* the *Nicomachean Ethics.* The *Eudemian* ethics, the *Politics,* the *Colonies* and the *Constitutions* and lot of books on other subjects. His ideas about criticism of literature are still taught in M.A. classes of the universities. As such M.B. Foster remarked *"He was a master in almost every department of knowledge. There is probably no parallel in the history of mankind either to the vastness of his intellectual achievement or to the extent of his subsequent influence"* (in political theory). Dante calls as Guru of intellectuals. In the opinion of Author it can he said that Aristotle was one of the greatest political thinkers of the western world both as a pragmatist scientist and due to his vast knowledge and subsequent influence.

According to Dunning the capital significance of Aristotle is in the history of Political theories, lies the fact that he gave to Politics, the character of independent science. Similarly Maxey regards Aristotle as the first political scientist. As such Aristotle, not Plato is regarded as the father of Political Science perhaps because he was a realist and practical.

PLATO AND ARISTOTLE CONTRASTED

If Plato was idealist and preeminently a radical thinker, Aristotle was decidedly resist and conservative in his political speculation. Plato is Painter and artist and deductive thinker. Aristotle is scientist and realist follows inductive method. Plato started with abstract notions of justice and virtue and on the basis of these ideas setup an ideal state. Aristotle thought inductively by comparing the working institutions large number of city states actually existing in his time. Both differed in family background intellectual make up and differed in their reasoning process. Plato proceeded from the universal to particular and concrete to the universal. Plato holds the reality lay in the ideal *i.e.*, ideal of thing while Aristotle believed that it lay in the concrete manifestation of things. Aristotle thought himself as a systemize of already existing knowledge than as a founder of new philosophy. The reasoning of Aristotle is less imaginative and more logical realist, pragmatic and scientific than that of Plato and his speculations and judgements are probably sounder than those of Plato. To him politics and ethics are not so closely mixed as with Plato. Plato subordinated politics to ethics but Aristotle made Politics an independent science; so he wrote on poetry, ethics and metaphysics, on art and literature, on economics and politics, on physics and mechanics on astronomy and logic and no physiology and medicines etc. separately. He was a realist philosopher, so he paid regard for popular opinions and current practices and defended existing institutions of family and slavery etc. He avoids extreme view and placed emphasis on moderation and followed a middle path with pragmatic output. Plato was influenced by his teacher Socrates and aristocratic setup while Aristotle was influenced by his father's profession of medicine.

Differences

As such political philosophy of Aristotle is empirical and descriptive in comparison with radical and abstract nature of Plato's philosophy, so in spite of many reflections and certain inconsistencies; the central theme of his politics is moderation, golden means or balance. According to Catlin, *"After Confucius, Aristotle is the supreme Apostle of common sense and olden means."* Moreover, the digressions or confusions of Aristotle lead for the opining of new chapters in political science. He tries to reconcile ideals with actualities and in doing so he travelled far away from his master and denied the scope of political sciences and dealt with most of modern problems.

Theories of Aristotle are based on historical knowledge. He condemns Plato for paying insufficient attention to history and for imagining schemes of Government without due references either to the nature of human animal or actual form of Government. This shows Aristotle's deep knowledge.

Aristotle as First Political Scientist and his Contribution to Political Science

According to Sabine, *"the true romance of the Republic is the romance of free intelligence, unbound by custom and untrammelled by facts."* But Aristotle gave due importance to fact as his biological training and scientific studies made him a careful and systematic observer and as said before politics became empirical and inductive in his hands. As such he may be considered as the father of study of comparative government. In this way new method of first knowing the constitutional history and then arriving general conclusion is his great achievement. According to Sabine, *"Aristotle is the founder of historical method which has been on the whole sound; and the most faithful that the study of politics has evolved."* To quote Karl Fredrick *"He (Aristotle) was the first man in the world's literature who applied a deeply inductive experimental or comparative method to the diverse phenomenon of the state."* Similarly Maxey also calls him as first scientist. It is his one of the chief contributions to political science.

Aristotle not only collected facts but also stressed the problem of value and importance of ethical judgements. Aristotle judged the importance of the facts in terms of the end of purpose of the state because politics was to him the culmination of ethics. Unlike his idealist teacher Plato, he was the first realist in his political thought. While Plato argued in the imaginary world of dreams or of idealism. Aristotle dealt with reforming of actual. This is the reason that Aristotle was honoured with the title of father of political science and that honour was not bestowed upon his teacher Plato. His love of facts checked him from being too radical and remained confined to reformation as he believed that ideal must conform to actual facts. Thus he followed middle path and separated ethics from Politics.

Difference in Form and Method

Aristotle was descriptive and was empirical than Plato so he did not have the bold sweep and courage of Plato to destroy all that stood in his way. He is more cautious and moderate *i.e.,* to say he is reformatory and not revolutionary. As such he never completed his ideals state for which he proposed in book III because his ideals were sunk in the mid-stream of realities. Hence, Prof. H.G. Sabine remarked *"What all he wrote was a book not an ideal state, but on the ideals of state."* But in this way, he brought Plato's ideal down on earth and accepting his general view of proportion and harmony adopt it to the practical politics of the city state. This new line brought him rich dividend. This revolt against Plato opened new world in political science and made it independent subject.

Other Differences

To quote Maxey, who points out difference between them in logical way, he says *"As Plato is father to the idealist, romanticists, revolutionists and utopians of political philosophy, so Aristotle is father to the realists, scientists, pragmatists and utilitarians."* All who believe in new worlds for old are disciples of Plato, all who believe old world made new by the tedious and toilsome use of science are disciples of Aristotle. He adds "Where Plato lets the imagination take fight. Aristotle is factual and dull; where Plato is eloquent, Aristotle is exact; where Plato leaps from general concepts to logical conclusions. Aristotle slowly works from multitude of facts; where Plato gives us an ideal commonwealth that is the best which his mind can conceive; Aristotle gives us the material requisite out of which by adopting them to the circumstance, a model state can be constructed."

DIFFERENCE BETWEEN PLATO AND ARISTOTLE

Ideas about Rule of Law

A great drawback of Plato's philosophy is that it is cut up in two halves. In *Republic*, he supports the absolute rule of philosopher Kings unchecked by law or public opinion. But in *Law*, in his second best state, he realizes necessity of laws and public consent grudgingly. But Aristotle not only restores law to its proper place but also establishes sovereignty of the law in the state. He takes hint form Plato and puts emphasis on law by saying Man, when protected is the best of animals but when separated from law and justice, he is worst of all. He believes that in making of law, the collective wisdom is superior to that of even wisest rule. Aristotle supports law not as a necessary evil but as a mark of good state. Sabine says "Even the wisest ruler cannot dispense with law and because the law has an impersonal quality which no man however good can attain." The law is reason unaffected by desire of objective truth.

Constitutional Rule better than rule of Enlightened Despot

Unlike Plato who believes in the rule of autocratic philosopher Kings Aristotle believes in constitutional rule as constitutional ruler, rules over willing subjects because he rules through law and constitutional rules and regulations and not by whim or caprice of ruler or rulers. It is a rule in the public interest as against a personal or factional interest. Thus, he supports constitutional rule. Probably Aristotle was correct as historically rule of despot has been replaced by constitutional rule.

Aristotle Practical. Plato confined Political science to the narrow limit of ideal state but Aristotle widened the scope of political science by including study of actual states also. He holds that political science should teach the art of governing and organizing all types of states good as well as bad. He even discusses how the tyranny may be preserved. In his writings, he used inductive method. Aristotle defines and describes the features of various forms of government and gives the causes of their decay and the best way to preserve them. He not only divorced ethics from politics but as per Aristotle the complete art of statesman must take government as they are and do the best it can be the means it has. It might even divorce itself from moral considerations altogether and tell the tyrant how to succeed in tyranny. *"In this way widening of the scope, definition and political science is Aristotle's profound contribution to the subject."* Probably he was the first Political scientist who gave independent state to Political Philosophy.

View on Constitution

According to Aristotle, a constitution is an arrangement of citizens, or a kind of life. A constitutional form of government is the expression of the kind of life which the state is designed to foster. As change in form of government would signify a change in constitution or the underlying kind or life that the citizens are trying to realize. He is shrewd enough to observe that political constitution is one thing and the way it works is a different thing. A given form of government would work in a different way if a new class gains power. He observes that political structure of a state depends upon social and economic structure of society. He recognized the importance of influence economic and geographical conditions on political organisation and activity. In addition to it character of constitution and its actual working depends upon the way in which deliberative, judicial organs and magistracy are constituted. His views are Pragmatic while Plato's views are visionary.

Importance of Aristotle

His work contains many maxims of great value. For example, Man is political animal and state comes into being for the sake of life and it continues for the sake of good life etc. which though he borrowed from Plato but he gave them classical expression. He holds that purpose of state is to widen knowledge, promote virtue and secure justice for all and not conquest or making state rich by exploiting other nations.

Importance of Law

Aristotle puts emphasis on constitutionalism, making law sovereign and governments as the servants of law. These conceptions gave inspiration to St. Thomas, Richard Hooker, and Buarke etc. He asks and states that the main problem of politics is the reconciliation of individual liberty and state authority. Unlike Plato, he laid a stress on the value of public opinion and believed that masses are better judge, and not the expert and therefore masses should be the final judge, and not the experts' judges or expert bureaucracy. In short, he gave sovereign power to people to whom officers are accountable. He holds that aggregate value and ability of the masses are greater than a handful experts of law or experienced bureaucrats. He favoured a vague sort of democracy and believed that permanent exclusion the multitude form all offices is dangerous because it produces widespread discontent. Thus is comparison to Plato, Aristotle gives more rights to common people.

Views on Democracy

Aristotle hated democracy but he possessed keen insight about democratic setup and went to deep thinking of democracy; If he opposed democracy, he did it frankly and perhaps he was a far greater democrat than the modern democrats, who pay lip service to democracy and wield powers which even philosopher guardians of Plato may have never reached to those Olympian heights of cruelty, despotism and utter neglect of general public in the name of democracy. According to him, democracy is that form of government in which the poor who constitute the majority are supreme. It may be also defined as the policy based on the principles of civil equality and freedom. He holds that equality and of common man. He supports Elections to be conducted on the basis of adult suffrage or by lot or rotation without any proper qualification. In democracy tenure of office remains of short duration, so that all may get opportunity to share them. Thus, Plato believed in philosopher King but Aristotle gives final power to citizens.

Division of Power

Aristotle stated, deliberative, Judicial area and magistracy are the organs of the government which lead to similar conceptions of executive, legislative and judicial Montesquieu is indebted to Aristotle for his theory of separation of powers. He shows by his political insight the realisation of the influence of economics on politics. Aristotle conceived the conflict of exploiter and exploited *i.e.,* between haves and have not which been developed later on by Marx. His classification of governments and the discrimination between the various forms of oligarchy and democracy ultimately on economic backgrounds. Aristotle shows that prosperity and stability are secured easily in a state where extreme wealth on one side and appalling poverty on the other side did not exist and strong middle class exists, which avoids extreme path and follows path of golden mean.

Practical Wisdom

Aristotle's conception of forms of government are sound and even applicable today. His conception on revolutions shows his clear insight, and minute observation. He was in a sense forerunner of Marx in conceiving that conflicts are produced due to economic causes. He pleaded main cause of revolution is inequality and perverted ideas of justice. He tells us in detail about the causes of revolution and also suggests remedies, by which these may be prevented and in this respect, he was probably forerunner of Machiavelli. His thought had exerted a profound influence on medieval political thought and that of Christendom. Dante calls him as master of them that know. According to Dunning, *"The capital significance of Aristotle in the history of political theories, lies in the fact that he gave to politics the character of independent science, which he achieved by separating politics from ethics which were blended in Plato's thought."* As such Foster says *"There is probably no parallel in the history of mankind either to the vastness of his intellectual achievement or to the extent of subsequent influence."* His claim to be called first political scientist: Aristotle doctrine of golden mean is a precursor of modern notion of checks and balances. He refuted ideal state of Plato and his conception communism of wives property. He believes in the wisdom of masses or multitudes and as such he may be said father of popular sovereignty and also of individualism, because he is more individualistic than Plato. As per Karle Fredric, Aristotle is the founder of logic, political science and of system of scholastics. Generally he gave inspiration to conservative and aristocratic critics of egalitarian democracy, to the Olympian heights. Aristotle remained realistic and preached not for idealism but for best attainable. In short due to his keen, intellects he laid the founding of real political science and won the title of father of political science and he has been called as the first political scientist by Maxey. He is regarded as first known Political scientist by majority of Political thinkers.

Aristotle is of the opinion that the state is prior to individual as Man is a political animal destined naturally for political life. He states that state exists for the sake of good life and not for the sake of life only. Thus, Aristotle's ideas are very convincing and of everlasting value.

POLITICS NATURAL TO MAN

Aristotle came to conclusion that man is a political animal destined by nature for political life. It implies that state is a creation of nature and it is natural for a man to live in the state. He says man leading a solitary life can either be beast or a God *i.e.*, in other words that state is a natural institution and not based on convention as sophists supposed or as thought by contractualists later on such as Hobbes, Locke and Rousseau etc. It is strange that these thinkers based origin of the state on contract and not on natural origin as is supposed by Platos and Aristotle.

Aristotle like Plato believes that man cannot live a solitary life far from society. It is inherent in his nature to associate himself with his fellow being and form family and associations. As soon as man feels necessity to mix his fellow being and form association, necessity of state arises and state comes into existence. Thus both believe that state is necessary and natural for man.

Necessity of State

To meet the bare necessities of life that is of procuring food and protection of life in hunting or in agriculture, man requires help of other fellow beings. Neither hunting nor pastoral activities nor of arming, can be carried on by a lonely man. It requires assistance of others. Further God has created man and woman and their sexual instincts as well as desire of continuing their race, forces them to come together and to form a family. Without the association of male and female, neither there can be satisfaction of sexual instinct nor further continuation of race. It is natural that male and female feel pleasure in company of one another which they cannot feel in a solitary life. As such bare necessity of food and continuation of race forces human beings to live together and form association and as soon as contact with other human beings are formed, state comes into existence.

State Natural

Political Korimonia are an association of unlike persons who by nature associate together to satisfy their common social and economic needs, desires and racial instinct by mutual exchange of expression, love and goods and services. The association of male and female for perpetuation of the race and of master and slave or employer and employee for the production of subsistence, gives rise to family or household or economic organisation which has its social, moral or economic use. So long they are satisfied by bare needs, it may suffice for them. But when the urge to seek fuller life seizes the different households, they come together and form a city or state which is enough to be self-sufficing to meet their essential needs. It is in the family or household that three essentials to the building of a state originate and develop *i.e.*, fellowship, political organization and justice. As such state which comes into existence for the sake of life, develops and continues for the sake of good life. It develops as naturally as household or family. The instinct of association of human beings suggests the naturalness of the state.

Importance of Family

The institution of family is first foundation of state and it is natural because it is a expression of man's instructive life. In family, man learns the virtues of civic life and according to Plato and Aristotle for the development of good life, state is necessary because it provides all the conditions and the environment necessary for the development of moral life. According to Foster, "*The lower form of society, the village for example, proved inadequate, not only because they do not supply the needs of his animal nature, but also because they do not supply the needs of his rational nature. The latter can be supplied only in a political instinct, for example from purely economic society.*" Family is necessary as child learns his first lesson in family.

State is Necessary for Progress

To Aristotle, state is a kind of association of individual with a factional unity of varied and reciprocal parts made one by the pursuit of common aim in which their nature, their habits and their training all lead them all to join. In other words state is thought as an association of individuals bound by spiritual chains, about a common life of virtue, while yet retaining the individuality of separate properties and separate families. God or nature has made man a rational being and he has been provided with the faculty of speech and expression and benefit of mutual exchange of thoughts. Without the civilizing speech of expression, speech and organized association, man would merely be a brute and not a rational animal. For this purpose state is necessary and is prior to individual. A man can satisfy his moral and intellectual carvings, only through the medium of state and as such for the sake of good life and for the moral development of man, state is necessary. Man is a man *i.e.,* rational being only, it he lives in the state, because only in state man can make progress.

The state is natural in a sense that it is an institution for that moral perfection of man to which his whole being, or nature derives through various forms of society, only in state human being rise above the state and an isolated man is a like cripple who cannot make its proper development. Individual is natural, integral and organic part of the state and states is the end or destiny of human life. The state is a natural association for it develops from natural associations of family, household and village.

The Ends of State

Aristotle holds like Plato that man was essentially good, and function of state was to develop virtue and his good faculties. Unlike Green, he holds that the function of state is not only to hinder hindrances to good life but to play a positive part in the development of man. He believed that individual identity cannot be destroyed in the organise conception of state and states that the function of state is the promotion of good life and as such it is a spiritual association to develop a moral life. He holds that the state like individual must show the virtues of courage, self-control and justice. He stated as self-contained ethical society, the state lives the same life as the individual like him, it a acknowledges a moral law and like him it forces itself law of evolution. It has the same end, and it attains the same happiness in pursuing that end. He believes that there is not much difference between family, who stands in different relation with different classes. The household fulfils their physical needs, while state fulfills intellectual and moral needs of citizens. To Aristotle state is prior to man, and the state has no end other than the promotion of the happy or virtuous life of the citizens.... it is necessary for the development of human personality... Thus, according to Aristotle the state has the positive function of promoting good life and it exists for the promotion of virtue and noble actions. Fundamentally, it is a partnership of men for life of virtue and not for only removing hinderances or prevention of views. Thus state is necessary and natural.

Aristotle stated "From hour of their birth, some are marked for rule and some for subjection." He further remarked for that some should rule and others be ruled is a thing, not only necessary, but expedient. Thus, Plato and Aristotle both opposed democracies based on equality and liberty in different ways. But supported rule of philosopher King and by aristocracy with their arguments, so both require deep study.

His views about slavery: Thinkers like Antiphone and Alcidamas maintained that slavery is unjust because it exists by convention and not by nature and rule of master over slave is contrary to nature because nature has created all men equal. American declaration states "life liberty and pursuit of happiness as natural rights of human but Aristotle defends support and tries quite opposite to natural to defend slavery. Before proceeding further, it may be pointed out hare that historically Aristotle is quite wrong because history produces ample examples where Mamluks *i.e.,* Turki slaves ruled over Egypt and a slave dynasty ruled over India. Further Abraham Lincoln says *"if slavery is not crime, nothing is crime"* but passion follows the reason and so in his passion to justify slavery, Aristotle advances various Hypocritic reasons to defend slavery.

According to Prof. Barker, Aristotle believed that the constituent elements of the household have, three relations of the master and slave, husband and wife and parent and child. The fourth element is of acquisition. He believes that family property contains two parts — Animate and Inanimate; and slaves come with an inanimate property like tame animals and birds; He states that life is action not production, therefore the slave is a servant in the sphere of action. He went to defend slavery to extreme limit and says *"He (slave) belongs entirely to him (master) and has no life or being of his or own her than that of so belonging."* In a passion to defend slavery, Aristotle forgot that even slave possesses should and body like his master.

Aristotle's Views on Slavery

Aristotle unlike Hobbes and Lincoln and Rousseau etc., believes that man differ from each other in their physical and intellectual fitness. Those who are intellectually more advanced than the others, are designed by nature to leas others. The intellectual must control and rule the physical. He states to quote Maxey *"many persons are intended by nature to be slaves from the hour of their birth, they are marked for subjection."* He hypocritically holds that some men are of serviceable nature and are better off when they are ruled by other men. They lack capacity of self-determination which a ruling class must possess and some persons lack independent power of judgement so it may be presumed that nature has intended them for slavery. Not only this, but he also strongly holds that slavery is beneficial to slave because it enables him to share the virtuous and good life of master, he is, as it were brought up into and elevated by the life of the family. Aristotle states *"since then some are slave by nature and others free men"* so slavery is natural. He justifies slavery on the basis of theory of Natural Inequality, theory of aristocratic rule, racial superiority and theory of specific functions.

Aristotle thinks that slavery like family if village and state is natural as it enables citizens to get time for state duties. He holds that some are fitted to rule while others are fit only to carry out orders because men of superior intelligence rule the inferiors. He is of the opinion that the Greeks are superior to barbarians so are entitled to rule over others on the basis of theory of specific functions, he states "The function of the intellect is to order, while the function of body is to obey" so function of man of superior intellect is to order and of slave who is of inferior intellect is obey and this may cause mutual help and mutual benefit to both.

Criticism

Passion follows the reason and in defending slavery Aristotle is seeking a laboured justification for slavery in order to make free his fellow citizens from manual labour for providing material and economic basis on which the structure of family and state was to be based. To quote Maxey from dawn of state to the latest labour driver, assumptions of superiority have always been made by those, who live by the tail of others. Having the power to rule, they doubt not, that they are superior beings having a just right to rule. There is but one answer to such reasoning, and that is to be found in the logic of force and cannot be justified.

Further his conception of slave as an instrument of action and not as an instrument of production shows his arbitrary division and useless argument for slavery.

Aristotle's contention that only a person who does not possess virtue can be slave is false, because such a being is nowhere to be found. It is true that some persons have a greater capacity for virtue and others less, but it is absurd to think that nature makes some persons as four footed animal, so that they should be used as inanimate being; is nothing but sheer nonsense. Even for arguments sake, we suppose that God or nature did not endow some men with humanly virtue then how can it be judged. During Alexander's regime Aristotle may presume that others should be treated as slaves but when Turkey may conquer Greece, they may also use the same arguments for the justification of Greek slaves. As such arguments of Aristotle are baseless, partial, guided by self-interest and racial prejudices. His defence of slavery shows that he does not believe in racial, human or sex equality but in exploitation of man by man.

Arbitrary Division

Aristotle divides that human beings are two classes into master and slaves but this division is arbitrary as even slaves became kings and ruled over vast kingdom, then how such division can be justified. Historically changes take place and Greeks who were rulers became slaves during Roman and Turkish rule, so there is no criterion for this arbitrary division of human beings into two classes. Superiority depends on circumstances. History proves that the proud Greeks were subjugated by Romans and Turks. Romans subjugated English race and later on Romans were subjugated by barbarians, celestial empire of Chinese bowed to Japanese arms and Japan had to bow to America, which race or nation possesses superiority over others can never be decided except by force, which may bring even the extinction of human race now with the help of atomic destruction weapons.

Racial Prejudice

He holds that non-Greeks can be made slaves but why not Greeks? Are they endowed by nature with more eyes or hands than others? If, not, then there is no justification to make other slaves and it shows his racial prejudice. There is contradiction in his views. On one hand, he desires human treatment to slaves and at another place, he treats them as inanimate beings who cannot apply reason.

Illogical Reasoning

His contention that some persons are that by nature slaves is not convincing as nature has made nobody a slave and no one has been created as a slave as poet says:

"If we look through all the earth, Men we see of equal worth." He says that some persons are born to command and others to obey. But how can we know the persons, who are born to command. Moreover if this contention is to be believed then majority of the humankind will be converted into slaves.

Status quo

His defence of slavery is based on his conservative outlook of maintaining status quo and Greek superiority. Aristotle's justification is quite contrary to democratic notion of equality, liberty and fraternity and declaration of human rights by U.N.O. as such his justification is quite outdated in present setup.

Autocrats Exploitation and Disharmony

Permanent division of society in two classes *i.e.,* in exploiter and exploited class may breed class war and may cause disturbance and disorder and perpetual conflict.

Unnatural Distinction

Further Aristotle holds *"Nature ordains that the superiors should command and inferior should obey"*, but society is divided in many classes and modern division of society is very complex. In such complex hierarchy one may be superior to other in one respect and other may be superior in another respect, then to decide, that who should command and who should obey is a difficult thing to decide. His theory is inconsistent, unnatural, unjust and unscientific.

In the end we have to agree with Lincoln, *"if slavery is not crime, nothing is crime,"* because to degrade a man to inhuman level is a crime against humanity and God and nature, who created him as human being. All tyrants and believers of the inequality, take shelter behind Aristotle's in human ideas which brings untold sufferings to humankind so his views on slavery cannot be accepted.

According to Aristotle "The cause of revolution is always to be found in inequality but he suggests remedies and ways of preventing revolution. He states also many other causes of revolution in different types of Govt. and means to prevent them. As such study about revolutions is very important.

Aristotle's encyclopedic knowledge about the constitutions and government and of frequent changes lead him to think about revolutions and their causes and to suggest remedies to remove them. In book V (in some editions of book VII and VIII) he discusses these problems. His analysis of causes of revolution and suggestions to remove them, which are useful even now. As such, he has been considered as the founder of realistic-school of Political thought: and forerunner of Machiavelli and Montesquieu etc. The general trend from oligarchy and tyranny to democracy according to him occurs due to social and economic changes as a result of factional contest which occur on account discrepancy between the practical abilities of the different classes of citizens and the actual authority of the persons of ruling elite class.

He suggests methods of checking revolutions even to tyrants and comes near to Machiavelli and separates ethics from politics. His part I, deals with his suggestion to oligarchs, democrats, aristocrats, monarchs and even to tyrants as how to keep themselves in power while in part II he deals with the philosophic bases of good and stable government.

Aristotle's Conception of Revolution

To Aristotle revolution means a change in the constitution of the state whether great or small; or the constitution may remain unchanged but political power may change hands. In short, he deals with minor changes and excludes great revolutions like American, French, Chinese or Russian revolutions, etc. According to him even a revolution may make oligarchy more or less oligarchic or a democracy more or less democratic, thus according to Aristotle change of autocratic monarchy into a constitutional monarchy comes with in the preview of revolution. A revolution may be directed to change the form of government *i.e.*, oligarchy to democracy or may be directed to any particular person or set of persons without any change in the form of government. In short, he supports Hellenic conception which supposes every constitutional change was social and political revolution. According to Sabine, part of political which deals with revolutions reveals Aristotle's political penetration and mastery of Greek Government and Greek ideas.

Causes of Revolutions

Aristotle believes that dissatisfaction with the existing state of affairs, widespread or limited to small group is the general cause of revolutions. It may result in violence which may be suppressed or may succeed in overthrowing the present regime. He thinks that while diagnosing the cause of revolution following factors may be taken into account:

(1) The temper of those who make it.
(2) The motives of the revolutions.
(3) The cause sand occasions of revolution.

The cause or source of revolutions according to Aristotle may be found in one sided or perverted notions of justice that different men entertain. Corresponding idea of justice and morality differs with various governments. To quote Aristotle, everywhere inequality is the cause of revolution but inequality, in which there is no proportion for example a perpetual dictatorship. Among equals, it is always the desire of equality which is responsible for rebellion. As men desire equality and grudge against injustice that arises when only a few people possess privilege. Thus, the apportionment of political power is basic necessity for the security of the state.

Democrats put emphasis on equality and believe that men are created equally by God or nature, but oligarchess hold as men are unequal in wealth, ability and birth, so there should be proportional equality according to birth, ability or wealth. This difference of vital desire of the average citizens to have honour, gain, equality of opportunity and rights. As such stability of state depends on the satisfaction of this craving of equality, upheaval in proportionate equality is mainly the cause of revolutions. To avoid this, mixed form of Government containing both democratic and oligarchic elements is the best.

According to Aristotle inferiors' revolts in order that they may be equals and equals that they may be superior. Revolutions are often caused by gradual process but sometimes they occur suddenly and sometimes only due to trifling causes and sometimes failure to attach due importance to small changes proves fatal. Power corrupts a person or group and creates arrogance in one, and resentment in others. Efforts to combine dissimilar elements or people in a state cause instability and perpetual dissension. Admitting of disloyal and dishonest persons as officers of the state, who oppress public, also creates dissatisfaction and resentment and sometimes brings revolution.

Revolution may be caused due to (i) love of fame and honour, (ii) insolence, (iii) fear, (iv) contempt, and (v) undue importance of individuals. Terrorization on the part of rulers to maintain their office or power or privileges is a sure cause of revolt. Election intrigues debase the purity of government and bring about a change of some fine. Political differences friendship or dynastic and family feuds result in formation of factions which upset the constitution; Universal desire for privileges, and difference of outlook about interpretation of justice, liberty and equality, particularly in case of immigrant foreign races bring revolutionary changes sometimes. Notions of justice, liberty and equality are differently due to different selfish motives. To quote Sinclair, Since justice and friendship are the moral basis of the state, injustice and ill will are the most potent cause of discontent and instability. The absence of proportionate equality of a fair deal, leads to a lack of justice; and splits the city into two factions. There can be no fellow feeling when one section of the community is convinced that its rights are being denied to it and that justice is not being done to it.

Differences

The democrats oppose oligarchic rules because they think that undue privileges are granted to oligarchs and are denied to them. Similarly in democratic rule oligarchs complain that they are not allowed privileges, which they are entitled to possess on account of their superiority of birth, wealth or ability. These differences in conceptions of justice causes revolutionary temper.

Specific Causes

Aristotle also deals with the specific causes of revolution in different forms of government. Oligarchs are overthrown due to revolts against their aggressive rule or by rivalry and factions which leads them to play the demagogue. Revolutions arise in monarchy due to undignified rule or contemptuous behaviour of the King. Fears terrors and courts dissensions caused conspiracies against the throne. Tyrannies are generally overthrown by the influence of neighbouring state of a opposite character. Aristocracies, are over thrown due to jealousy caused by narrowly restricting power and honour of state to a limited circle and because of imbalances in different elements. Oligarchies are overthrown by the excesses and acts, who widen the differences between rich and poor and attaching the former individuality and collectively which results in combination of rich oligarchs against the popular Government.

He states long list of particular cause of revolution such as given below:

(1) Arrogance of rulers or ruling class.

(2) Universal craving for privilege and prerogative.

(3) Administrative inefficiency and corruption.

(4) Election intrigue.

(5) Universal craving for privilege and gains.

(6) Underserving importance to few.

(7) Assumption of undue power or privileges.

(8) Tact's of wrong doers in administration to foment trouble to serve as a smoke screen to hide their own misdeeds.

(9) Disproportionate increase in territory, economy and social setup.

(10) Contempt for public opinion.

(11) Disloyalty of administrators.

(12) Rivalry among ruling elite class.

(13) Dynastic and other feuds.

(14) Dissimilarity in elements in the state.

(15) Dissensions and rivalries between different races.

(16) Neglect of small changes.

(17) Free immigration of foreign races of different outlook and social setup.

(18) Struggle for power between rival parties and forces.

(19) Neglect and carelessness of ruling class.

(20) Inequality and injustice.

According to Dunning, *"He shows insight of discovering causes of revolution in social and economic sources,"* Maxey state, *"one or more of the factors enumerated by him will be found to have been among the provoking forces of virtually every political revolution of which history has any second."*

Prevention of Revolutions

Aristotle not only dealt with revolutions but suggested remedies to check them which may be summarised as below:-

Aristotle is of the opinion that to prevent revolution too much reliance should not be placed on devices to deceive that people. No one as a class should feel that it cannot hold power and no class of citizen should have monopoly of power.

(1) According to Aristotle best way to prevent revolution, is to preserve friendly atmosphere, to act moderately, to avoid extremes, to counteract dissatisfaction and not to wrong in the ambitions, in a matter of honour and for the common people in matter of money. Aristocratic and oligarchic rulers can give stability to their rule by wisdom and by keeping on good terms with their subjects.

(2) Aristotle believes that revolutions can be checked by inculcating the spirit of fairness and reverence of law both for ruler and ruled. Unlike Machiavelli he is of the opinion that it is unwise policy, for the ruler to rely on their capacity to deceive the people.

(3) Ruler should be ever vigilant and trouble should be nipped in the bud as soon as it may begin.

(4) He believes that political power should not be allowed to concentrate in one or few hands but honours should be awarded on the basis of distributive justice. Office or honours should be awarded on the basis of merit and no class should feel that it can never be in a position to acquire political power.

(5) Foreigners and strangers should not be given important political offices.

(6) The highest office of honour should be given only on consideration of the faithfulness to constitutions, administrative capacity, honesty and integrity of character, but each citizen should have his due.

(7) The best way to satisfy classes and masses is to give them honorary offices as it makes them to work for the benefit of the state without financial loss to the state.

(8) He feels that men are spoilt by the power, so he proposes that smaller offices should have long tenure and higher offices should

have a short tenure. This is followed even now and Presidents and Governors are appointed or elected for short tenure.

(9) Administration should be carried on in such a way so that office holders may not get chance of bribery and illegal gratification and of illegal gain etc.

(10) He proposes that access to power should be slow and gradual and no one should be allowed to rise in power suddenly, because higher offices require experience and mature judgement.

(11) To gain political stability and popularity, financial and administrative machinery should be open to public scrutiny. This suggestion of Aristotle is followed even up to now, as in America scrutiny is made by congress and in other countries by parliaments and by courts and commissions etc.

(12) In order to curb internal revolt and dissensions, threat of powerful external enemy should always be kept hanging so that internal situation may submit to the dictates of ruler. This suggestion was followed by Machiavelli and now nearly all government follow this suggestion. U.S.A. frightens public by fear of communism, communist countries of capitalist countries and China fear of U.S.A. and of other capitalist countries and of Russia. India projects dread of China and Pakistan projects dread of India. Thus most of the countries of the world project of fear of other countries to control internal trouble.

(13) Patriotism of people should be kept to extreme limit.

(14) The ruling group should keep unity and should not give rise to faction. This is a suggestion which has been observed more in breach as is case in China and was in Congress party of India and is in other parties of India also.

(15) Sound defence against foreign invader makes the Government stable and popular. As such most of the states are resorting to destructive weapons.

(16) Distribution of wealth should be closely watched as economic power affects the political power. This idea was deplored later on by Marx.

(17) In Oligarchies, the rights and dignities of poor masses and in democracy property and rights of the rich should be respected.

(18) He favours even restriction to private life of individuals such as friendship and marriages, if they lead to revolt. This suggestion was followed by Alauddin Khilji in India.

(19) Aristotle believes that Oligarchies and aristocracies should not grant concession in constitutions, so that it may be converted into democracies. Democratic and oligarchic spirit should remain within its limits and as such polity or mixed form of Government is the best because it avoids extremes. Stability can be maintained by giving to each his due by proportional equality.

(20) Tyrant should follow divide and rule policy; employ specially family spies, encourage quarrels and should keep people busy and poor. He should show devotion to religion and should punish through others.

Importance of Education

Finally, he believes to calculate loyalty among the citizens, education should conform to the constitution of the state. If citizens possess same education as constitution demands, they will be faithful to constitution and no revolt may occur. Thus, in suggesting ways and means of curling revolution, Aristotle is forerunner of Machiavelli.

Tyranny

In discussing revolutions, Aristotle preaches even to preserve tyranny and in suggesting ways by which a tyrant may maintain his power, he supposes even Machiavelli and keeps aside ethical consideration.

Aristotle holds that a tyrant maintains his power on the basis of vigilant watch over the unruly elements by an efficient system of espionage specially through women spies. He dazzles his public by his victories in war, so that the public may forget his cruel acts and mass destruction. It shows Aristotle's clear sightedness. Napoleon, Hitler and Czars of Russia and all dictators maintained their positions by diverting the attention of public to foreign glories. But it is a risky game and so Nepoleon, Czar, Hitler and Mussolini all were overthrown as soon as they were defeated and now dictators do not take such risks but maintain their power by giving illusion to public of popular election, in which dictator's party is always successful due to being in possession of the powers of the state as now state has become all powerful and persons in power are only to manipulate the elections. In order to maintain his power, tyrants create quarrells among the various classes of subjects. People are kept hard at work, so that they may not conspire. He destroys powerful and wealthy persons and takes precaution by all measures to prevent people from real knowledge and checks intelligent discussions. He keeps intelligence to lowest level, so that people may not think intellectually for overthrowing a tyrant. He shows fear of foreign danger or adopts other means to maintain patriotism at highest level by hook or crook. He creates imaginary dangers to keep people under his thumb and uses propaganda to keep himself in power.

Tyrant is disliked by men, who like liberty but slaves and women support him because they are benefitted. A tyrant should destroy intellectual life but he should improve material well-being. Tyrant should show favour to himself and his supporters but should punish others. He should be impartial both to rich and poor. Tyrant should appear to do everything for public good and show sympathy and concern to the people to gain the goodwill of the people. He should refrain from taking material gain due to his power and position. Tyrant should appear enthusiastic in service of good and in promotion of the arts and culture. He should clock his feeling and activities and self-confidence, behind the interests of state. Tyrants' friends should remain austere and wide awake as he may deceive them at any time. To quote Aristotle, Let his disposition be virtuous and if he must be wicked, Let him be half wicked only. All these ideas show his deep insight and perhaps all tyrants have used some of these ideas to maintain themselves in power.

Distributive Justice

According to Aristotle, distributive justice plays important part in the stability of state. Complete or absolute justice to him, means excellence in character which lies in conforming to laws. In narrower sense it means observing the rules of equity and justice. Particular justice contains corrective and distributive justice. The corrective justice mainly deals with voluntary commercial transactions like sale, hire and furnishing of security etc. Distributive justice means giving to all what is their due in form of wealth or virtue and in form of political rights etc. Every form of government has its own notions of justice. In democracy, it is based on free birth, in an oligarchy it is based on riches in monarchy it is based on birth or descent and in true aristocracy it is based on virtue. He says, in virtuous state, honours, offices and powers are assigned on the basis of virtue. An ideal citizen possesses wisdom, Military strength, property and efficiency in some particular direction. Distributive justice awards office, honours and other prizes according to social performance and contribution to society and prevents encroachment by one member upon the sphere of another.

He is of the opinion that offices should not only be open to virtuous few, but to all citizens. He believes people make contribution collectively and so should be proportionately rewarded. He prefers collective wisdom of people in electing and judging the office bearers than their appointment by a few, in such a system every class contributes something and thereby becomes entitled to some power. Stability required some supporters than enemies. He desired to reconcile principle of democracy with his philosophy of justice and thereby evoked a liberal constitution of present time. In short distributive justice assigns his due according to his contribution to the society and in proper allocation to each person according his to his worth or ability and importance. Thus, he favours Govt. based on law in which all citizens share some power.

Criticism

Aristotle's criticism of distributive justice is based on the conceptions of small city states and cannot apply to modern big states. His notion of distributive justice is based more on duties than on rights and he imposes duty of paying proportionate taxes. Similarly his conception about revolution is outdated as now revolution cannot occur except by faction within the ruling party as public is quite helpless before atom bombs etc. In spite of all this, his conception of state in which power is shared by all classes and his ideal of koinonias of fellowship and golden mean etc. are important.

According to Aristotle "The more perfect the admixture of political elements, the more lasting will be the constitution. He avoids extremes and sticks to principle of golden mean. This may be considered conservation of today. He concludes control by middle class is best. Thus, Aristotle propounded ideas which are relevant even now.

Aristotle Aims for Life of Virtue and Happiness

Aristotle holds true happiness is more after found with those who are most highly cultivated in mind and character and have only a moderate share of external goods. Then among those who possess external good to a useless extent but are deficient in higher qualities. Thus Aristotle believes that the best and happy life for state and individual is having enough external goods for performing good action. He subordinates politics to ethical purpose, and refutes the views that power is good in itself on which politics is conducted. He states War like pursuits, though generally deemed to be honourable are not the supreme end of all things but only a means and good lawgiver should enquire how states may participate in the good life. He believes that peace has her victories no less glorious than war and true ideal of people and state is to gain life of virtue and complete happiness.

Best Government According Aristotle

In discussing about the best form of Government, Aristotle comes to conclusion that a political institution, must correspond to the character and needs of the people concerned as such ideal state can be possible only in ideal conditions and best state should be ruled by absolutely by virtue. If one man is of pre-eminent virtue, form of state may be royalty. If few, it may be aristocracy which are the best form of Governments. But it is difficult to find a man of pre-eminent virtue or a few selfless men of pre-eminent virtue, so taking into account the frailty of human nature as it is, he favoured a vange form of moderate democracy.

After studying about 200 Constitutions become to conclusion that same type of state cannot be best everywhere all times. As such, he classifies states as which is the best absolutely, according to ideal but which can be attained, and attained actually by men and which is the best under a particular set of circumstances. Leaving aside the first type of ideal state, he discusses about the state which can be actually attained according to circumstances and conditions prevailing at that time. Aristotle assumes golden mean as criterion of goodness besides Plato's theory of virtue. In human beings excess of wealth make people haughty, arrogant and unsubmissive while extreme poverty makes people slavish; degrading and submissive and unable to oppose tyranny. The arrogant rich knows only how to crush the masses and submissive poor people know how to work slavishly? In a state where there is extreme poverty and richness, there can be no real state as there cannot be friendship between the two which is essential principle of Politics so he suggests the principle of golden means to avoid extremes. It is to be noted here that Sanskrit proverb also says that extremes are to be avoided and he comes to consultation that best government is that in which middle class is stronger than either or both of the extremes. The middle class people neither plot against others, nor are they plotted against, and they pass their tenure of life peacefully and give stability to the state. Thus, he favours rule of middle class.

Aristotle believes that stability is the touchstone of the best state. Democracy in which poor dominate is tolerable, oligarchy due to superiority of talent or power is better but polity where middle class rules, is the best and superior to all the rest. In such a polity the citizen have a sufficient property and moderate ways of living. He desires that maximum number of people should participate in public life as he wishes that all the citizens of state should have civic virtues. Political knowledge high moral and intellectual qualities as against Plato's small number of guardians. Such constitution is his average or best attainable constitution.

Classification of States

He prefers state in following order (i) Ideal monarchy, (ii) Pure Aristocracy, (iii) Mixed aristocracy, (iv) Polity, (v) Most moderate democracy, (vi) Most moderate oligarchy (vii) The two middle or medium varieties of democracy or oligarchy and (viii) Tyranny.

In Aristotle's preference though polity comes fourth but he calls it as best a practicable state. This show that unlike Plato he was aware of human weaknesses and selfishness, he did not long for philosopher Kings but makes a realistic approach. He believes mixed constitution brings stability and harmony, happy balance of oligarchic and democratic elements of quality and quantity. The oligarchic elements in polity bring prestige of birth, wealth status, education and experience while the democratic elements strengthen it with numbers. He desires to give balance of power to middle class, who may be more intelligent than masses and may not work for the vested interests and may keep welfare of masses in view. He wished something like platonic arrangement, yet he desired to give some power and functions to all for which than may best be suited. Like Plato, he believes that rights and duties should be proportionate to qualifications but yet he favours to give chance to all classes in participation of Government to keep practical balance to check extreme. He desires to check in the cycle of political changes in his polity which according to him goes on with endless chain of succession. Thus he favours mixed government with check and balances in which middle class gains upper hands.

After discussing about forms of the best which are best under different circumstances, he discusses about population, territory, topography character of the people of city states and so on. In this discussion he also follows his formula of golden mean. In his ideas he was greatly influenced by setup of Greek city states.

1. Population. Aristotle holds that there must be certain minimum of population to make the state self-sufficing but he does not lay down maximum or minimum bumper. He says population should be such so that citizen may know each other and may elect right persons. This conception of Aristotle points out he inclination towards city states.

2. Territory or size. He states that size of state should be neither too large nor too small; it should ensure a comfortable but not luxurious life. Size should be small enough to permit the holding of periodic assemblies for deliberative purpose which may be known at a glance. He believes for the best state personal knowledge and personal intercourse with one another is necessary, so that unity of purpose and interest may be maintained. The territory of state should be difficult of access to foreign invaders but easy of checking enemy. It should be on the bank of sea to encourage important but not to near so as to encourage foreign trade or sea adventures. To Greek mind big empires were foreign to their conception and Aristotle confined his thoughts only to city states thought Alexander whom he taught, created first world empire in western countries.

3. Character of people. For characters known to history, Aristotle take Greek virtues as model and state in character and ability state should resemble Greek who combine the spirit and heroism of northern races and intelligence of ordinates.

4. Classes in the State. According to Aristotle necessary classes in the state are agriculturists, artisans, warriors, wealthy people priests and administrators, to make itself sufficing. He is not in favour of granting rights of citizenship to agriculturists and artisans but to all other classes, he allows citizenship. Land should be in the possession of citizens see top perform different function in different periods of the time according to laws. They should fight in army in their young age and should work as administrators in old age and should work as priests in a very old age. Thus he gives importance to age and experience like other thinkers of ancient times.

5. Education. Like Plato, Aristotle believes virtue is teachable and he places emphasis on education. He believes that tone of society and character of people to a considerable extent depends upon education which cultivates, intellectual, moral and physical excellence and enables a citizen to do his duties efficiently. He prescribes a system of uniform, compulsory and public education which is more cultural than practical.

6. Other things. He mentions other things about his best state as best means of defence against foreign attack, water supply, to topography, fortifications and arrangement of streets and communications etc. He believes that popular assembly for deliberative work which should be composed of all citizens and to whom the ultimate decisions of government must be submitted, and a system of magistracy *i.e.* executive body and a system of judiciary is necessary. In this way he is forerunner of three organs of Government. This idea was developed by Montesquieu and is followed in U.S.A. and in many other countries.

He believes in extreme democracy in which all the offices are open to all citizens endangers the stability of state. To minimize this danger, polity in which minimum property qualification may be prescribed is the best because it will bring the rule of middle and stability. He desires reasonably, equality of property rights between the citizens. He disfavors all aggressive ware because the ideal of state should be virtue and not power. State should possess the capacity to achieve and infuse virtue in citizens.

In short Aristotle's best state is secure form attack possessing golden mean the superiority of middle class, devoid of desire for territorial or trade expansion, homogenous, virtuous and cultured, unambitious community, self-sufficient but not aggressive, independent and medium size ruled by a true aristocracy. He places emphasis on law in his ideal state and refutes that laws and morals are matters of convention. The features of the ideal state of Aristotle tally with the ideal of best state as depicted by Plato in his *Laws*.

Criticism

(1) Aristotle's conception is guided by the ideal of Greek city states and did not conform to modern great states like U.S.A., U.S.S.R., China or India etc.

(2) He did not mention about actual governmental machinery in his ideal state.

(3) He leaves subject of education unfinished.

(4) His ideal of states failed to save Greek city states form ruin and his ideas of small states cannot be accepted now.

(5) His book remained unfinished so his conception about ideal state is incomplete.

In spite of all defects, he gave us ideal of democracy and of mixed constitution bases on rule of law and on checks and balances and is founder of three departments of state *i.e.,* legislative, executive and judiciary. He forms a precedent upon which to a large extent rests modern system of Government of U.S.A. models emphasised on middle class rule, based on rule of law, as he thought law is reason unaffected by desire. Thus he is founder of many conceptions which are still followed in modified.

Aristotle thinks perhaps rightly that the virtues of citizens are relative to the constitution. According to same writers his views are conservative as he defends slavery etc. In spite of all this, it has to he accepted that he was a very great thinker and his views on citizenship, property and family are valuable and realistic.

Book III of the *Politics* deals with the fundamental question of Aristotle's idea of citizenship. According to him, state is an assemblage of citizen. He believes that neither descent nor legal privileges make a person as citizen. Aristotle believes that a citizen is a person who participates in the administration of justice and in legislating as a member of the ruling body. As such citizen is a person who takes part in the administrative, deliberative and judicial organization of state, In Greek states only those persons who took part in deliberation, magistracy and administration of justice were called citizens. Thus he favours direct democracy of Switzerland type and did not believe in the myth that people who did not possess right of any kind of participation are citizens.

Citizenship

According to Aristotle essence of citizenship is that he must be a functioning member of the state and not only a adherent or dumb follower. Thus main qualification of citizenship is to rule and to be ruled in turn. To Barker Citizenship is not determined by residence or by rights of private law but by constitutional rights under the system of public law; a citizen is one who permanently shares in the administration of justice and in the holding of office. He excluded labourers and mechanics from citizenship because these people due to their dependent nature cannot develop the capacity is to rule. According to him an essential qualification of a citizen is to have property to ensure leisure, *i.e.*, economic self-sufficiency to make him free from cares and worries from the necessities of life, to give him time for proper discharge of duties of citizenship. Manual work degrades the soul of a man and makes him unfit for political speculation and discharge of civic functions. He did not allow workers' rights of citizens, because they neither possess capacity nor ability to discharge civic functions.

Criticisms

(1) Aristotle's conception of citizenship divides the states in three hostile classes *i.e.* citizens, non-citizen and slaves, antagonistic to one another.

(2) His conception of citizenship can only be applicable in city states or in direct democracies and not in representative governments or in modern vast government like China, India, U.S.A. and U.S.S.R. etc.

(3) Aristotle did not present views about rights and duties of citizens.

(4) It is said that conception of Aristotle about citizenship is too narrow and unsuitable for modern age.

Conclusion

The greatest criticism about Aristotle's conception of citizenship is too narrow but these critics forget that by citizenship, Aristotle means power to participate in deliberative organization or in judicial functions and if such high notion of citizenship is taken into account then modern citizenship is most narrow because only a few judges and members of parliament can be called citizens. For example in a country where a family who enjoys heredity,

Prime ministership, and supreme court judges and members of parliament and Secretaries or high officials rule with the help of Police and draconian laws can only be called citizens and all other non-citizens. While Aristotle excluded persons who did not possess power to participate, now all voters are considered citizens, then of course citizenship becomes wide but it an empty boast because it possesses none of the privileges granted by Aristotle to citizens and in a country where booth capturing is a rule right of vote means nothing. Thus, struggle for office and power and terrorism prevails now where ruling elite class only enjoys power.

Aristotle's View about Family

Aristotle believes that family is an institution established by nature for the supply of every day wants. It is natural outcome of the sex instinct and impulse for self-preservation and self propagation: It is essential for economic security and well being of the association. Family is not only a biological and economic term, but it is indispensable school of human affection. The child is not only nourished by the mother and looked after by father but child learns his first lesson of love and affection in his home. He says let us remember that we should not forget the experience of ages. However he provides social control.

Unlike Plato, Aristotle did not hold that is the household unit. In State there is only one relation of ruler and ruled but in household there is relation of husband and wife, parent and children, master and slave and these relations are quite different, from the relation of ruler and ruled. In family affection dominates and so mostly welfare of all is kept in view but in state mostly ruling elite class enjoys all benefits.

In the end, Aristotle emphasises for the need of property as or family.

Property

Aristotle defines property as the stock of inanimate instruments necessary for household. His definition of property as stock of instruments means that it is necessary and indispensable for the proper functioning of the household. To quote, Maxey *it is nature's own way of assuring that wants, where in that to live.* A man needs food to keep himself alive, clothes to protect himself and house to live and all these things come within the limits of property.

Nature or God himself has equipped man with the instinct to acquire property and as such private property must exist. Private property is necessary for a person to lead a comfortable and dignified life.

Aristotle is in favour of property but he wants to limit it to the extent that it may be sufficient to satisfy minimum wants and as such he fovours property to a certain limit only. Private property spurts a man to greater activity and efficiency and for new ventures.

He values money as a means or instrument for good life and did not value possession of money as an end in itself. He agreed with Plato and Christ that excessive love of money is root cause of all evils and disfavoured placing of system of production and distribution in the hands of those, who operate it for the sake of profit. But vehemently criticized idea of common ownership because he believed common ownership of property leads to common neglect and it is only magic of exclusive possession that turns sand into gold. For him property is source of great pleasure as it is a form of self-love and of self-esteem, respect and dignity.

He values property essential for the development of generosity, literary enthusiasm and hospitality and as such essential for the development of moral and virtuous life. He believes that private property is a mirror in which an individual finds himself reflected. Private property enables a man leisure to think and contribute something to civic life. Not only this Aristotle goes a step further and even defends unequal distribution, of property but confines this difference to a limit so that it may not create antagonistic class and may not result in class war. In short he favours property to enable a family to lead a comfortable and dignified life, but dislikes extreme poverty and extreme rich capitalist class.

He believes that private property gives pleasure to all men and women. He is of opinion that private property develops the art of managing people which is useful for the state. Thus in short, Aristotle favours limited private property to enable him to develop virtue and make himself self-reliant and self-supporter in all civilized states including Russia and China etc., to lead a decent life. As such right to private property has been granted as basic fundamental right all over the world.

According to Aristotle "The law is reason unaffected by desire, so his views on sovereignty of laws, constitutions and their classification are very important. He supports rule of law because he thinks law represents body of rules which have been determined, beyond the passion of men."

Aristotle defines constitution as the arrangement of the offices of state determining which of its members shall hold different offices, especially the highest; it is a plan or scheme in accordance which government is carried. In short, it exphasizes that the constitution makes the state and the nature of the ruling class determines the nature of constitution. As such according to Aristotle constitution is not merely a legal bases of state structure but it expresses the whole of the national life. It is a way of life of its citizens, it is the ideal for the realization of which citizens are united in the forming of a state. It is true that Aristotle attaches utmost importance to constitution but it is not an exaggeration, as is proved by revolutions of America, France, Russia and China etc. Where whole structure of society has changed with the change in constitution. In India where Constitution is based mainly on 1935 Act, only change that has taken place is that Indians have replaced a few Britishers who help previously most important offices.

CLASSIFICATION OF CONSTITUTION

His Distinction between State and Government

Aristotle was first to point out distinction between state and Government. State was the assemblage of body of citizens, and Government consists of those citizens who help the supreme political power of the state *i.e.,* they execute and perform the political or ruling function. Govt. may change with the change of those, who help highest offices but state only change with the change in constitution, as after Rajiv Gandhi, Indian Govt. has changed but constitution is same.

Sovereignty

Aristotle was of opinion that sovereignty lies into elective government. He is one with Dicey, who says in England parliament is sovereign because it can change anything without the concurrence of any other authority. He believes that sovereignty should go to most virtuous. To Aristotle, location of supreme power in the state is very important consideration. He believes that the aggregate value and ability of a part of that mass. It may be possible that the majority of the citizens may not be able to give judgement on the technical details of administration, still they have enough commonsense of deciding to whom they should delegate political power and authority to make laws. They possess enough commonsense to choose their rulers and bring to book to those who misbehave. As such he is vaguely in favour of giving ultimate sovereignty to citizens though persons work may be carried out by the best administrators and talented. Thus, he favours sovereignty of people and gives ultimate power neither to parliament as in England nor to Supreme Court as in India or U.S.A. but to people.

Sovereignty of Law

In order to prevent the abuses of sovereignty of people, he placed above it sovereignty of laws. He favoured laws because he holds law represents the body of rules which have been determined beyond the passions of a man. It represents the rule of reason and it is based on traditional wisdom, so it gives stability to the state. As law represents the practical wisdom and experience of ages, so it is essential for proper conduct of man and for the proper working of governmental machinery. By law Aristotle did not consider law as 'will' of the sovereign or rules promulgated by ruling elite class to perpetuate its rule but practical experience and wisdom of ages and rule of reason. He discards the conception of Plato who prefers rule of philosopher Kings and supports law as unfortunate necessity. Aristotle gives preference to law and as such, he is the first man to defend constitutionalism and is forerunner of St. Thomas Acquinas, Holles, Hobber, Locke and Burke and Montesquieu, Colnes Marshall and Dicey etc.

Usefulness and Importance of Law

Aristotle believed that men not only require proper training at an early age but the watchfulness of perpetual discipline throughout life, in order to be kept within the bounds of morality and virtue. No amount of moral exhortation will suffice to enable a common man swayed by passion and self-interest to restrain and control himself, to curb a man's selfishness and passion coercive legal authority is necessary. The brute in a human being cannot be prevented and kept under control merely by pious and moral teachings, it can only be controlled by fear of punishment. The fear of law in said to be the beginning of wisdom. Man only listens advice or reason in shape of law because it is supported by force. A judge or king or ruler is more easily corruptible because he is liable to be swayed by prejudice, greed, passion and lust for power or sex. Law cannot be corrupted because it is passionless. The passionless authority of law does not take place of a magistrate, but it gives to magistrate's authority, a moral quality which it could not otherwise have.

Plato said man acting legally is best of all animals when separated from law and justice, he is worst of all. Subjection of law leads to perfection of man as such Aristotle stated life in subjection to constitution is not to be regarded slavery but as the highest welfare.

Classification

The Government in a state could be constituted on the basis of (i) birth, (ii) wealth, (iii) number. A monarchic government based on birth suffers from the defect that one ruler may be most wise and efficient and benevolent but his son or successor may not inherit these qualities as generally it occurs in history. Ashoka was great king but his successors were incompetent, same is true of Lous XIV, Harsha, Harain UI Rashid and Alexander etc. Their empires banished as soon as they closed their eyes due to incompetence of their successors. A Govt. based on wealth may not be good as wealth is no criterion of a man's moral or intellectual talent and efficiency. Third basis of number is better than the two because wisdom lies in multitude and it is easier for a single man to err than for numerous persons to make a mistake. However Aristotle classifies government based on number who hold sovereign power and on the basis of the ends or ideals in view. Whether it is for general welfare and good or corrupt and for selfish motive of rulers.

Efficient or moral form	*Corrupt form*
1. Monarchy with supreme virtue as its guiding principle.	1. Tyranny representing force, decent and selfishness.
2. Aristocracy representing a mixture of virtue and wealth.	2. Oligarchy representing the greed of wealth and selfish motives.
3. Polity representing martial and medium virtues, power resting with the middle class people.	3. Democracy representing the principles of equality with power in hands of the poor.

To Aristotle's monarchy, representing the rule of one man based on hereditary succession for common good; and tyranny is its perverted form. An ideal person who may create rule of philosopher King or Rama Rajya is not easily available even if such a man may be available then it cannot be true for his successor. Who, over it may create luxury and arrogance and it may be used for selfish ends and not for common good. He recognizes five kind of monarchy *i.e.* Spartan type, oriental hereditary, disposition old heroic guardian. Aristotle's difficult to be realized as in human nature selfish motives gain supremacy over motives of common welfare and as such aristocracy degenerates into oligarchy. Polity is government of all, for the good of all, but as poor persons are always more numerous than the rich, so polity gets perverted into democracy which to Aristotle means rule of the benefit of poor. Aristotle considers polity having mixed form of Government and supremacy of middle class as the best rule. Here it may be noted, Aristotle by democracy meant direct democracy, as such his ideas did not apply to modern representative democracy. Aristotle holds if a rule is by more than one man, wealth is the deciding factor. Aristocracy always degenerates into oligarchy in which rich persons rule for their own benefit and polity degenerated into democracy in which poor persons rule. Aristotle believes that in a state four elements always struggle for power *i.e.*, (i) Birth, (ii) Virtue, (iii) Wealth and (iv) Liberty and it depends on efficiency of the group in which only determined and efficient persons succeed. Here Aristotle lays emphasis on economic factors and efficiency and capacity and will power of the ruling elite class.

Cycle of Change

Aristotle believes in famous cycle order according to which Governments are not static but dynamic. Every form of Government change but history is a very complex phenomenon, so changes do not follow any set rule any fixed manner. So conception of Aristotle that change is inevitable law of nature is correct but his conception that monarchy changes into tyranny and tyranny into aristocracy and aristocracy into oligarchy and oligarchy into Polity and Polity into democracy is not correct. As due to French revolution monarchy changed into democracy and Czars tyrannic rule of Russia changed into communist rule of Lenin and Stalin or in Indian rule of British Imperialism changed into dynastic rule of Nehru family. Thus, complex changes take place in historical process. Various forms of Govt. such as parliamentary, Presidential, Federal or unitary or Imperialistic rule or communist rule etc. were not known to Aristotle, so his ideas about fixed change of circle cannot be accepted.

Criticism

(1) Aristotle did not regard democracy as good form of Govt. but now it is regarded as best form of Govt.

(2) Many forms of Govt. such as constitutional monarchy, Dictatorship, Totalitarian Govt. or one party Govt. such as of Fascists and Nazis were unknown to Aristotle, so his classification is unsuitable to modern age.

(3) It is wrong to say that Democracy is Govt. of poor people in U.S.A. and in capitalist democracy bourgeois and in communist democracy workers rule so Aristotle's conception does not apply either to capitalist or to communist democracies of modern age.

Evaluation. Aristotle is pioneer in the classification of states and to great extent his observations are important and relevant even now.

Plato's ideal state is idealist, difficult to be realized but Aristotle's state is pragmatic but it does not fully conform to Plato's ideal state so it is second best state.

According to Barker in his old age Plato realized frailty of human nature and his imaginary of philosopher King gave way to state based on supremacy of law. Constitutionalism or supremacy of rule of law a forced conclusion on Plato due to weaknesses of human nature and he considered such state as second best state.

But to Aristotle state based on law is an ideal state and as such there is similarity between Plato's second best Aristotle's best state.

1. Law. The first resemblance between the second best state of Plato and ideal state of Aristotle is regarding law. Both believe it, as a necessary condition for moralized and civilised life. In conception of law, Aristotle goes a step further than Plato and supremacy of law is accepted by him as a work of good state and not merely as a concession to frailty of human nature as supposed by Plato. To quote Sabine *"even the wisest ruler cannot dispense with laws because the law has an impersonal quality which no man however good can attain because low is passionless reason unaffected by desire."* Both believe when perfected man is best of all animals but when separated from law and justice, he is worst of all. Thus, both put emphasis on law and favour state based on rule of law, but Plato gives first preference to a state managed by Philosopher King and second preference to a state based on law while Aristotle prefers state based on law.

2. Communism. It is true that Aristotle vehemently opposed the communism of Plato as stated in *Republic* but Aristotle supports views about property as stated in *Statesman* and *Laws*; in these books Plato speaks of common ownership but recognises private ownership of property. Aristotle also recognises private ownership of property to a limited extent only to enable a man to lead a moral and comfortable life and for the sake of lust of possession only. Perhaps like Plato Aristotle would also like common meal because eating together would promote stability and integrity of the state, but Aristotle discards communism as propagated by Plato.

3. Effimism. Plato and Aristotle both favour uplift of women and allow education to women. In Greek city states women did not possess equal rights with man but both thinkers went against Greek conception and favoured emancipation and equal rights and education etc. for women and favoured their participation in public life. Keeping in view of ancient days, their ideas are very progressive in comparison to Manu etc.

4. Ethics. Both of them believed in an ethical purpose as the chief and of state. They believed that real purpose of state is to achieve the best possible for its citizens. The state above is self-sufficing as it alone provides all the conditions within which the highest type of moral development takes place. Thus, both believe not only in necessity of state but consider it necessary for good life.

5. Education. Plato and Aristotle both believed that virtue is teachable and put emphasis on education. The main function according to them should be a scientific course of education designed to cultivate moral intellectual and physical excellence in its citizens forth proper discharge of the civic duties. A system of compulsory, uniform and public education is the first necessity of an ideal state. They believe that education should conform to the ideal state. They believe that education should conform to the ideal or ideals or constitution of state. It is meant for leisured citizens for developing moral and mental culture rather than professional or practical utility. They put emphasis on physical training and on character building virtues etc. Emphasis is laid on gymnastic and music because the former helps in bringing beauty, grace and symmetry in the body and later in producing a sound mind.

Plato gave more space to education than Aristotle but according to Sabine Aristotle was unable to devote much space to education due to his premature death. However, both favour education to inculcate virtue and to fulfil their duty to state.

6. Ideal of City States. Plato and Aristotle both confined their ideal to Greek city states only in all details. In spite of the fact that Aristotle saw a great empire created by his disciple Alexander but he remained unmoved and clanged to city states as an ideal. Both favoured small states based on participation of citizen.

7. Democracy. In statesman and laws Plato favoured mixed government consisting of the principles of monarchy and democracy. Thus, though Plato condemned democracy due to poisoning of his teacher Socrates but in the end gave some support to democracy and this support in spite of condemnation of democracy by Aristotle was given to a greater extent by Aristotle and Plato. He favoured the maxim that wisdom lies in multitude, and supported a vague form of democracy. He favoured a constitutional rule in which government is based on consent and for the general welfare. Thus though both of them criticised democracy but both showed some inclination towards it. However, Aristotle was more inclined towards democracy than Plato.

8. Similarity in details. Ideal state of Aristotle resembles to second best state of Plato in details. Both say that state should be a agricultural and propose Assembly council of elders and magistrate etc. in identical language and terms.

9. Exclusive citizenship or Aristocratic temper. Both opposed aristocratic temper and desired to give rights of citizenship to upper class and leisured class. Both excluded agriculturist and appetite class from citizenship while Marx favoured them. None of them gave rights to slaves and non-citizens.

10. Classification of a State. So far classification of states is concerned views of both Plato and Aristotle are identical in second best state of Plato and ideal state of Aristotle with minor differences here and there.

11. Direct participation. Plato and Aristotle both mean by citizenship direct participation in the affairs of the state. If direct participation in government affairs in considered as real citizenship then only legislatures and high officials and judges come within the preview of citizenship and about 99% population of India comes to the conception of no citizenship, a conception which may give rude shock to all concerned. Now a days there is clamour for Govt. service in India because Govt. servants are rulers while people are dumb driven cattle.

12. Slavery. Both considered leisure necessary for citizenship and as such they were unable to guess about a state without the existence of slavery. Plato kept mum but Aristotle went even to the extent of defending slavery. Their views about slavery cannot be accepted now when U.N.O. has declared human rights.

Conclusion

Ideas of Aristotle's ideal state resemble to Plato's second best state. Plato was speculative and Aristotle was practical, so there are minor differences. But on the whole Aristotle's best state is similar to Plato's second best state.

Plato seeks a superman but Aristotle seeks a super science which will create a state as good as can be, so he prefers state leased on law so how states are generally based on constitutional law.

Plato and Aristotle are the two leading and great thinkers of western political philosophy. The former has been called first utopian and the latter has been called as first political scientist by Maxey. Dunning calls *Republic* of Plato as a work essentially brilliant a romance consisting of series of brilliant metaphysical where in politics has been incidentally discussed. Sabine calls *Republic* of Plato as a romance unfettered by laws and custom. Plato believes ideal is the real and ideal state constructed in the Republic is meant as model for all times and for all places. He gives the ideal of the state without worrying much about the practicability of the ideal; thus, Plato is theoretical while Aristotle is practical.

Comparison

According to Sabine, *Aristotle is soberer, if less original than Plato.* He has an empirical and practical approach and always keeps in mind about practical realisation of his ideals in realistic world. His central theme is golden men, balance, moderation and reconciliation. According to Maxey Plato can live out conceptual commonwealth to conform with the absolute perfection of his dreams because he sees human nature as infinitely plastic and infinitely perfectable, but Aristotle sees human stature as plastic only within the orbit of its inborn potency and perfectable only to the extent of its ability to build on things as they are. As such Catiline states after Confucius of China, Aristotle is the supreme apostle of common sense and golden mean. As such Aristotle has been considered as first Political Scientist.

Plato's Ideas

Plato is mainly deductive philosopher and used inductive facts casually due to frailty of human nature. He believes that the ideal can be reached by rational man. He desires to development to achieve the ideal through education. He believes through education in ward eye of the individual will fully Understand the inner sight and will attempt to achieve the ideal of good. He did not realise that and is passionate being and passion follows the reason.

Plato believes that persons differ in natural aptitude and ability and human nature is composed of three psychological characteristics called reason, spirit and appetite. He divides society on, these three bases and holds in guardians, reason, in military, spirit and in workers and artisans in which appetite will dominate. He comes to conclusion that ideal can be achieved, if power may be bestowed to philosopher king, who possess reason but he fears that they may spoil the whole show due to selfish motives of benefiting their family and hoarding wealth. To avoid this, he proposes that philosophers should not be allowed to have family and private property. Here it must be kept in mind that even in Indian philosophy, Brahmans and saints and Muslim fakirs and Jain monies etc., are not allowed to keep property and accumulate wealth but to lead an ascetic life of devotion to God and man. As shrewd observer Chanakya says that if a Brahmin strives for hoarding of wealth and remains unsatisfied, he is ruined, though common ownership has never been proposed by Indian Rishis and sages.

Aristotle was a pragmatic and empirical thinker so his approach is different. He also desires to attain an ideal state like his master Plato but after studying about 200 Constitutions and being aware of about frailty of human nature, he confines himself to best attainable constitution. He comes to conclusion that extremity in all things as such he had supported, golden mean and proposes, a state in which middle class may dominate. But Aristotle aware of human weakness, so he makes his middle class to rule according to laws. Thus, Aristotle supports sovereignty of laws unlike Plato whose supermen, *i.e.,* philosopher king is not featured by laws. According to Wayper, *"He began that method of observation and of deducting general conclusion and actual practices, which has, as it were anchored political thought to earth. His interest in politics is concerned with the best in good in existing circumstances, his conviction that we must take state ss they are, and do the best as we can with them."* His belief that political thought must combine a knowledge of political good and a political mechanics, his insistence on the value of law or disembodied wisdom his realisation that some constitution would not grow in certain soil, all played a great part in the development of political thought. Aristotle favoured golden mean. His motto was that we should not aspire for ideal but must make the best use of abstract ideal, to be translated into reality by philosopher king, who will sweep away all existing institutions and genetics and education to create a new and better race of men in a perfect social order, Aristotle builds fabric of materials already existing, thoroughly tried, well understood and laws for use by any intelligent statement who dares to try his skill moulding them into practical, the ideal to preserve and, strengthen that state. Yet both thinkers display the same ethical order, the same passions for order, the same law for moderated the same devotion to justice and reason, the same confidence in education, the same faith in humanity and same concern for the realisation of good life.

Criticism

Pepper and some others accused Aristotle for vulgarising political science. There is some truth in this as Aristotle was compelled to be realistic because he had to earn his living by drafting constitution for innumerable city states that came up like mushrooms in his times. Here we came across with the truth of Marx that method of earning livelihood decides thought, so Aristotle moulded his attitude to earn his livelihood, but this made him practical and pragmatic thinker.

To quote Sabine, *"In originality and boldness of speculative constructions, he was by no means equal to Plato and the underlying principles of his philosophy, were all derived from his master (i.e., Plato)."* In the power of intellectual organisation especially in the ability to grasp a pattern or a tendency in vast complicated mass of details, he was not only superior to Plato but the equal of any thinker in the later history of political science. According to Prof. Bowle, the philosophical premises are similar to Plato's but Aristotle does not argue about them; where Plato is set on obstructing planned state in the light of assumed principles and will after brush aside practical objections, Aristotle is constantly testing his hypothesis is by the facts. In the words of Maxey *"As Plato is father to the idealists, romanticists, revolutionaries, and utopians of political philosophy, so Aristotle is father to the realists, scientist, pragmatists and utilitarians."* All who believe in a new world for old are disciples of Plato; all who believe old worlds made new by the tedious an toilsome use of science are disciples of Aristotle. As per Sinclair main quality of Aristotle is sense of possible his conviction that one half at least of politics is making the best what you have. Plato seeks a supermen and ideal which in not realisable, but Aristotle being a realist seek super science which may contain wisdom of ages and may guide the path of state, to best idea attainable under the circumstances. Probably he favours Govt. based on rule of law of mixed type which he calls polity based on domination of middle class and rule of law.

Chapter 4

Greek Political Thought after Aristotle, Epicureanism and Stoicism

(Zeno, Crates, Aristippus)

With the decline of city states, Greek Political thought also declined. Plato and Aristotle were giants of political thought but after them, Greek political thinkers were pygmies but to continue chronological order their description is necessary.

Change is the inevitable law of life. Nothing is stable in this world. Greek's power reached to its Zenith with Alexander the great, who created a world empire. Similarly Greek political thought reached to its Zenith with Plato and Aristotle who were the most learned and best champion of philosophy of city states. Conception of a thinker and even of a country change with the change of political social and economic circumstances and its political setup and environment.

With the decline in Greek glory and power there came the defeatist philosophy of Epicureans and cynics. According to Sabine, Failure of *Plato and Aristotle to influence the insecure future was their magnificent failure.* But it was natural, philosophy of Plato and Aristotle was the philosophy of proud race who despised others as barbarians. In the arrogance of power, Aristotle totally forget humanity and supported slavery as natural and beneficial to all with the decline of Greek power, Greeks themselves became slaves of Romans and as such it was natural to Greek thinkers to put emphasis on equality rather than on naturalness of slavery as such change in political thinking was logical and natural and according to environment.

When a man or country possess nothing to boast in deals or glory, it finds solace or consolation in sensual pleasures or in religion. It is the human nature prevailing everywhere. Later, Moghuls were unable to boast about victory so they gave themselves entirely to sensual pleasures. They left all is beauty and forget their duty. Some is true of Rajputs as paintings of Khajuraho depict to what extent sensual pleasures captured the mind of these Rajas, who vulgarized even temples, Roman pleasures are proverbial and even glorious British empire went to the same path as according to Bernred Shaw, in Britain every man is after money and every women is after marriage. Thus, no country escapes form changes and during glorious days it captures arrogance and in declining period, philosophy of pleasure *i.e.,* epicureans and of universal outlook etc., *i.e.,* stoicism and finally, religion as a last resort of solace.

With the decline of Greek glory negative altitude was in the logic of history, so it is difficult to agree with Carlyle, it was a sudden change but it was a startling change in which whole structure of thought changed, that cannot be denied. During glorious days Greek identified state with good life because slaves and workers and agricultural class worked and they enjoyed life. But now glorious positions and highest offices were available to Romans and not to Greeks, so both Epicureans and Stoics preached for individual good and self-satisfaction instead of self-sufficiency and good of state. As highest offices which bring happiness to life were not available to Greeks so they paid attention to individual happiness. Thus Greeks thought changed according to environment.

Impact of Alexander's Empire

With the creation of Macedonian empire of Alexander the great, which was followed by Roman empire; narrow philosophy of Greek city states was not possible. Plato and Aristotle's philosophy of ideal of citizenship of a city state was replaced by the ideal of citizenship of the world. To quote Gettel *"universalism and individualism replaced city patriotism."*

With the disappearance of city states, public offices lost their charm as in a great empire only a few commanded and others had to obey. Under these circumstances, Epicureans and stoics have to search happiness in ideals of personal character and private happiness in place of devotion to the city state. They diverted their attention towards ethics and religion.

Cause of Decline of City States

Plato and Aristotle treated slaves, foreigners and even agriculturists and artisans with contempt and excluded them form citizenship. Their support to give rights of guardianship to woman was an attempt to disguise and to keep ruling power confined to the narrow circle of guardian class. As guardian class was small, so they allowed women to participation in the affairs of the state. Majority of the population among whom neither man nor woman were given office were bound to develop an attitude of indifference towards the city state. Without the support of majority of population, no state can be stable, so ruin of city states was hidden tin the every pages of the republic of Plato and Politics of Aristotle.

Rise of Stoicism

Aristotle defended slavery and considered Greeks, superior to other races. But this conception was impracticable for Alexander, who created a world empire. It was not possible for Alexander, either make all persons to whom he conquered as slaves or to treat with contempt, the rulers to show he made alliances, so he had so mix Greeks and Orientals and had to develop idea of common citizenship and to refute slavery. Idea of equality of men under an universal law, give rise to stoicism.

Impact of Big Empires

Rise of Alexander gave rise to Roman Caesars, the Papacy and Roman empire of the middle ages. With the change in atmosphere, philosophy of city state was bound to change. Narrow ideal of citizenship and conception of Greek superiority yielded to the ideas of universal brother hood and to the conception of equality.

Foreigners flocked in Athens and this affected outlook and culture of the city state and instead of narrow outlook Greeks had to open eyes towards an open world state. In this way, Epicureanism and stoicism etc. came into existence.

Rise of New Ideas

Failure of philosophies of Aristotle and Plato gave rise to Epicureanism and Stoicism or Cynicism. They derived ethics from politics and preached for vigorous political life as advocated by previous writers. They both championed the cause of securing the happiness of the individual. They both claimed to have derived their ideas from Socrates. This period was of building of civilisation and one of empire building but not of political speculation. As such this period is devoid of any great political philosopher as Sautner regards Epicureanism as philosophy of escape.

Epicureans who followed motto of eat, drink and be merry. To them, Government was based on individual self interest and law as an agreement of utility. They were succeeded by Stoicism, who possessed cosmopolitan outlook and believed in equality and liberty.

The two schools of thought *i.e.,* Epicureanism and Stoicism which developed after Aristotle were fundamentally philosophical in character. These thoughts were individualistic as they inspired individuals to seek self-satisfaction and individual happiness. It was unrealistic in outlook as individual had to learn to live with others in a brotherly and social atmosphere. Stoicism developed conception of law of nature and is more important than the former. They taught suppression of the emotions and the subordination of immoral desires to the demands of reason.

EPICUREANISM

It was founded by Epicureans at Athens in about 306 B.C. and may be said development of Cyrenaicism which was established by Aristip-us, who claimed to have derived it from Socrates. Epicureanism taught that highest end of life was the attainment of the greatest amount of pleasure or happiness and interpreted happiness negatively to mean absence of worry, anxiety and pain. This could be achieved by making oneself independent of state. As such Catlin remarked that Epicureanism is philosophy of free will.

The Epicureans believed that society is based on selfish interest, in which each person seeks his own good which usually conflicts with that of others. As the selfish good of one person is endangered by the selfish pursuit of another so they enter into tacit understanding of neither inflicting harm nor suffering injury. Thus, in their philosophy we find germs of famous social contract theory. They believed that the state and its institution are based on expediency. Law is to be obeyed if it secures peace and order and facilities intercourse and happiness. They preached obedience to any form of Government which may bring peace and security and happiness.

They believed in the Pope's poem, which states:

For forms of Govt. let fools contest.

The government which governs best, is best.

As such they cared least for forms of Government.

But showed preference to monarchy.

In short their aim was greatest happiness to be achieved in life. Up to the time you live, happily. Drink Ghee even by taking loan. Because this mortal body cannot be got again. Thus they preached the philosophy of *"eat, drink and be merry."*

They based government on individual self-interest and defined law as an agreement of utility. According to Sabine for individual men, it was source of Peace and consolation.

STOICISM

It influenced Roman political thought and remained most influential from 300 B.C. to 200 A.D. It declined with the rise of Roman legal ideas.

Stoicism was founded by Zeno about 300 B.C. who was Phoenician and one of his parent was Semitic. He was pupil of Crates, who was leader of cynic school as such it may be considered as development of cynicism.

Like Epicureans, Stoics also believed that the aim of life was to achieve human happiness. But while Epicureans desired physical and sensual pleasures, stoics advised pursuits of intellectual pleasure based on reason and not on feelings. They were on par with basic concepts of cynicism of perfect self control, independence of circumstances, self sufficiency and life according to nature. They developed the concept of law of nature based on reason and cosmopolitan outlook.

The concept of nature is the central theme of their political thought. In order to live the best life man must be one with mankind. All men are equal and so men should lead a free life based on reason. Thus Stoics believed in liberty, equality and fraternity and can be said forerunner of these concepts.

In their view life according to nature meant life according to law. The law of nature is common, universal, divine and good rule of reason, which governs universe, combined in a natural association. Civil law should follow natural law which is sovereign and universal. According to Sabine "The fundamental teaching of Stoics was religious conviction of oneness and perfection of true moral order."

They believed private life is more important than public life and condemned participation in political life. They believed in the general perversion of mankind and thus justified the existence of Govt. as conception propounded by Christianity. Stoics gave to the world notion of equality based on spirit of freedom and the notion on universal brotherhood based on universality of natural law. This philosophy greatly influenced Cicero, Sanlce, Aurelius and Emperor Marcus etc. Doctrine of original sin and of brotherhood was supported by Christianity. Modern cosmopolitan outlook and ideas of equality, liberty and fraternity are their basic contribution. Christians developed ideal that all human beings are created by God and preached for universal brotherhood.

Contribution of Greek political thinkers is great and valuable which is given here in brief.

In Europe or in West, political philosophy began with Greeks. The Greek city of Athens created praiseworthy civic ideals. Plato and Aristotle were two giant thinkers, their breath of vision and loftiness of conception, not only influenced European political thought but political philosophy of the whole world.

1. Patriotism. The Greek city life controlled the whole social structure of the society and developed one religion and civic feeling. Education conformed to the set-up of the state and as such it helped in the development of oneness and patriotism. Intense patriotism led Greek persons to sacrifice their lives against Persian invaders for the sake of their country Battles of Themopole are still famous.

2. High civic sense. Greek thinkers thought about ideal and Greek conception of citizenship meant participation in the fairs of the state. They meet together occasionally, compromised their differences and developed a feeling of oneness and unity of action which helped in the development of civic sense, Civic sense is a great boon of Greek civilization and so word civics originated from Greece and teaching of civics began with Greek thinkers.

3. Idealistic but practical. Greek thinkers thought about ideal and preached virtue but always possessed practical outlook and even Plato tried to put his ideas into practice. According to Barker, their thought is pathological and not psycho, logical.

4. Harmonious mixture of ethics and politics. Greek took politics as an ethical state. Plato believed in the supremacy of justice and virtue and desired to achieve his ideal through the state. Aristotle was empirical thinker but he too had to yield to the ethics and to him also ideal of state was to help in achieving perfect life. Thus, they tried to make state as an ethical institution.

5. Common life. Greeks enjoyed life in common and to them state and society was one. In Athens, its members used to live a common life and there was no separation in their religious, social, political and economic conceptions. To Aristotle constitution meant a mode of life. As such, they developed common feeling and common outlook and patriotism to their states.

6. Secular and rational. Greek thought remained free from mysticism and religious superstitions colouring as such it was rational and secular. Indian, Muslim and Christian political thought is mainly religious but outlook of Greek thinkers was secular.

7. Democracy. Greek city were ruled not by kings but by citizens who participated in civic affairs by rotation. In Egypt, China and in India and in Iran etc. prevailing form was monarchy but in Greek city states, it was democracy. It was not only democracy but direct democracy. According to Pericles, no man is born to office and no man buys office, but by an equal opportunity, he is shifted down to the position to which his natural gifts entitle him. Thus, Greeks believed in equality of opportunity to hold office.

8. Liberty and authority. Greeks loved individual liberty. Plato and Aristotle developed an organic conception of the state. They brought conception that state is not an organisation but as organism, a moral organism. This brought them to the development of organic and idealist theory of the state but Epicureans held, man should first satisfy individual desires. The Greek conceptions that each citizen should have free development and should have some share in the business of state is still important.

9. Freedom of conscience or freedom of thought and expression. Athens encouraged freedom of conscience or thought and Socrates gave life but did not submit against conscience. Plato developed ideas quite contrary to prevailing ideas but still, he was regarded a great thinker. Thus freedom of expression and of thought and conscience prevailed in Greek city states to a large extent.

10. Love for freedom. The stoics preached for the equality of their country from the core of their heart. Persian invaders caught a Tartar in Greeks and love of freedom compelled Persian invaders to go back and Greek's city state remained free.

11. Equality. The stoics preached for the equality of mankind. Notion of equality was prevalent in Greek states to such extent that leaders were looked down upon by masses and Socrates was sentenced to death perhaps because he favoured rule of superiors than of masses.

12. Justice. Greeks placed much emphasis on justice and stated the truth that justice is the interest of stronger. But better definition was given when injustice was defending to "give every man his due." Plato's conception of justice is hidden, to which perhaps political philosophers have failed to conceive. Actually by proposing rule of guardian class, who is stronger is wisdom and of military guardians, who are physically and temperamentally strong perhaps he is persuading rule of stronger class. In very mysterious ways, Plato supported rule of stronger class superior in wisdom or power or courage and urges all others to do their routine work *i.e.,* to work as hewers of wood and drawers of water. In a very mystical way, he pleads for the justice of stronger class. However credit goes to Greek thinkers that they devoted so much attention to the justice and finally preached universal brotherhood.

13. Education. The notion that virtue is teachable and the pride place which education occupied in Greek conception is still very important. To Greek thinkers' education did not mean only knowledge but knowledge which creates virtues in man and makes them fit to perform critic duties in life and makes them good citizen.

14. Sovereignty of law. Greek thinkers paid great regard for law. Plato in Statesman and Laws and Aristotle in politics pleaded for sovereignty of law. He even placed sovereignty of Law even above the sovereignty of people. According to him obedience to law was not slavery but highest good.

15. Constitutionalism. Each and every city contained its separate constitution and considered it as sacred, so constitutionalism originated in Greek. Aristotle is said to have studied about 200 constitutions and he is stalled to father of constitutionalism.

16. Effinimism. Plato and Aristotle both supported cause of women. They gave higher place to women than Roman or Persian or Arabian or Christian thinkers. Thus, they championed the cause of fair sex.

17. Theory of international relations. Greeks evolved common law for foreigners' common rules of war and Olympic games and even a loose confederation, so ideas of world citizenship or of common rules and universal brotherhood etc. originated with Greeks. World games are still called Olympic games.

18. Natural law. Stoics' basic then depended on nature and they propagated ideas of law of nature. They preached for equality of man and universal brotherhood.

Thus, Greek political thought gave lasting and universal ideas and till the beginning of 20th century, all political thinkers drank deep from this rich fountain of knowledge and wisdom and idea of universal brotherhood and ideas of world state, of natural justice and of universal citizenship which are now cherished by U.N.O.

Epicureans and Stoics supported universalism, equality and brotherhood etc. and thus influenced Christian thought and modern ideals of U.N.O. As such their conceptions with some modifications possess some impact on Political Thought.

Chapter 5

Roman Political Thought

Saneca, Cicero and Justanian

Roman Political thinkers borrowed their ideas from Greeks but according to Sabine belief in justice is the crowning glory of Roman jurisprudence. Similarly Dunning says the justice genius of the Romans evolved that body of rules which constitutes the basis of Roman law. Romans developed theory of imperium and believed on Imperialism. Roman conquerors and rulers created a vast empire and imposed Roman law which is still followed with amendments in lot of countries of the world. Romans evolved a common official language Latin like Sanskrit and a universal legal system Jusnatural which was regarded higher than enactment of a particular state and common citizenship. As such Romans gave legal system and empirialist state. They believed law is the expression of passionless reason with ethical and or religious basis. Ideal of universal brotherhood and Imperial state is also their contribution. Saneca, Cicero and Justanian the law has given more main figures who contributed to Roman thought who may be studied briefly.

Roman mind was consolidative *i.e.,* legal and not speculative as such Polybius himself a Greek and Cicero are poor comparison to Plato and Aristotle. It is true that Romans did not contribute much to political philosophy but the political institutions and the legal system of Rome moulded western political thought and conception of justice and legal system. Whole of Italian and Swiss law and substantial parts of the laws of France, Germany, Poland and of South American states are based on Roman law, when Christianity became the state religion, church of the Roman. Empire became centre of Roman Catholic religion. It is true as said by Mclewin that Romans did not contribute much to political philosophy but profoundly influenced political philosophy, legal and juridical system. As such we have to study political career of Rome.

POLITICAL CAREER OF ROME

Rome started her political career as a monarchic city state but achieved greatness as a Republic and declined as an imperial and despotic power. Monarchic form of Government was replaced due to conflict of patricians and the plebians and it started her aggressive career. It founded one of the greatest and most stable and longest empire which world has ever seen. To solve the problem of political nature, it evolved a political system and universal legal system. Roman empire existed about 2000 years and influenced whole of Europe.

Roman Political Institutions

It will be interesting to give a brief description of Roman political institutions, Plebians *i.e.,* common people succeeded in getting a Comitia centuriats and about 500 B.C., a Republic was setup. Two consults replaced King and these were assisted by Proctors, and censors and later on by the Tribune, the people's representative. Romans conquered many other states which were governed by Perfects. Later on military dictatorship was established and popular assembly lost its power. As such ideals of democracy, liberty and autonomy were replaced but the ideals of unity, order universal law and cosmopolitan outlook gained ground. They evolved a common official language and a universal legal system and common citizenship, which were followed to some extent by British, French and Russian empires.

Impact of Greek on Rome

The development of Roman law was influenced by intellectual impact of Greece upon Rome. According to Molluruain that the arrangement of Roman law in the form of twelve tables was largely due to influence of Greeks; the tables were based on the laws obtained from Greek city states; Greek influence on Rome increased vastly when Romans conquered Greece. It became a fashion in Rome either to send his ward for study to Greece or to keep a Greek tutor. Greek political thought gave ethical and humanistic basis to their legal system.

Development of Rome Law

Foreigners flocked in Rome and to decide the cases of conflicting nature, a special magistrate decided the case on the basis of common practices, supplementing them with rational and ethical consideration. At the end of his term, he collected his decisions and published them. New proctor took into consideration the edicts of his predecessor and added his own. Thus, a new law of Jus Gentium came into existence.

Jusgentiuem was different with the Roman law, called Juscivile, which applied to Romans only. Jus Gentium was common to whole while Jus civile was applied to Romans only. In formative stage doctrine of political relations were held and taught by Greek thinkers of those days, which were combined with principles drawn from Italian customs, to be handed on together to the new people of Europe as the basis of their law and politics. This combination and transmission together constitute the chief role of Rome in the drama of the growth of western political thought, a role second to none in practical importance.

Later on principles that were considered to be inherently reasonable irrespective of them being found in law gave rise to Jus Naturale. Jus Naturale began to be regarded higher than the enactment of a particular state. It began to be regarded higher than Jus Gentium which was based on generally recognized principles. It became according to Sir Fredrich Pollock an ultimate principle of fitness with reference to the nature of man as a rational and social being which is, or ought to be the justification of every form of positive law. Jus Naturale thus became touch stone of ethical criticism of positive law.

Development of Law under Roman Empire

Thus, Romans produced Jus civile, based on twelve tables and applicable to Romans, Jus Gentium applicable to foreigners and the people of Roman empire and the Jus Naturale which belonged to philosophers and influenced the work of jurists and Proctors. Under the Roman empire these three systems were mixed into one universal law applicable to all subjects of the empire and so these have come into existence. The Roman outlook became wider, humane and less narrow when to its practical character was added ideal of justice borrowed from stoicism and developed it. According to Sabine, *"Belief in justice is the crowning glory of Roman jurisprudence."* They believed "Justice must be done through hewers may fall."

Roman Concept of Law

To Greeks, Law was the expression of passionless reason and its sanction was ethical or religious. In the beginning Roman law was also a mixture of religious regulation and customary rules. But in a vast empire containing people of diverse faiths, it was not possible to keep the relation between law and religion and so it became secularized, positive and secular to a great extent. However, the Roman law was not product of llegislation in modern sense of term. Roman justices and philosophers conform to the higher law of nature. They were deeply influenced by humanistic doctrines of Stoicism. According to Sabine, *"Roman law preserved the spirit of civic phrase, that we are servants of the law in order that we may be free."*

Social Contract and Theory of Natural Rights

Roman conception that king is source of law, during close of middle ages drifted to theory that King is the agent of people and was used for the sovereignty of national King. Teachings of Stoicism that all men are born free and that all men are equal in natural rights were used by the opponents of royal power in constructing the theory of social contract and natural rights that served the basis for revolution and democracy. Moreover, conceptions of Jes Jentium and Jus Naturale was worked out by Grotious in international law. Thus, we find germs of social contract of natural law and international law, in Roman juristic conception.

The idea of contract played a great part in Roman legal theory and even the creation of law took from the social contract. The laws were made by magistrates in connivance with popular assemblies. According to Gettle, *"Law was not a command imposed by sovereign upon his subjects, but a contract arranged among the constituent organs of the state after negotiations."* The private law of Romans was based on the idea of contractual obligations between the individuals. Romans thought even worshippers worship God in bargain for certain benefits from God.

Popular Sovereignty

Romans like Dicey thought that the state is legal sovereign but the political sovereignty resides in people as a whole. According to Gettle, "*the early Kings, the republican magistrates, and in theory at least emperors, received their authority from the citizens and acted as their agents, and were responsible to them for exercise of their duties. The will of emperor had that force of law because in theory people have delegated to him their entire authority.*" This delegation is irrevocable and therefore revolutions are unjustified. Later on with the development of power of King, this conception gave place to divine authority of emperor, who delegated his authority to state officials. Thus ideas changed due to influence of circumstances and environment.

Imperium

Roman empire began under monarchy but they never believed that any individual had a particular and absolute title to rule over them because of any hereditary claim or divine antecedents. Any Roman could fill the office of the own ruler but once chosen, the King held office for life. During life tenure, he could not be deposed constitutionally and subjects were to own their allegiance to him. He possessed the absolute power of the state. He was the high priest and held imperium for peace and war. Power was gift to him but this gift was absolute and irrevocable. At his death, however imperium returned to the burgesses on the representative, the proctors. An inter-Rex was appointed for a temporary period through whom power came to next Rex *i.e.*, King chosen by people. This idea is interrelated to their conception of popular sovereignty and should be taken as complementary to one another.

Conception of Universal Brotherhood

With the expansion of Roman Empire, they developed wider outlook. They developed ideals of human brotherhood and of equality of men before law. The cosmopolitan outlook of Rome and theistic-Christian conception of the brotherhood of man laid the foundations for the modern point of view of universal brotherhood and modern ideas of U.N.O.

Another contribution made by the Romans was the principal of colonial rule and local self-government or municipal administration. Limited local self government was permitted to the provinces. Dependent people also realized the value of Roman order and ghost of Rome haunted during middle ages. Roman law and language spread all over the world. Roman law is taught to Indian students in Indian universities even up to now. The Christian Church organized itself on the model of Roman empire Caesar, Imperium and theory of world unity influenced the course of political philosophy. Roman law and its legal system influenced whole mankind.

ROMAN CONTRIBUTION TO POLITICAL THOUGHT

Concept of secular law which has its sanction in the will of ruler is the main contribution of Romans to the theory of law and jurisprudence. It brings us to the idea that state is distinct from society, and it is more of a legal structure than an ethical association. Romans also propounded the idea of legal personality of the state. Romans also believed that mixed constitution is the best. They also propounded the contractual theory of law which meant laws were a contract arranged among the constituent organs of the state after negotiations.

Imperium which means lawful but not necessarily actual authority is their special contribution. It meant authority is a trust on the public will. However, greatest contributions of Romans are in the field of law and jurisprudence of which whole world is indebted to them.

(1) Next to law, Romans contributed to building of a stable empire. By building roads and defence walls, Romans compelled subject people for submission. They developed conception of integrity of empire and commerce but replaced liberty by the notion of peace and order and protection of Govt. established by law.

(2) Unity. By uniform political and legal system and common official language, they developed a sense of security in the Roman Empire.

(3) Centralised Despotism with local self-government in colonies and provinces was keynote of Roman administration.

(4) Cosmopolitan outlook and international law and conception was to be developed by Romans as stated before.

Polybius 204 to 102 B.C. Polybius brought out importance and advantages of mixed Govt., so his ideas may be studied properly.

Polybius was the first political philosopher, who wrote on Roman government and its constitution. He was a Greek hostage, who was born in 204 B.C. and died on 102 B.C.; up to this time, Romans conquered Greeks. Polybius wrote his History of Rome in which he admired Roman polity which enabled Rome to become a great political power. He began his history by dealing with the cause of the origin of the state. He briefly narrated the various types of government *i.e.,* monarchy, aristocracy and democracy in Aristotelian manner and declared difference between the three types were external rather than internal or ideal. He displayed that pure forms of these are unstable because of the rivalry shown by the elements in the states representing other two types. He recognised a natural cycle of change in the form of government in the state. According to him change took place in them following cycle; monarchic, tyranny, aristocracy, oligarchy and democracy and mobocracy and, then the new cycle again. After that analysing philosophically, the constitution of Rome had declared that it was of a mixed form and therefore better than a constitution of pure types because it embodied a system of checks and balances among the different organs. These ideas effected makers of American Constitution which is based on checks and balances.

Classification of Government

Following Aristotelian conception he classified government into Monarchy. Aristocracy and Democracy with their perverted forms of tyranny, oligarchy and extreme democracy. Earliest type of government was monarchy, first based on force, but later on approved by popular approval Monarchy degenerated into tyranny. This was overthrown and followed by aristocracy based on virtue and intellect. Aristocracy degenerated into oligarchy, which was followed by democracy, which too degenerated into ochlocracy or mob rule or Mobocracy which means anarchy of mob violence.

Mixed type most Stable and Best

He believed that the best safeguard against political revolutions was the incorporation in the constitution of the best elements of all the three pure forms of government, a thing which has been achieved by the Roman Republic wisely and advantageously of Roman constitution, the consuls represented the mobs, and the senate represented aristocratic element and the popular assemblies represented democratic element. Each one of the elements, Polybius checked, watched and controlled other two elements. Polybius based his ideas on Aristotelian conception. His democracy is identical with Aristotle's *Polity* and *Ocholocracy* with his extreme democracy.

Conception of Polybius was to a great extent correct as is proved by subsequent historical facts. British constitution and Roman constitution were considered best due to their mixed character. His ideas of checks and balances holds, the field in U.S.A.

Dictatorial and communist states did not accept his conceptions due to different social setup but decline of dictators and Russian power has again proved utility of mixed constitutions. As now it had to be admitted, that he was the first political theorist to bring out the importance and advantage of mixed type of Govt. which was grasped by Montesquieu and in modified form incorporated in many constitutions.

CICERO (106 TO 53 B.C.)

Cicero was a great orator and his thoughts contain synthesis of Platonic and stoic ideas. He believed time is right reason. He believed in Res Populi *i.e.,* authority proceeds from People and it should be exercised according to law on moral grounds only. Conception of natural law is his great contribution. He believed in democracy and rule based on popular sovereignty in which office holders act merely as agent of public.

Cicero was born in 106 B.C., when political constitution of Republic was failing. His purpose of writing was to commend national virtue of public service and to recast them with old method of government.

He wrote about a century after Polybius and he was the greatest Roman representative of Stoice school of Political philosophy. His age was the age of military dictators like Morius, Sulla, Pompey and of Julius Caesar etc. But Cicero was an ardent supporter of republicanism and wrote to increase the power of senate and magistrates. Like Polybius, he also believed that mixed constitution is best one. His *De Republica* written on Plato's *Model* and *De Legibus* represent a frequent appeal for the revival of old spirit by restoring old constitution with its healthy system of checks and balances.

Importance

Importance of Cicero's writing does not lie in his originality of thought but in the manner of their expression. Characteristically, he was not a political philosopher but a lawyer and statesman, whose works are reflection on politic rather than on political science. Sabine holds that Cicero lacked the originality to strike out a new theory for himself with Roman experience and in defiance with Greek sources. According to Foster, *"much that he writes, is directly inspired by Plato and Aristotle."* He himself stated that his works were compilation but according to Sabine, an idea once embedded in his writings was preserved for all time to the reading public and became immortal.

Cicero championed the cause of moderation, concord and constitutionalism. Like Polybius, he believed in mixed constitution and the theory of cycle of constitutions. He took these ideas from Polybius but amended them in the light of his own understanding of Roman history. Cicero brought Jus Naturale of stoics and supported Natural law and human equality to be realised in Roman Empire. His ideas have everlasting influence and are treasure of mankind.

Following the footsteps of Plato, Cicero in his *De-Republican* has painted the picture of his ideal state. He copies Plato in supporting justice as main theme but unlike Plato, his ideal is co-related to reality. Plato was idealistic thinker of city state, but Cicero influenced by Stoic philosophy has the practical sense. According to Dunning. He confines himself to the consideration of Roman state and its history as illuminating and embodying the ideal of political science.

Like Greeks, Cicero believes that state is the natural outcome of the social instinct of man and supports stoic conception of the state as a rational and desirable institution. But he differs with stoics and thinks the state as political institution is distinct from the society in general and separates state and government and places the ultimate authority in people and government acting as their agent. He holds commonwealth as moral community and regards commonwealth as people's affairs, in which a group of persons possesses the power of the state and its law.

Difference with Plato

Plato confines political authority in guardian class, but Cicero believes in Res papuli in which people are involved. Politically authority when legally and rightly exercised, is the corporate power of the people. The magistrate are merely creatures of law. The motto of state is to supply its members with the advantage of mutual and just government. As the law and state is the common powers of the people. He regards state and its laws subject to natural law or law of God. Force is an incident and is justified only because it is required to give effect to the principles of justice and right. He believes that authority proceeds from the people, it should be exercised according to law and moral grounds only. His ideas achieved universal acceptance and profoundly influenced the western political thought.

Classification of States

In classification of states, Cicero followed footsteps of Polybius and like him, he also believes in cycle of revolutions. He considered monarchy best, aristocracy next and democracy least desirable. In order to check revolutionary cycle, he preferred a mixed form of Government, combining the best of all forms and avoiding weakness of other forms. He comes to conclusion that the Republican system of Rome is a perfect example of the checks and balances for good and stable government. Monarchy gave place to tyranny and brought its ruin. The patrician aristocracy was over bearing in its monopoly of power and came to ruin. As such he follows footsteps of Polybius but his idea of check and balances is more mechanical than Polybius.

Natural Laws

His most profound contribution to political philosophy was his conception of Natural law. In developing his conception of natural law, he followed the idea of Plato that the principles of right and justice are internal and took from stoics that a supreme universal law existed in nature. To quote Dunning. In Greek philosophy the distinction between right and law had been recognized but right had been regarded as source and content antecedent etc., largely independent of law... Cicero reversed the earlier Greeks' conception of the relation between law and rights and proceeded to make right in every sense subordinate to and dependent upon Law.

Conception of Natural law was taken by Cicero from stoic philosophy, but through him its idea spread in whole Europe and held field up to 19th century. He believed that single universal law governs the whole universe. It is based on rational and social nature of man divinely bestowed upon him. To quote Sabine, it (natural law) is same everywhere and unchangeable binding upon all mean and nations. Legislation that contravenes it, is entitled to the name of law. For no ruler and no people can make right led to the name of law or wrong, Cicero stated true law is right reason consonant with or nature diffused among all men, constant and eternal; which summons to its duty by its command and hinders from fraud by its prohibition...To invalidate this law, by human legislation is never right. He terms it as law of God and states that God is the author of this law, its interpreter and its sponsor. The man who will not obey it will abandon his inner self. Thus, he places emphasis on natural law in most forceful language. He discarded theory of inequality of Plato and Aristotle and gave crowned glory to natural law.

He believes that Natural law governs the entire universe to which all human beings have an obligation to conform. Inanimate things obey it due to natural necessity, animals due to instinct and man should obey it due to reason. He felt that a citizen's obligation to state law is not absolute but conditional. But his obedience to natural law is unconditional and absolute. Man is not bound to obey state made laws, if these do not conform to natural law. He goes a step further and states if state laws to not conform to natural law these laws do not deserve to be called laws. According to Gettle, *"Cicero believed that moral principles are as applicable to political matters as they are in private matters and that true law is right reason, comfortable to natural, universal and eternal."*

Belief in Equality

Stoics believed in equality of nature and Cicero puts emphasis on the natural equality of men. He believes that men are better than brutes due to reasoning faculty, and that makes them equal in the eyes of God. His conception of equality is against the philosophy of Plato and Aristotle who believed in the inequality of mankind and Aristotle even defended slavery. His conception of equality according to Dr. Carlyle is the dividing line between ancient and modern political theory. His belief in equality brings him nearer to us than Plato or Aristotle. He agrees with the Stoic conception and believes in the citizenship of world without any distinction of caste, creed race or religion.

His concept of equality of man, supremacy of law universal brotherhood and natural law are indicative of novelty and modernity of his thought. Natural law and equality of man are the basic assumptions on which our democracy is based. His conception of natural law and universal brotherhood are the basis on which modern international law and hope of a world Government and U.N.O. is based though in a vast course of time these have changed considerably.

Cicero and Aristotle differ in many respects and according to Dr. Carlyle, no change is so startling as a change from Aristotle to Cicero.

(1) Aristotle stated that some should rule and others should be ruled and so restricted his rights of citizenship to a narrow circle though his circle is greater than Plato. But Cicero believed in the equality of man. Slave is not as Aristotle said, a living tool but a wage earner hired for life. He believed that some measure of dignity and respect is due to every man. Like Kant he believed that a man should to be treated as an end and not as means.

(2) Cicero gave preference to democratic mixed Government but Plato and Aristotle condemned democracy and preferred Monarchy and Aristocracy.

(3) Plato's outlook was fascistic, Aristotle's conservative but Cicero's outlook is democratic.

(4) Plato paints idealistic picture of his state but Cicero's approach is practical.

(5) Aristotle and Plato dealt with city states but Cicero dealt with great Roman empire and so his outlook is broad based on universal brotherhood.

(6) Greeks were ignorant of natural law. Cicero gave a concept of natural law applicable to whole mankind and said state laws are subject to natural law of Govt.

(7) Plato gave prominence to philosophy, Aristotle supported law but Cicero supported, rule of law is right reason, conformable to nature, universal and eternal *"a state is nothing but partnership in law."*

(8) Greeks thought right is source and content its antecedent to and independent of law. But Cicero differed and reversed the process.

(9) Cicero believed in liberty unlike Aristotle who believed in slavery. He stated liberty has no dwelling place in any state except

that in which the people's power is greatest and surely nothing can be sweeter than liberty; but if it is not the same for all, it does not deserve the name of liberty.

(10) Aristotle believes in rule of philosopher Kings, Aristotle in rule of limited class of citizens but Cicero's rule is based on popular sovereignty and office holders act merely as the agent of public, who delegates authority to them for discharge of their duties only.

(11) Cicero unlike Plato and Aristotle believed that state is not prior to individual and King is representative of law.

(12) He identified Roman law, based on the principle of equality and justice, with the stoic law of nature.

(13) According to Cicero Authority proceeds from the people and should be exercised through laws on moral grounds. Thus, we may conclude in the words of Gettle, *"His ideas of natural law and justice sank deeply into Roman legal thought and influenced the later imperial jurists and imperial writers. And his idea of world unity and of universal law and authority remained central principle of political thought throughout Medieval age and to some extent in modified form even now."*

According to Dunning the juristic genius of Romans evolved the body of Principles which constitutes today the laws of European law. According to Sabine belief injustice is crowning glory of Roman jurisprudence.

Greatest contribution of Roman political thought is in juristic field of law. It is still taught in Western and in Indian Universities to the students of law and all over the world in majority of countries. As such it will be interesting to know about the development of Roman law.

Roman law grew slowly. In primitive stage it grew with religious percepts, customs and rules of equity. With the passage of time distinction began between divinely functions and rational customs of men. About 450 B.C. the customary rules of Romans were codified into the Twelve tables. It brought symmetrical classification and clearness into the laws. Codification hitted hard the clearness of the laws. Codification hitted hard to the powers of nobles, who were the sole interpreter of laws in their own interest as Cicero stated laws govern the magistrate.

Common men called Plebians now knew their laws, and future laws passed in their favour were also recorded and became part of codified law. It gave inspiration to legal thought in Rome and yielded place to secular authority and manmade laws. The Twelve Tables were supposed to contain all laws and gaps were supplied by adding new body of laws passed by legislative bodies with the consent of the people. This gave rise to Roman diction that Roman laws represent the will of the state. In the beginning these were passed and modified by plebiscite but later on by senatas consults and constitutions of the emperors. Lawyers were jurists and not philosophers.

Growth of Jus Gentium

Roman state grew into world empire and Twelve Tables were wholly inadequate and narrow to foreigners and dependencies. Narrowness of Twelve Tables was broken down by the edicts issued by Practors, responses drafted by Juris consults and the constitutions proclaimed by emperors. In this way law not only expanded but it also rationalised. During this period practors and jurisconsults laid down new judicial principles of general application and the important notions of Jus Naturale were recognised.

Foreigners with the expansion of trade company in Roman Empire flocked to Rome. To decide their cases special magistrate was appointed. As these had to deal with foreign merchants of different nations so a common law known as Jus Gentium came into existence. Practor Perigrinus in it embodied principles of natural equity and customs and laws common to nations subject to Rome. Principles of equity representing abstract principles of justice, dictates of reason of universal application brought into existence, conception of Jus Naturale, Jus Gentium meant laws common to all nations as slavery was prevalent during those days among all nations so it was acceptable to Jus Gentium. But as nature has created all men equal so slavery cannot be accepted or supported under Jus Naturale.

Direct Effect about the Growth of Jus Gentium

Nattleship holds that the Jus Gentium meant the usage of world of all mankind. It was intended to express common usage and customs, picked up in war commerce or travel. Sabine on the other hand holds that Jus-Gentium was and never was anything else, but a portion of the positive Roman law with commercial usage and other sources of law, more specially the praetorian edict, had clothed in a concrete form; the Jus Gentium was that part of the private law of Rome which was essentially in accordance with the private law of other nations, more especially that of Greeks.

Fusion of Jus Gentium and Jus Naturale made Roman legal system comprehensive and more liberal; Legal appeals from all parts of Roman empire were sent to professional Juris-consults and their opinions were considered as good as law. The Jurists had to lay down general principles of universal application and were responsible for the creation of a scientific system of jurisprudence like code of Justinian. Jurist were stoics and so notions of brotherhood of man and the universality of law prevailed in their rules. They believed that law is an impersonal reason.

Corpus Juris or Code of Justinian

Next to *Bible* and Christian teachings, code of Justian made profound influence on the Western world. This code contains these main things:

1. The institutes 533 A.D. It contains legal notions gives ideas of Marcian and Florentines. The legal jurists collected their opinions of various legal problems which came to have force of law as these expression expressed opinions of best legal minds.

2. *The Digest* published in 533 A.D. contained select passages from the legal pronouncements of collected lawyers.

3. Novel. A collection of collected lawyers.

4. A collection of imperial laws and decrees relating to public and private laws from the beginning of the empire.

(a) The laws of nature. Gins divided law as Jus Gentium *i.e.* law of notions, jus civile *i.e.,* the actual law of Rome called civil law and Jus Naturale *i.e.* law of nature emptying abstract principles of right. As per Gins Jus Natural law presents ideal law. It is a law which nature has taught to all mankind. Ulpian says law of nature was ideal law, while Jus Gentium and Jus Civile are supporters of it.

(b) Property and slavery. Aristotle defended slavery but Gins holds that slavery is unnatural and artificial. Ulpain regarded slavery as wickedness of mankind. Cicero and Sancea pleaded for the humane and kind treatment to slaves.

Regarding property. Roman jurists believed during primitive golden age *i.e.,* in Satya-Yuga of India, there was no property. They believed that property came it existence due to greed of man. They supported its retention because in every known stage of human history property always existed and is necessary for human existence.

(c) The civil law. Law has been defined by great jurist, Salmend "as will of sovereign body as interpreted by judges." It is not necessary that it should be related to morality or justice. But Roman conception of law was based on ethical principles of morality and mystical Gains stated Law is right reason embodied in state. Ulpian said law stood as a criteria to judge what was just or unjust and enabled man to do good and just. As per Justinians institutes justice represented a constant and perpetual disposition of the will which renders to each one what was his due. Thus Romans believed that object of law was to make man good. Justice is fixed to give every man his right.

(d) Source of political authority. Romans sought source of political authority in imperium which meant that people delegate authority to rulers as Gains said the people are the source of all legal authority. Thus, ultimate source of authority were people, who delegated their authority to ruler *i.e.*, Rex Legius possesses the force of law because it was finally based on the will of the people. The people gave all authority, *i.e.* Imperium and its powers to the ruler. Thus, lawyers gave us new theory of delegation of authority or Imperium by the people to the ruler. Authority once delegated cannot be taken back, so authority of King became supreme and he became not only fountain of law above law. Thus, on one side Emperor got authority as delegation from people and on the practical side he became supreme, but the ultimate source remained people.

Importance of Roman Law

Romans made everlasting contribution in the field of jurisprudence and law. Roman law served as the basis of common law of the church. It influenced whole legal world. In western Europe and in America all the countries have been influenced by it. It is still taught in India and all over the world, law of nature now took shape of international law. According to Rudolf Stammler, *"Belief in justice is the crowning glory of Roman jurisprudence."* As quoted by Sabine, *"A conception of Natural law and belief in justice and equality of man etc. are important contribution of Roman Political thought."* Roman law was taught even in India during British period and it continued to be taught in Agra University and in Uttar Pradesh even up to 1965.

Chapter 6

Christian Political Thought

St. Paul and St. Augustine

The rise of Christianity gave new conceptions to political thought based on Bible and teachings of St. Paul and of St. Augustine. Rise of the Christian church as a distinct institution entitled to govern the spiritual concern of mankind indecently of the state affected political thought and activity of western world. They propounded theory of two swords and stated render unto Caesar the things that are Caesar's *i.e.,* worldly affairs and the things that are God's *i.e.,* spiritual things to church. Thus, church become supreme in religious and spiritual affairs and emperor and king in worldly affairs.

Christ was a Jew who was born in Jerusalem. After his crucification, Christianity took its rise in the eastern part of Roman empire when it was at the height of its Zenith. Christianity spread rapidly. In 313 A.D. Emperor Constantine gave support to Christianity and in 380 A.D. emperor Theodosius declared Christianity to be the official and only lawful religion of the empire. As the Roman empire was very great so it became the official religion of the majority of the people of the Europe.

The Christian church in its early organization was local and democratic. Soon it became centralized having its headquarters at Rome. With the decline of the power of Roman Empire, power of Roman church increased. With the end of Western Roman Empire in 476 A.D. with the deposition of Domulus Augustulus, church became symbol of unity and rallying point of Christian nations. The conception of a church representing an entity separate from the state was original contribution of Christianity to political thought. Sanicass representation of Govt. as remedy for human evil influence Christian thinkers.

THE GROWTH OF POPACY

The belief that in Roman Church was founded by chief apostle St. Peter who increased the prestige of Rome and in 4th century General Council made the bishop of Rome as the highest court of appeal against the bishops of other countries. The belief in divine and eternal character of Roman empires supported by the idea of kingdom of Christian whole world led to a spiritual conception of world empire which was embodied in Christian Church and the Popacy, with the change of capital of Eastern empire to Constantinople made the Pope supreme at Rome, who also exercised temporal power in the adjoining territory of Rome and later on became supreme over whole Christendom till the rise of Protestant states. Pope and Roman catholic church still influence thought of Roman catholic Christians.

Roman Empire and Roman Catholic Church

Roman Catholic Church resembled with the Roman Empire. According to Dunning, *"Not only did each city has its bishop, the limits of whose size corresponded with those of city territory but the civil province was also an ecclesiastical province."* The Church was as authority as an empire had been. To quote Bryce, *"The crown law intended by its authors to reproduce and rival the imperial jurisprudence, a correspondence was treated between its division and those of corpus juris civils."* During medieval period church wielded the powers, but later on a great controversy arose and Roman empire which possessed touch, of universalism. Both wielded similar administrative powers, Empire represented physical and church of spiritual power.

Popacy and the Holy Roman Empire

The attack of barbarians ruined the Roman empire. Lombards even desired to attack Rome, but Pope made appeal to France leader Charles Martel. He and his son Popin defeated barbarians as well as Muslim invaders and so out of gratitude, Pope crowned his son Charles as emperor of Holy Roman Empire, who gave importance to Church. Charles was a great and mighty ruler, he as a Roman emperor made Church very powerful.

Legacy of Greek and Rome

In Greek conception there was distinction between state and society and no separation between religion and politics. But rise of Christian Church gave colour to new religious outlook and new power of Church came into existence. So far stoic ideas and ideas of Christianity are concerned, these were similar to a large extent. Stoics and Christians both believed in equality, universalism and brotherhood of man. Main difference in their outlook was that Christian Church gave new religious ideas based upon spiritual and other worldly outlook. According to Bowle, Christians made a distinction between the spiritual and earthly interests of man and thereby brought into the world a new piety, and a new hope and a new promise of salvation and a new sense of sin. Christianity introduced an element of purpose in human life and social organization, it taught man has a mission to fulfil. It gave belief in progress, respect for individual, and an humanitarian outlook. When Christian came into power, they emphasized the sacred duty of state to suppress all other faiths. During Greek age motto of thinkers was to bring their beliefs into harmony with reason and of modern age is to bring in harmony with facts but medieval age, it was to conform beliefs to Church. As such church claimed power and with the fall of Roman empire, it became dominating power and it requested obedience to church as well as to the King which gave rise to the idea of two swords or of two powers, spiritual and of worldly affairs.

Doctrine of two Swords

Stoics believed that a man must render obedience to duly constituted authority, faith in the divine government. St. Paul, the greatest of Christianity saints referred to natural law as written in men's hearts and revealed by reason distinct from the law of the state.

The duty to obey to duly constituted authority was emphasized in his famous words, "*Render unto Caesar the things that are Caesar's and unto God the things that are God's, St. Paul echoed these words "Let every soul be subject unto high powers. For there is no power but of God, the power that he is ordained of God. Whosoever therefore resists the power, resists the ordinance of God and they that resist shall receive unto themselves condemnation.*" In this way obedience to secular authority as well as to church became fundamental principle of Christian political thought.

Romans believed that Emperors and other officers rule because people delegate their authority to the emperor and rulers; but St. Paul's famous saying that state or civil government derives its power not from people but from God. As Government or authority is created by God, so to disobey the authority of ruler is to disobey God. As such it became religious duty of Christians to obey the authority of ruler and Christianity upheld the divine right of Kingship, though not of Kings. According to Gettle, the Christian writers in adopting the stoic rather than epicurean attitude towards the state and in adding the Christian conception of the divine order in human society, laid the foundation political thought of the following thousand years. Thus, doctrine of two swords which resulted in the controversy of church and state dominated political thought of whole medieval period. The Christian apostles believed that political authority is of divine origin as a result of the fall of man from original innocence to the depremed conditions. The civil authority has its origin in human sin but it is not sinful itself. It has been established by God for the maintenance of justice and peace and order. It came into existence due to disobedience of Adam in eating forbidden fruit and remains into existence due to depravity of human nature as controlling and correcting agency. Thus, they considered government as a necessary evil to curb the evil in man. Hence all people should obey the duly constituted authority because of its divine character. King being the vicar of God, had wielded his authority as a trust. According to St. Paul King was not the lord of people but their first servant. He stated, *"Whosoever will be the chiefiest shall be servant of all."* Thus, during medieval period of kingship was regarded as a trust.

Christian's thinkers gave divine sanction to civil government to curb the anarchism. Secondly, the empire adopted Christian faith and gave it a high place and so church in order to show gratitude by exalting the position of empire to divine origin. Moreover, Christian Church itself inherited the Jewish theory of divine kingship. This theory of divine origin of kingship discovered the early theory that king exercises authority delegated by people and consequently contractual basis of political obligation.

The famous saying of Christ *"Render unto Caesar the things that are Caesar's and unto God the things that are God's"* means sphere of life beyond political one. It implies that man has two fold duty, one to civil authority and other to God. In case of conflict between the two, one should obey God *i.e.,* Church rather than civil authority *i.e.,* emperor or king.

In this way church came into conflict with Roman emperors who desired unlimited and undivided devotion to the state and they began to prosecute the Christians. Christians suffered hardships and martyrdom but survived. Greek thinkers like Plato and Aristotle believed that a man could realize values through the membership of the state. But the Christian principle separates the spiritual power from temporal sphere and takes the ultimate values of life out of political sphere. According to Bowle, *"it pulls out the individual out of the organic community of the city or temporal state and sets him into a world beyond them."* It undermines the whole structure of the more primitive, less individualized community and the psychological solidarity which had kept earlier societies strong and stable, if St. Paul preached obedience to civil authorities but he said that Christians should seek settlement of their disputes not in pagan courts but in Christian courts according to Christian law. It meant setting up of state within the state and to lessen the power of the state by setting a rival authority. Christian conception of rendering unto Caesar things that are Caesar's and unto God's means that man has dual nature and subject to two authorities. It means that physically a man owes allegiance to state and spiritually to church. As soul is more important than body so whenever a conflict between the two may arise, man should obey church rather than state or king. Stoics also believed membership in the state of birth and the world at large. But Christian idea is based on the conception of body and soul and is quite different from stoic idea because it places church at a bigger level.

In the beginning Emperor prosecuted Christian preacher but when Christianity became state religion they evolved the idea of mutual help and so it was stated that human beings owe their duty both to king and the church. In the beginning, Church was merely a department of the state but as the power of Roman empire declined and consequently power of Roman emperor became extinct, Church became all powerful. The problem of relation between church and state arose which gave rise to doctorine of two swords.

Sword implies rulership. According to early Christian thinkers, God gave one sword to the emperor and the other to the Pope. Main duty of civil authority was to maintain peace and order and dispense justice while the business of clergyman was to look after the spiritual welfare of people and to give them eternal salvation. Jesus Christ desired harmony between the two powers and mutual assistance but power demands absolute power and so conflict arose between the two about supremacy.

Conflict

It began with Pope Gelasius. He said in letter to the Roman Emperor Anastasins, "Augustus emperor, this world is governed by two powers by bishops and by kings of these responsibility of the priests is weightier, since they have to render an account to God, even for kings themselves...You bow your head to the bishops, who are charged with the administration of holy things; you address yourself to be conducted in the ways of salvation; and in all that regards the reception and administration of the sacraments, your acknowledge that far from having any power to command, you are bound to obey them...in all such concerns you have no right to subject them to your will...The ministers of religion obey your laws in all that belongs to temporal order, because they know, you have received your powers from above."

This doctorine of two swords could have worked successfully if both kings and bishops would have worked within their own sphere. But in feudal setup it was very difficult to divide the spheres and so conflict of superiority between the secular and temporal authority arose which occupied the whole thinking of medieval thinking. According to Sabine, *"In the eleventh and twelfth centuries political writing was in main controversial, catring about the contest between the Popes and the Emperors over the boundaries of secular and the ecclesiastical authorities."*

The views of medieval thinkers on law, slavery and property.

Rise of Christianity gave conception of dual authority and doctorine of the swords as stated before. But other notions also changed with the rise of Christianity. Conception of different writers will be delt separately with their descriptions but ideas of early Christian thinkers may be stated here briefly.

The Christianity believed in the universality of God and brotherhood of man. This conception saved surfs from degeneration into slavery. It also gave rise to the ideas of individualism.

(A) Justification of State. In the Epistles to Romans, Christian thinkers declared that the object of state is justice and justice is a sacred thing, so any institution which deals with justice is also sacred. As such officers of state should be obeyed and authority of state should be respected. But in spiritual matters church ought to be obeyed and in case of conflict church possesses predominance over the state and its authority not resisted by passive resistance.

(B) Law of nature. Christian thinkers believed in the conception of stoics about law of nature and recognised distinction between manmade-laws and the law of nature. Law of nature was revealed by reason and was with it. State made laws are changeable but natural law is definite and constant. St. Paul's dictum, "Do by nature the things by law recognizes law of nature." The early Christian thinkers identified natural law with divine law.

Property. The book of Act supported the idea of property which resembled to communistic idea and even New Testament regarded communism as the ideal form of society. But it differed from compulsory idea of communism of Plato. It places emphasis on the equalization of property and on philanthropy of rich towards poor through charity and neighboureness. Christian thinkers restricted themselves to the virtue of charity and did not preach its complete abolition, though they cherished the ideal of common property as an ideal.

Slavery. The New Testament recognised soul in the all human beings, identity of human nature and equality of men. As such, they ought to have condemned slavery. But neither St. Peter nor St. Paul showed enthusiasm for the abolition of slavery. Early Christian thinkers saved their conscience by ordering that soul remain free in spite of bodily or physical bondage which is unnatural. Origin of slavery was sought in sin of men and so it should be tolerated as God's will. External slavery is a discipline by God for the good of the soul of the slave. Christian teachers though emphasized on human treatment to slaves but tolerated it for centuries though it was against Christian teaching. However it saved serfs from degenerating into slavery and treatment of slavery became less cruel with those who followed Christian teachings.

ST. AUGUSTINE (354 to 403 A.D.)

The Main Political Ideas of St. Augustine and Assessment

The most important political ideas of St. Augustine centre round the doctorine of two cities, the earthly city and city of God. The city of God realizes two values *i.e.,* of justice and peace. According to

Hearnshaw medieval thinkers depended on the *Bible,* the Roman Law and the Politics of Aristotle. St. Augustine's, ideas and his book *De Civitate Dei i.e.,* city of God according to Maclanain made its influence felt all over the Christian states. St. Augustine wielded a tremendous influence on medieval thinkers and next to St. Paul, he is considered as greatest Christian thinkers of medieval age.

St. Augustine 354-430 was the most important figure after St. Paul in Christian Church. He was the son of a pagan father and Christian mother. He was educated at Madawara and Carthage. He was converted to Christianity by St. Ambrose of Milan and he became Bishop of Hippo in north Africa. It may be said Machiavalism began with him. He became Bishop and died in 430 A.D.

He believed in an age which was extremely critical the fate of civilization and catholiasm was in balance. In 410 A.D. Attic and the Goths sacked Rome and this ruin of Rome was attributed that ruin to the new faith of Christianity. Superstitious people thought of Rome occurred as Romans forgot their old gods like Jupitor and Neptune etc., and adopted Christianity as its faith. St. Augustine took up the cause of Christianity and wrote his famous book 'De Civitate Dei' in which he defended Christianity against pagan rules. This book not only explains the fall of Rome but depicts the polity of future and lays down the structure of St. Augustine's city of God. He wrote confessions which has been called mine of ideas. His confessions influenced even Loy Tolstoy and Mahatma Gandhi.

De Civitate Dei

St. Augustine wrote this book in about fifteen years and divided it in 22 parts. The first ten parts are connected with the defence of Christianity against pagan attack and remaining twelve deal with the construction of city of God. In his book *De Civitate Dei,* the city of God held that if Christianity could not save the Rome, it at least saved it from the horrors and misery of the sack. To refute the pagan attack, he stated that Rome was also sacked in 390 B.C. when paganism was practiced. As such he said sack of Rome was due to eternal will of God. The sack of Rome was neither due to divine will to pave the way for the establishment of city of God. He stated that the rise and fall of nation occurs due to will of God. The story of mankind depends not upon chance but upon the eternal purpose of the God. There is divine will behind everything as it was predestined.

He stated that every cloud has a silver lining as such evil of Rome would be attended by the emergence of city of God in which Christianity would be adopted by all and after which no catastrophe would appear. He made a bitter attack on paganism and said that it is neither useful in this world nor helpful in the other world.

In his 11-12 books he pointed the picture of city of God. He stated that city of God will be an eternal city and will be neither sacked nor destroyed life earthly cities. City of God's latest and most perfect terrestrial–manifestation was the Christian Church. He painted a highly glorified picture of city of God. He painted the picture of city of God by mixing together the ideas of Plato and Cicero and presenting them in a setting of Christian theology. City of God was founded on self love of God while other city was founded on self love. The former was for promotion of good while latter for the promotion of evil. One aimed at justice and other for power. By city of God, he not only meant heaven but also earthly portion. The church is the part of it because only in church virtue and goodness of the city of God prevailed. Church's weapon was state to be used for the promotion of good as such they were interdependent. City of God was a kingdom on earth based on Christian virtues. He was influenced by Plato, Cicero, stoic and Christian saints. The conception of city of God is based partly on the constitution of the universal brotherhood of man preached by Greeks and Cicero. Cicero concluded universal society but St. Augustine allowed citizenship only to those possess grace. All members will form one society because of their common love and worship of God. Citizens of God will enjoy community with God and with one another in the city of God.

His city of God is closely connected with the Roman Catholic church. Conception of justice of St. Augustine is based on the idea of Plato that an individual is just if he fulfills his duties to family and conforms to the order of society. The state to Augustine is not final society. There is universal society to be found outside the state *i.e.,* in universal order as such justice of state is relative and not absolute. Absolute justice is to be found in universal order. Thus, his conception of justice is more absolute than Plato's conception of justice.

His Views about State

St. Augustine disagreed with Hellenic thinkers and Cicero that justice was the basis of the stated. He state that justice could prevail only in Christian state while there may be non-Christian states also. He holds that justice was an attribute of Church and not of state which is superior to state. According to his conception origin of state lies in the gregarious instinct of man and his sin resulting from original sin. He holds that state is due to sin represented a Godly remedy for sin but it did not represent sin. State has been created by God. Though state has been created by God but earthly state represents the kingdom of Christ. He felt necessity of state to fulfill the needs of property and buildings for the church. As the state owes its existence due to will of God, it should be normally obeyed but in case of violation of law of morality and religion it should be disobeyed. He did not believe in sovereignty of state.

Property and Slavery

According to St. Augustine keeping of private property is legitimate and justifiable. He holds that property right grows from the state and is not a natural but conventional right.

St. Augustine did not believe like Aristotle that man is slave by nature. He defends slavery as a punishment for human sin as a result of original sin. Slavery could not be abolished because it was divine retribution for sin. His theory did not explain the cause of individual slavery. If slavery is caused due to original sin then all must be slaves and not only a few unfortunate persons. As such it may be stated that his justification of slavery was against Christian teaching of fatherhood of God and brotherhood of man.

Influence

St. Augustine next to St. Paul is the greatest figure of Christian church. He wielded a tremendous influence in medieval age. According to Lord Bryce, it is hardly too much to say that Holy Roman empire was built upon the foundation of *De Civitate Dei.* Many medieval thinkers were influenced by his ideas. *De Civitate Die* gave to Christian Church a basis on which to build its greatness. On account of *De Civitates Die* of St. Augustine church became a universal power and challenged not only Holly Roman Empire but also for a time worsted it. According to Sabine *"his De Civitate Dei was a mine of ideas which moulded the thought of medieval rulers like Charlemagno and Otto the great."* His conception of Christian Commonwealth formed the basis of universalism of middle ages. According to Maxey, *"Civitate Dei became the work of the hour, and was widely read by laity and clergy alike."* It may be added that wielded influence throughout the middle ages. In pleading superiority of church, he created a great controversy. According to Hearnshaw, *"idea of superiority of church lead to dissension, disintegration and disaster,"* but St. Augustine concluded *"The happiness lies in the city of God."* According to W.E. Benste *"He helped to transmit ancient heritage to the new world that was being born."* As such St. Augustine was greatest thinker of Christian ideology next to St. Paul and he wielded great influence on medieval Christian thinkers.

Chapter 7
Medieval Political Thought
St. Paul, Pope & Greagory VII

The Christian thinkers supported universalism and stated that Christians are obliged to obey church in religious and spiritual matters and rulers in worldly affairs. As in medieval age people were religious minded so Church wielded a great influence over Christians.

According to Barker, *"The note of all political thought is universalism."* It assumes the existence of a single universal society, the inheritance and continuance of the ancient Roman empire; and on its ecclesiastical side the incarnation of Christ in a visible church. Roman empire, which included under its sway nearly all civilized society of Europe introduced idea of unity. He believed that their Roman empire is divinely bestowed and is eternal and universal. Some belief was cherished by Christians when it became official religion of Rome. St. Augustine echoed the same feeling by saying that pagans established Roman empire due to divine will and it was to be converted into a universal church as it is divinely ordained. Influence of Roman empire also made church universal. Citizens of Rome believed in centralized secular and a centralized ecclesiastical power and their relations were maintained on the famous theory of two swords. Christ said, "Render unto Caesar the things that are Caesar's, and unto God the things that are God's." The whole empire was considered Republican Christiana in which people come to do dual duty to obey state in secular matter and to obey church is spiritual matters. Thus Christians were obliged to obey both Pope and emperor.

Change is the inevitable law of life and old order changeth yielding place to new and so barbarians attack the Roman Empire. The Roman Empire which was considered eternal shattered before the barbarians like a chaff before the wind and in a large number of small kingdoms came into existence. Consequently local churches took place of universal church. Charles Martel, his son Pepin and Charlemango saved the Roman empire, so they were considered Emperor by Pope. Charlemango was a great and mighty ruler but after his death universalism on secular side was not possible as his empire became divided in his successors. In Italy, there was anarchy, so Pope called German rather to say Austrian King Otto I to conquer Italy and end monarchy. He did so and he was crowned as emperor of Holy Roman empire. Thus, on secular side there was Austrian empire building the title of Emperor and on ecclesiastical side it was Pope. According to Voltaire, empire was neither Holy nor an empire but it held its sway up to the time of Nepoleon and up to the beginning of 19th century when it was destroyed by Nepoleon Buonaparte. Hilderband or Pope Greagory VII restored the universal authority of Church and claimed superior power than Emperor. On the other hand Emperor claimed highest authority, so conflict for supremacy of power took place between the two and continued for a long time *i.e.,* up to 1630.

In medieval thought sole purpose of life was spiritual salvation to which all earthly activities must be subordinated, Salvation of soul was possible only by following the teachings of church or in other words key of salvation of soul was with the church. As such church wielded all authority to verify all life in every aspect whether it may be social, economic, political or intellectual according to universally binding principles of Christianity. Church attempted to regulate political sphere in reprimanding the Kings for their wrongs and insisting upon right behaviour. In the economic sphere it insisted on regarding property as a trust, on just and fair prices, the prohibition of usuary and laid stress on charity and help to needy and powerless persons. In social sphere every sphere was governed by church as they Baptist the child, performed marriage ceremonies, punishment and forgiveness for sins like adultery etc. On intellectual side, they controlled all ideas against Christian teachings and prosecuted the non-believers and those persons who were considered dangerous were burnt alive and ladies were burnt as witches. As the principle of unification of life prevailed so every aspect of life was dominated by Church and more or less similar ideas, outlook and way of life prevailed in whole Christian world. Similarly monarchial government prevailed both in Church where Pope was supreme and for secular side King was supreme.

According to Maitland, *"the medieval thinkers believed in the essence of the social organism which lies in unity, that this unity must be represented in governing part; and that the object can be best attained if that governing part be in itself a unit and consequently a single individual."* Dante stated that *"the unifying principle of Body politics is will and that for the purpose of presenting a unity of wills"* the regulating and governing will of one man is best.

Roman empire was fragmented into small kingdoms but idea of St. Augustine. St. Equina & Dante etc., whose thoughts will be dealt later on all supported universalism during middle ages, so it is true that universalism was the keynote of medieval political thought. Roman empire still prevailed in the shape of Roman Empire and of Pope's supremacy in Roman Catholic Church, so it is said ghost of Rome haunted middle ages and even Kings called themselves Caesar in the fashion of Roman Emperors.

Medieval Christian thinkers believed in universalism, and in supremacy of Church, monarchical governments, in holy Roman Empire and in representative government. They developed guilds and corporations in the medieval age of feudalism.

In medieval age there is much confusion and little political philosophy. According to Hearnshaw, *"medieval thinkers were like students writing essays on political theory from text books three in number the Bible, the Roman law and the politics of Aristotle."* As such genuine political thought during medieval period was replaced by mysticism and ideals of universalism when Europe was fragmented into different small states. He wrote about the universality of church and quoted Aristotle, a thinker of city state when no separate church existed. The discrepancy between theory and fact was due to unscientific, unhistorical and uncritical outlook. Intellectual side was controlled by church and was dogmatic. Religion was the basis of knowledge controlled by rigid orthodoxy. It was born of the complex interaction antagonistic forces of the church, Holy Roman Empire, Feudalism and Nationalism.

Medieval ages were unprogressive because these were dominated by barbarions. For example, Mr. Adams states a German warrior was astonished at 'seeing ducks apparently swimming on the floor of the ante-chamber in which he was waiting and dashed his battle axe to the beautiful mosaic to see if they were living. As such intellectual thought remained barren up to 11th century. The young nations like children were learning their intellectual alphabet and were labouriously spelling out the works of former masters. However, part played by the middle ages in the development of the Western civilization as described by Prof. Adams, "*was to form the organically united and homogeneous world and of the heterogenous and after hostile elements which the ancient world supplied, and so to furnish the essential conditions for an advance beyond any point was possible to the ancients.*"

Universalism

Rome had established a great Empire to which they thought universal, eternal and extending to all civilized world. Christians dominated idea of universalism from stoic ideas of Rome. According to Barbers, "The note of all medieval thoughts was universalism. It assumes the existence of a small universal society, which on its side is the inheritance and contravention of ancient Rome and on ecclesiastical side the incarnation of Christ in a visible church."

Supremacy of Church

In the beginning Church was simply a welfare or religious department of the state. But with the decline of Roman Empire, power of church increased. When there was anarchy Pope called Charles Martel for his help. Charles Martel and his son Popin saved Pope and Rome. Popin's son Charlemange ruled himself as an Emperor but after his death kingdom was divided. Otto saved Pope and he was crowned as an emperor of Holy Roman Empire by the Pope. This meant Pope gave the title of Emperor of Roman Empire to greatest Christian ruler and became supreme.

Further it was said that St. Peter gave spiritual power to Pope and temporal power to Emperor. As soul is more important than body, so Pope is superior than King or Emperor. Another argument was that when Emperor Constaintine left Rome and changed his capital to Constaintine, he gave all power to Rome. As such different arguments were advanced to prove the supremacy of church which will be dealt later on. However, it cannot be denied that for a temporary period, church worsted his enemy and became supreme. According to J.M. Figgs, *"In the middle ages church was not a state. It was the state, or rather the civil authority that acted like a police department of the church."* To quote Barker *"The sovereign power might exclude the temporal power from things spiritual, he could not being sovereign, exclude the spiritual power from things temporal."* Pope Innocent III according to Sabine, claimed "a power of revision and supervision over all the other forms of authority, whether ecclesiastical or secular." Thus, Pope claimed superiority, so this age is considered unpolitical.

Monarchical Conception of Government

During medieval ages people believed in the centralized administration under one head, so both church and states or empire adopted monarchical forms. Pope was the head of the Church like a monarch, Emperor of empire and king of the state and feudal lord of his land. Thus, everywhere monarchial form gained an upper hand.

Holy Roman Empire

Holy Roman Empire came into existence when Pope called Otto I of Germany for his help and Pope crowned him as an Emperor in 962 A.D. It remained into existence nominally up to the time of Napoleon. It figures in political thought because it was an attempt to establish universalism in secular sphere and to establish peace and harmony between the Emperor and Pope. But the attempt did not succeed and conflict between Pope and Emperor fill the pages of political thought of medieval ages. Thus, according to Dunning, *"therein was dogma of two powers."*

Representative Government

During medieval period Teuton races dominated the medieval age. They brought ideas of representative government which will be dealt later on.

Feudalism

One of the chief characteristic of the medieval age was feudalism. According to this system, serf or the farmer was at the lowest ladder, who owed allegiance to feudal lord and, feudal lord to King and King to Emperor or Pope. But actually feudal lords dominated the whole scene and wielded great powers. So it is called feudal age.

Development of Guilds

During this age guilds of artisan and trading classes developed who controlled and managed their own affairs. These guilds were numerous to control the different trades. These were like our caste panchayats who controlled their own social and economic affairs. In India, trades depended on castes so castes committees controlled them but in Europe trade decided his membership of guild. Idea of autonomy of guilds gave birth to the idea of Guild socialism.

Corporations

Medieval ages developed autonomous institutions such as universities, or local self government, who were autonomous in their internal administrations, these were called corporations. Defence of autonomy of these corporations helped in the ideas of development of pluralism. In brief these were the special features of Medieval period. Thus it different from Greek and Roman setup.

Medieval thinkers believed in representative governments and in constitutional monarchy and developed conceptions of legal rights for private persons which are still followed with some modifications and amendments.

Growth and Concept of Law of Nature in the Middle Ages

According to Adams, the Germanic people thought with them fresh vigour, youthful outlook, a new set of ideas and institutions which combined with the old gave birth to new civilization. The Greeks and the Romans placed emphasis on the state but Germans had a very high idea of personal independence of the value and importance of the individual man compared with the state. A Teuton was very jealous of personal independence as is depicted by the proud spirit of personal or individual war. They considered revenge as the duty of injured person. The unit was individual man and civil liberty was regarded as one of the most precious rights to be jealously guarded by a Teuton. The private rights were considered inviolable and limited the sphere of the state.

Representative Government

Teutonic races introduced the representative institutions and spirit of local autonomy which had a profound effect on the growth of medieval and subsequent growth of political institutions and ideas. The primitive tribal organization was incompatible with the highly centralized and despotic government of the Roman empire. Attack Teutonic divided Roman Empire into a number of loose knit kingdoms whose organization was tribal. The series of local institutions and feudal organization saved the empire from complete anarchy. German possessed following characteristics.

There was National Assembly consisting of all the treemen of the tribe. Its main function was to elect a chief and to decide necessary matters referred to it. Sometimes it used to assemble, to decide cases which might be placed before it. In addition to it Teutons possessed local representative assemblies in the hundreds or in the cantons which decided matters of local importance and acted as judicial bodies. He survived till the revival of Roman law at the end of the middle ages. In England they provided basis for the rise of House of commons and establishment of local self bodies like city councils and borough councils etc. The germs of our modern legislature and local Assemblies lie in the Teutonic ideas of representation of middle ages. The system of Government of the Teutons represented a device that combined central control with local self government and possible control over vast areas.

Constitutional Monarchy

The early Teutons freeman had the right to choose their own Chief or King. Though later on, it gave place to hereditary kingship in other countries but in Germany it was preserved for centuries. In England monarchy became hereditary but parliament claimed the right to choose successor in case of disputed succession and even to depose unpopular Kings or tyrants. Generally primogeniture or law of succession of eldest son was in vogue but it was not so strong, as to rule out the principle of election by people. With the development of Christianity idea of rule of King due to grace of God was also added. As such King inherited his throne, owed his office to popular election and ruled by the Grace of God. They broke the principle of state absolutism. The King was subject to law, it was the corollary of his ruling by grace of God. Principle of election was used in the choice of emperors, so long Holy Roman Empire remained into existence.

Legal System

Teutons developed conception of legal rights in their capacity as private persons. It had a personal basis and claiming the right to be tried according to his own law. It was promulgated by assemblies acting as courts. Feudal customs were declared to have the force of law, and case law, based on common notions of justice, which helped in the development of unwritten law. In England this common law is still retained though in Europe, it has been replaced by Roman law.

Representative local self government, elective or constitutional monarchy and a system of common law and ideals of individual liberty are the greatest boons which Teutons gave to the humankind and which had a profound influence on the development of representative and constitutional governments. In the words of Sabine, Teutonic people can be given credit of the idea that *"the people was corporate body which expressed its corporate mind through magistrates and natural leaders. In short notions of individual liberty or rights, representative Govt., Common law and of constitutional governments are their main contributions"* With some modifications and amendments these are still followed, so their contribution is very important.

Feudalism of Middle Ages

Disruption of Roman Empire gave rise to various petty local kingdoms. As the fall of Moghul Empire created local nawabs and jagirdars in Rajasthan and U.P. etc., so fall of Roman Empire brought into existence numerous feudal lords. According to Prof. Sabine, *"feudal institutions dominated the middle ages as completely as the city states dominated antiquity."* Thus, Feudalism prevailed in middle period.

Feudalism has its forms a political feudalism and economic feudalism. Political feudalism means decentralization of the governmental authority. In this system maintenance of peace and order and of deciding cases and of keeping armed forces rested with feudal lords.

In this system at the top where Popes and Emperors next was King who was unable to deal with feudal lords, with individual persons and with lesser nobles. He death with feudal lords and feudal lords dealt with subordinate lords and subordinate lords dealt with the individual or agriculturist who was called serf. Serf was at the lowest ladder and he had to pay tax and owe its allegiance to his immediate lord. His condition was pitiable. Serf used to hold his fief from his immediate superior called his suzerain. Serf was called Vassal and his immediate superior was called suzerain. The relation between them was personal and natural, Vassal had to take on oath of fealty to his lord and to respect his rights and immunities. Vassal on the other hand had to pay certain dues, attend his court, and to do military service whenever required. According to Sabine this feudal organization maintained *"an aspect of mutuality, of voluntary performance, and of implied contract which has vanished from modern relationship."*

Suzerian of serf owed his duties to feudal chief and he was vassal and feudal lord was his Suzerain early in the same way as he was of Serf, Feudal lords owed allegiance to their Kings. These feudal lords possessed power maintaining peace and order and maintaining justice in their territories. Army, court and state revenues were with the feudal lords and King was unable to interfere in their internal affairs. It depended on the ability of King as to what extent he was able to keep feudal barons under his control. Strong Kings were able to keep feudal lords under their thumb but if King was weak and feudal lord was strong, they used to care a fig for King and sometimes feudal lord of the same King fought with one another and even with his own King. Thus, though King theoretically supreme was sometimes unable to do what he desired as sometimes feudal lords were very powerful.

On economic side it was a system of land tenures in which those who tilled the soil possessed only right of life interest. In theory land belonged to King who gave to feudal lords as he was unable to till the land himself, feudal lord to his subordinate and subordinate lord to tiller *i.e.,* on certain terms. Serf was bound to lord and lord to feudal lord and feudal lord to King. Thus, there was herarcrachy who owed duties and obligations to one another. As church was also owner of land, so its bishops also became spiritual as well as secular feudal lords. Thus, feudalism prevailed not only in Europe but in Japan and in India also. Emergence of national states, rise of trading class and strong weapons gave a death blow to feudalism and modern nation states came into existence.

Invention of Gunpowder, Renaissance, emergence of national states of England and France etc., under strong kings such as Henry VII and Louis XI, geographical discoveries, commerce and Reformation gave death blow to feudalism in 15th century. New national states emerged with new political ideas of patriotism and democracy which brought medieval political thought to an end.

Chapter 8

Controversy Between Church and the State

St. Paul, Pope Greagory VII, Innocent III

According to Dunning the starting point of all medieval thinking in politics was dogma of two powers, the sacred authority of priest and royal power. This gave rise to controversy between Church and the state. St. Paul and Popes particularly Pope Greagory VII and Innocent III supported supremacy of Church. They argued Humankind owes its existence due to fatherhood of God and brotherhood of man and as such is one. As such church founded by God received mandate to govern. They argued Pope is supreme as he got mandate to govern from God and combines both spiritual and temporal power like Caliphate of Islam. But secularists argued that the secular authority is of divine origin and is not delegation of Pope, so he did not possess supreme power, so controversy began.

The arguments in the middle ages in the church state controversy.

Christianity began as a religion against the state but Emperor Constantine adopted it and it became the official religion of the state. In the beginning it was the department of the state and Emperor was the head of both church and the state. With the division of empire and decline of its power, church became all powerful. The barbarians who gave a death blow to Roman Empire themselves adopted Christian religion. Gradually Christian faith achieved a dominating place in the heart of masses and church became so powerful that even prince who defined its teachings were ex-communicated. This ex-communication from society forced even princes for submission.

Supremacy of Pope

When there was anarchy in Italy and Muslim invaders also threatened Christianity, Charles Martel his son Popin and Charlemagno saved it. Consequently Charlemangno became the Emperor as he was declared so by the Pope. In reality Charlemagno was one of the most powerful of the rulers ever produced by Europe but support of emperor gave sacramental sanction to his achievements. After the death of Charlemagno, his empire was fragmented and gradually national states grew.

When there was anarchy in Italy, Pope again called German ruler Otto I, who prominently helped the Pope and the Pope conferred on him title of the holy Roman Emperor, who was theoretically supreme in whole christiandom. Thus, Holy Roman Empire was created which remained into existence up to nineteenth century when it was destroyed by Napoleon Bonaparte.

When the holy Roman Empire was created, no attempt was made to define the relations between the Pope and the Emperor. It was difficult to decide whether the Emperor derived his authority from God directly or through the Pope and whether they were superior in their own temporal and secular sphere or the Pope was superior to Emperor? Claim of superiority between the Emperor and the Pope gave rise to fierce controversy. But in medieval period feudalism prevented the growth of central secular government. On the other hand church became centralized grew politically powerful and the act coronation of the Emperor, gave the Pope, the idea of claiming supreme universal power.

Pope Greagory VII was a very powerful Pope, he reformed the church and decreed that "we, *ecclesiastical should be invested with the symbols of office by a secular ruler under the penalty of ex-communication.*" The decree lead to the conflict between Emperor Henery IV and Greogory VIII. The Emperor got the Pope deposed by church council and the Pope ex-communicated him. Consequently the emperor had to go to the Pope at Canossa for forgiveness and had to stand barefooted in cold night for forgiveness. Thus, the Pope became victorious and the Pope became supreme in Christiandom.

In 13th century under Pope Innocent III, Papacy reached to its Zenith. Reason of supremacy was support of feaudal lords and the reforms of Greagory VII. He propounded justice *i.e.,* the Papal supremacy over the church the liberation of clergy from social bond of matrimony, the economic bond of Simony and the feudal bond of lay investiture. He stated that the sovereign Pope might exclude the temporal power form things spiritual, he could not bring sovereign exclude spiritual power from things temporal. As the clergies were not allowed to marry but to hold church property without the control of state and state was unable to interfere in their affairs though clergy was allowed to interfere in secular matters, so church became all powerful.

In 14th century power of feudalism declined and nation states became powerful. The contest between the Papacy under Bonface and French monarchy led to victory of the latter and the seat of Papacy was shifted to Aniguon and the papal control was shifted to Paris. This gave rise to another Papacy at Rome and mutual conflict between the Popes decreased their power and the growing national states of Spain, France and England refused to submit to a discredited papacy. Later on Papacy became one and centralized at Rome but it was never able to achieve its best power. Later on Protestant reformation gave a death blow to the power of Pope and the secular national states became supreme. In 19th century Napoleon Bonaparte abolished Holy Roman Empire which according to Voltaire was neither Holy nor Roman. Now Pope became only a religious saint wielding only moral influence on its followers. However during the medieval period whole political thought of Rome centered in the controversy of superiority, between the church and the Pope as such arguments of both sides may be stated here briefly.

The Ecclesiastical Claim for Supremacy

Right from 9th century onwards, the papacy laid claims to supremacy not only in ecclesiastical but also in secular matters. The supporters of church employed their learning in giving a historic basis to the claim of Pope for supremacy. In the Decretum of Gratian 12th century a sort of clerical hierarchy was worked out. The famous donation known as Donation of Constantine according to which the seat of imperial authority was transferred from Rome to Byzantine a grant of authority in themselves was given to Pope. It was made out as irrefutable case for papal supremacy of Pope meant supremacy of Pope exclusively in spiritual matters and supremacy over secular authorities also, arguments may be stated here briefly.

(1) Humankind owes its existence due to the fatherhood of God and brotherhood of man and as such it is one. As such church founded by God can be only true state, having received a mandate from God, the plenitude of all spiritual and temporal powers, they are being integral part of one might. The head of this world is Christ, but he must have an earthly representative to exercise this authority over the mortals and his representative is the who "is their priest and their king, their spiritual and temporal monarch, their law giver and judge in all cases supreme. As such the Pope combines the both powers in one as the caliphate of Islam.

(2) Both temporal and spiritual swords were given by God to St. Peter from whom they have descended to the Pope who is the representative of the God on earth. The Pope retained the spiritual power while gave secular power to the secular rulers, who is to exercise the secular power as his agent. The Emperor and secular rulers get their power through the Pope from God so they are the vassals of Pope. The Emperor being the highest of the Papal vassals pays homage by taking coronation oath. The secular power being delegation of church should be exercised under the supervision of church. The Pope possesses the right and is bound to exercise a direct control over secular rulers. He may transfer the imperial authority from one individual to another. Guardianship of Empire reverts to the Pope in case of vacancy. The Pope can bear complaints of lay rulers, can depose or ex-communicate them absolving their subjects from loyalty to them.

(3) The state is not of divine origin and it gets power through the church. State owes its origin to sin due to the fall of man and so it requires to be controlled by the authority of church. The temporal power is subject to spiritual because human laws are inferior to divine laws. Temporal offices are inferior to spiritual offices.

(4) The church possesses the right to set spiritual leanings of state and that cannot be done without interfering in the affairs of the secular authorities. As such church possess right to interfere in temporal matters.

(5) The soul is superior to body and as church represents soul and state represents flesh to church is superior to the state. The church is the sun and state are the Moon, so state authority is borrowed from, sanctioned by, and dependent on spiritual authority.

(6) As Emperor Constantine transferred power and prestige of Roman Empire to the church, so church is superior to temporal

rulers. All power must be centered in the church to prevent disintegration of Rome. This argument was valid in feudal regime of Europe as church was the only centralized force to save the Europe from chaos and anarchy as at that time it was ruled by too many European feudal lords.

(7) The secular power is invention of worldly man so it cannot morally compete with the divinely ordained authority of the church. As the officers of church represent the higher moral authority of church, so they cannot be controlled by secular authorities. But as the officers of the state owe their existence due to inferior secular authority, so they can be controlled by church in their moral actions. Officers of the state can be punished if they do not conform to morality by the church.

(8) It was argued that the church gave power to Charlemagno by coronating him as Emperor and similarly the Pope crowned Oatto as Emperor. If Pope can give power to the Emperor it can also depose the inferior secular ruler.

According to Dunning, *"with a wide basis in custom and public sentiment for the exercise of jurisdiction over many classes of legal controversies,"* with an exclusive control of such as could be shown to be spiritual in character; with the facility for extending his control that inhered in the doctorine that it embraced whatever action were in any way, tainted with sin, and with the power to enforce its interpretation of its authority by the deposition of secular rulers from power the medieval church was in fact, if not in theory a most potent political institution.

The Pope claimed the right to save the damned soul by the authority from Christ who said to Peter "And I will give unto the keys of kingdom of heaven! and whatsoever thou shalt bind on earth shall be bound in heaven and whatsoever thou loose on earth shall be loosed in heaven." With this powerful authority from Bible, church was able to control the rulers and ruled alike to the orthodox religious minded people and rulers of the middle ages. Thus, church became supreme in medieval age.

Criticism

(1) The Pope claimed supremacy over all matters whether these may be spiritual or temporal but it involved decrease in authority of bishops. The ambitions bishops had to sacrifice themselves and their ambitions for the realization of exalted position of Pope who

felt humiliation and some bishops revolted against the authority of Pope. It was revolt of one clergy Martin Luther and other clergies like Wycliff and Calvin which brought the downfall of the authority of the Pope.

(2) Every Pope was not Geregory, the great and the controlling of secular authority required a superman. As the other Popes were not equal to the task to their authority declined.

(3) Church owed ownership of landed authority under King, so their point of higher moral authority lost its ground of superiority.

(4) As the church by owning land itself became a secular power so its claim to punish king to whom theoretically all land belonged gave a death blow to the idea of superiority as it itself became a feudal lord.

(5) Church claimed to punish rulers in case of moral breach but in case of breaking of law by clergy, it claimed right that his clergy cannot be punished by secular rulers, now clergies were left with the wild punishment of the church which was against the motions of equality before law.

(6) The protection which clergyman enjoyed loosed their moral and consequently toned down general administration and their respect before general public. It cannot be supported that clergy men should not be punished by secular ruler for breaking law and morality.

(7) Sometimes Popes interfered in the matters of secular rulers which casted reflection on their impartiality as in case of Innocent III, he commissioned Philip of France to invade King John of England for his disregard. This antagonized England against the Pope.

(8) Greagory, the great proposed Celibacy for clergies and nuns but every clergy was not able to follow morality and consequently it lowered the prestige of the church. The corrupt practices and immorality which took its origin in church gave a death blow to the idea of supremacy of the church and it lost its claim of superiority.

(9) Lastly, in some cases church was unable to act promptly and impartially as in case of divorce of King Henry VIII of England which threw this mighty king and England against the idea of supremacy of the Pope and established supremacy of King.

(10) Lastly, discoveries of new world and countries where secular rulers were supreme in secular matters and rise of power of

trading class and ideas of socialism and scientific spirit gave a death blow to the ideas of supremacy of church. In Europe or in Roman Catholic world, the Pope or Church still wields some influence but in India it has lost its all power as fast of Jagadguru Shankaracharya remained a cry in wilderness to which no attention was paid by the rulers of India. They not only overlooked it but also condemned it. As such when religion has lost its complete hold on the minds of rulers of India, in a country which is said to be most religious minded, what to say of others except Muslim countries. As the religion lost its hold among Hindus and in Christian rulers now supremacy of the Pope was bound to go, though Muslim fanatism is still in ran etc.

The Secular Claim

While the Pope and supporters of Church claimed superiority over secular rulers including emperors confined themselves to the claim of superiority in secular matters only. Except Fredrick II, all supporters of secular authority confined themselves to the supremacy in secular matters only and did not claim for superiority of Church over the state in spite of the fact that early Church was under the Roman Empire. Only Marsiglio of Padua demanded the absorption of Church in the state. As such generally supporters of state claimed that the Pope's duty is to look after spiritual sphere only and in secular spheres, rulers derive authority from God and Popes could not interfere in secular matters.

Secular Arguments

(1) The secular authority is of divine origin and is not delegation of the Pope. The Kings are representative of God on earth and so they are responsible to him alone. The state owes its existence due to divine power and as such it cannot be controlled by Church.

(2) The medieval thinkers claimed that state has also a moral basis as stated before by Plato and Aristotle. As state is a moral institution so Church cannot control secular authority on moral grounds.

(3) The sacredotium and Imperium are two sides or Christendom and to maintain harmony state should be subordinate to church in spiritual matters. And church to the state in secular matters.

(4) According to New Testamant, St. Paul said, *"the powers that he ordained from God"* as such state also is divinely ordained and

secular rulers are responsible only to God and as such they are supreme in secular matters.

(5) With the revival of study of Roman law in 11th century and study of theology lost its monopoly. Bartolus, the leading jurist held that Emperor's sovereignty is inalienable and that to dispute it was sacrilege. It was also claimed by later jurists that "the emperors possessed the unbroken imperial power of the caesars." The Emperor's will have the force of law. It was held by them that Roman Emperors were supreme overall and as Holy Roman Emperors as independent of all including the control of church and are superior to all temporal rulers. According to Sabine, in long run, lawyers turned out to be the most effective defenders of secular cause.

(6) It was also said that Apostle said Fear God and, however, it meant that secular powers hold crown due to Grace of God.

(7) Peter Crasus argued that state is the private property of King and to deprive an individual his private property has no sanction in law. Anointing does not indicate superiority but it is simply a ministerial function.

Above argument show that church was on the aggressive side and claimed supreme authority in both spheres while secularists claimed authority in secular affairs only. In the beginning, church got an upper hand but decline of feudalism and rise of national states gave a death blow to the power of Pope. But for a long time according to Hobbes, "*the Papacy was the ghost of the Roman Empire, sitting crowned on its grave.*" In the beginning church got an upper hand as Maxey states, "*No lord was strong enough to prevail against hold upon the superstitions of classes and masses enabled her to rout all opposition.*" With emergence of national states and renaissance and reformation supremacy of Pope and Church declined.

Chapter 9

Supporters of Papal Supremacy

Greagory VII John of Salisbury, Thomas Acquinas

Hilderband later on Pope Greagory VII, John of Salisbury and Thomas Acquinas were main figures who supported supremacy of Pope to promote righteousness and believed in divine law of eternal justice to which Prince is obliged to follow, so Prince is subject to divine law.

Hilderband, later Greagory VII 1073-1080 A.D. was most pronounced champion of supremacy of papacy over secular authorities. He was a great reformer and tried for Monastic revival which increased his prestige. Pope Greagory VII dreamed "of a Pope sovereign orbiter of all disputes, holding in hands, the supreme mediation in questions of war and peace adjudging contesting succession in the kingdoms, deposing tyrants, and in short forming, instead of King or Emperor, the real chopping stone of the feudal organization.

He claimed both spiritual power and supreme temporal power are in the hands of Pope. He believed even the humblest priest is greater than the mightiest ruler because priest represents moral side. He allowed divine sanction to secular authority whose main function was to maintain justice by force as state originates due to force. Gandhiji also believed that state is based on force, same was view of others.

Pope Greagory VII desired to create the kingdom of Christ by means of promoting righteousness through the instrumentality of Government of the church which represented divine origin. He worsted his rival Emperor Henry IV, by absolving the subjects from their oath of allegiance to a temporal prince, who had offended the church. He meant by justice the undivided authority of the Pope over the church and right of the Pope of admonishing or banishing even a King if the later violated divine law. He believed that by purifying and exalting the church, he could spread righteousness in the world and for this he desired domination of Pope to create city of God as combined by just to whose school of thought. He belonged he made church supreme.

JOHN OF SALISBURY

John of Salisbury 1115 – 1180 was an English theorist. His book Poncractions or the statesman's book has been described by Dr. Dickinson as the earliest elaborated medieval treatise on Politics. Dr. R.L. Paule states that it is *"the first attempt to produce a coherent system which should aspire to the character of a philosophy of a politics."* Thus, Podicraticus is the first extended and systematic treatment of political philosophy during middle age.

Ideas of John Salisbury

Political Philosophy of John of Salisbury is ethical rather than constitutional. He states about monarchical form of government only and of administrative machinery of imperial type. He did not state much about the organization of government or about its forms of distribution of functions or inter relationship.

His most important conceptions are (i) Organic conception of society. (ii) The subordination of state to church. (iii) The theory of prince to law and distribution between the true king and tyrant. (iv) The theory of tyranniede.

John of Salisbury follows that the state is a commonwealth or a society united by a common agreement about law and rights. He compares the state with human body and believes in the organic theory of the state. According to his definition, state or commonwealth is a body which is given life by benefit of divine favour, and is moved by the highest equity, and is ruled by a certain moderating reason. It means state is like a human living being. It is created by God. Its different parts are bound by law and justice and it is governed by reason. The state is like a heart, the judges and governors etc. correspond to the eyes, ears and tongue of body. Soldiers are its arms and husband men are its feet. His theory resembles to caste system of Hindus according to which Brahmans come from mind, Kshatriyas represent arms, Vaishyas appetite and Sudras feet. However, he believes that body has purpose similar to state of these things that establish the right to religion in us, and teach us the worship of God. He states that those men who preside over the rites of religion should be honoured and revered as the soul of the body.

As the soul rules the head and other parts of body, so the Prince should be subject God and to those who represent him on earth. Subordination of state to Church is provided by concurrence of divine, clerical and popular elements in election of a prince. The king heads the Government due to divine will with approval of people and by the ceremony performed by priest.

John of Salisbury states that originally both the swords, spiritual as well as temporal were held by the Pope or Church. Christ, who possessed both powers gave them to Peter and used word. Keys which mean not only one but both the powers. The Church preferred to retain only one power and transferred the other to the secular rulers to be wielded on her behalf and at her will. John of Salisbury states that the sword (coercive jurisdiction in temporal matters), then the prime receives from the hands of Church, although she herself into sense hold sword of blood. She nevertheless possesses the sword but used it by the hand of prince on whom she confers the coercive power of the body, reserving the authority over spiritual thing for herself in the pontiffs. The prince, therefore, is in a sense the minister of the priestly office, and one who performs that part of the sacred functions which seems unworthy in the hand of the priesthood. This makes temporal power derivative and subordinate to Church. It seems that Pope Innocent IV formulated the theory of subordination of state to Church as divinely ordained on the basis of these thoughts.

His chief contribution lies in his conception that the prince is subject to law and its servant and holds that Prince was the minister of public utility and servant of equity. Power of all subjects assembles in him, so that he may be strong enough to seek out and perform what was necessary for the welfare of all. It means Kingship was a public office and as such his authority must be used only in ways consistent with the purpose for which it owes its existence. Its medieval age there were no supreme and constitutional courts or popular assemblies to check the unlimited power of the King and so he subjected king to moral restraint of law as other medieval thinkers did.

John Salisbury believes that law is not the positive law of the state but the divine law of eternal justice. He followed conception of natural law of stoics and stated it is eternal, immutable and independent of all human enactments and to such a law, all – monarchs must submit. A ruler who does not care for such a law is guilty of abusing his authority and instead of performing public welfare rules for his own selfish ends and becomes a tyrant. The only difference between a monarch and tyrant is that monarch rules in the interest and for the welfare of the public in accordance with the law of external justice. He depends for interpretation of law on priest or clergy. Only priest or clergy know about the eternal law of justice and can tell as how to act in conformity of that law so prince has to depend on clergyman for guidance as is consequently subordinate to him. Now same arguments are used by Judges for Judicial supremacy.

Distinction between a King and tyrant was also made by Greek thinkers but John of Salisbury gave a new conception of tyranicide. He states that tyranicide is not only just but also a meritorious thing to get rid of the ruler who behaves tyrannically. Support of Tyranicide is something unique to be propagated by a Christian because it is against the teachings of Christian religion.

However, King remains king so long he rules justly and public possess the right to remove unjust king or to punish him if he acts contrary to the constitutional laws and traditions. But he stated doctorine of tyranicide rather harshly, emphatically and stated naked truth in clear language. He shows that force in ultimate end, will never succeed for he who usurps the sword is worthy to die by sword. As such he meant that a King who rules not according to law, but by the power of sword is to be opposed by power of sword and should meet its doom through the sword.

His greatest contribution lies in his conception of law according to which a ruler should rule and relation of ruler and subject and his comprehensiveness and systemization of thought which affected even secular rulers of 16th century and even when the supremacy of church declined.

ST. THOMAS ACQUINAS (1227-1274)

St. Thomas Acquinas believed that function of Govt. is to make man virtuous for leading a good life and for seeking salvation. As salvation can be achieved through Church so head of Church *i.e.,* Pope possesses supreme powers. He argues that law is an ordinance of reason for common good. He believes divine law consists commands of God and is supreme to manmade laws. As divine laws can be enforced by Pope so Church and its Head Pope is supreme.

It was argued spiritual power is supreme so church which holds spiritual power ought to be considered supreme. Hindus consider *Vedas*, Muslims *Koran* and Christians *Bible* as revelations from God, so propounder of these revelations may be considered supreme but this argument was not accepted by kings who claimed divine origin, so with the rise of powerful national states supremacy of Pope got a death blow and his supremacy became confined to religious matters. In spite of all this according to Foster, "Acquinas was one of the greatest philosophers who brought synthesis" (doctrines of Aristotle, the stoics, Cicero and of Roman jurists). As such Foster is of the opinion that St. Thomas Acquinas represents, as no medieval author singly does, the totality of medieval thought.

ST. THOMAS ACQUINAS

Life

St. Thomas Acquinas is generally acclaimed as one of the greatest political thinkers. He was born in 1227 and died at the age of 47 in 1274. According to Foster, *"he was one of the greatest systematic philosophers of the world."* He holds that the distinctive thing about Acquinas was that he assimilated into the unity of a single system the different trends of thought which had previously been apart. He represents, perhaps as no other medieval thinker does the totality of medieval thought.

As such he is one of the best champions of the church and he ranks as one of the best philosophers and schoolmen of middle ages. He was born in Sicily in a noble family and inherited imperial traditions. He joined the begging fraternity of St. Dominie. An extraordinary intellectual man, he moved among Popes and Kings and travelled far and wide and observed affairs keenly. Thirteenth century was the period of scholasticism which as a philosophy of life was all comprehensive including moral, social, political economic and other problems. It was supposed that church dogma is unquestionable and infallible. Rational explanation was given to show that dogma was not contrary to reason. According to Hearnshaw, *"The scholasticism is a master key to the understanding of medievalism."* The 13th century was remarkable for a passion for the unification of knowledge and its achievement in this direction perhaps are most notable.

Environment

During 13th century contest between the Holy Roman Empire and Papacy resulted in the complete victory of the Pope. Spain and Portugal were conquered by Arab invaders. Aristotle and Cicero was revived and through Spain it reached in Europe. The classics translated into Latin reached to Europe and had a profound influence on the political thought of Europe and St. Acquinas. St. Acquinas thought had a strong Aristotelian bias. He gave a new birth to Politics of Aristotle and principally though him it was incorporated in the political thought of Europe. He fused the teachings of Aristotle's Politics with the teachings of St. Augustine's city of God in an amalgam which still remains the essence of catholic society and the state. In his book 'Sunma Theologica' containing three parts and about a million words, he embodied a great edifice of thought in which some of the Platonnic traditions and the teachings of Aristotle are united with the Roman law, the Bible the saying of Church fathers and other great theologians. As per Dunning, his doctorine presents the reconciliation of St. Augustine and Aristotle.

Work

His work was synthetic, architectonic in nature incorporating the best in scholasticism with best in Hellanism. He agrees with Aristotle that state is natural to man but he believes that happiness which is the aim of the state can only be achieved through salvation. He agrees that state is necessary to provide conditions of good life but for eternal good church is necessary. The church is the root of social omganisation and not the rival of the state.

Summa Theologica is not a book dealing primarily with politics, but it discusses law, justice, Government and topics like sin, incarnation, faith, resurrection etc. In his commentaries on Aristotle, he discusses about law and justice and in incomplete work De Regima Principum, he deals with the Rule of Princes. His Political philosophy can be gleaned from his books, *De Regima Principum* and *Summa Contra Gentiles* and *Commentaries on Politics of Aristotle* in a modified way.

According to Thomas the whole of Human knowledge makes a unity like a pyramid whose base consists of the various special sciences each of which has its own subject matter and philosophy deals with general reason. As such he and Aristotle are one in their conceptions. While Hellenic philosophers regarded philosophy as the summit of knowledge, Thomas holds that above philosophy there stand theology whose instrument is faith and revelation and not reason. There are things which could not be understood by philosophy or reason and here faith is necessary. He believes, according to Sabine that Theology completes the system of which science and philosophy from the very beginning but never destroys its continuity. Faith is fulfillment of reason. Together they build the temple of knowledge but nowhere do they conflict or work at cross purposes.

He agrees with Aristotle that in nature everything acts under an inner urge to realize its own nature or perfection and so a man has also a purpose. Aristotle holds this purpose is rational contemplation because his reason is the highest faculty, but Thomas says highest thing is soul and so a man should try to achieve salvation of his soul, which cannot be achieved by reason as such a man should have faith in religion.

His Views about State

In his social and political philosophy Thomas states that human society is a system of ends and purposes in which the lower serves the higher and higher directs and guides the lower and as such state is necessary. According to Sabine, he regards state as a mutual exchange of services for the sake of good life to which many calling contribute. He held like Greek thinkers that the state is necessary not only to check evil but without it, an individual could not realize himself fully and as such it has somethings of a natural character. He further agrees that the state is a positive organ of social welfare. He is modern in giving preference to nation state. Community of manners and customs can be found in a nation state than in a heterogeneous empire. He states that state justifies itself by education and by the provisions for the poor. From God legitimate authority to govern passes to the whole society. The people are sovereign and they may delegate authority to any form of government such as monarchy, aristocracy or democracy. According to him *"life in community enables a man...to live fully, with all that is necessary for its wellbeing."*

He believes that the end of state is the realization of good the virtuous life. But state can only achieve earthly happiness and not salvation. He believes that society and state should be organized with a view to an end beyond earthly happiness and for this, he advocates social legislation as main function of the state. But salvation and eternal happiness can only be achieved by church so it should be subordination to church achieve higher end to life. Thus, Acquinas corrects Aristotle by making church the crown of human life and greater than the state. He believes in Christian truth that man has also a supernatural end, namely salvation and further blessedness to which the end of his happiness of life is itself subordinate.

Classification of Government

According to St. Thomas Acquinas man's rule on man may be either result of sin which takes form of slavery or it may be due to social instinct and may take the form of civil government which may be sacraderoal or royal or political or economic. Of these first headed by the Pope is the best and highest. Form of government did not matter much but what matter is its work. He preferred monarchical form of government next and stated as God rules the whole universe so a monarch should rule. Moreover monarchical form of Government brings stability and unity of the state. Democracy is an impossible ideal. Further monarchical form of government brings unity, regularity, experience and an analogy with divine rule. Tyranny is worst. Monarchy can be prevented from degeneration if it is limited as such limited monarchy is the best. He opposed tyranicide as stated by John of Salisbury because it may be followed by mob rule which is the worst type of tyranny. He, however, held that the elected monarch may be deposed and he preferred elected monarchy. He believed that state exists for the welfare of individual and not individual for the state.

Supremacy of Church

He believed that function of the government is to make man virtuous for leading a good life and for seeking Salvation. As salvation of soul can be achieved by the church so a secular ruler could perform his functions only in co-operation with and under the guidance of church. The Pope as head of church must have landed property but he cannot be vassal to any secular ruler to his holding of property. As secular ruler can give only earthly happiness and the Pope can give salvation of soul *i.e.*, eternal happiness so he is supreme and secular rulers must be subordinated to him.

Law

According Acquinas *"Law is an ordinance of reason for the common good."*

Thomas Acquinas believes that main function of the state to make its citizen morally and to help them to realize the true end. Political authority must be exercised in accordance with law and a ruler who disregards law becomes a tyrant. According to John of Salisbury, the binding character of law follows from its rational or moral character and according to modern concept law means command of sovereign or will of the sovereign body. But Thomas Acquinas defined law as 'an ordinance of reason for the common good promogated by him who has the care of the community. Thus, according to him law should be based on reason and it should be for the common good and it should be enacted by the ruler. Modern definitions of law places emphasis on enactment of ruler but Thomas Acquinas puts emphasis on reason of common good also. His definition of law combines the Greek, Roman, Stoic and Christian point of view.

He held that law must be related to reason for command and it should be enacted by public or its representative and it should have obligatory power to force to obey those who are subject to law. He distinguished between four kinds of law (1) eternal, (2) natural, (3) divine and (4) human. Eternal is ordained by God which governs the whole universe. It governs celestial and territorial spheres, animal and inanimate kingdoms and heavenly bodies such as stars, the sun and the moon etc. In the world where human beings dwell who are, rational, it is interpreted by the reason of rational being and is called natural law. The natural law was written in the heart of man and though his reason enabled him to recognize and obey the eternal law. Man understands general principles of conduct due to his reasoning faculty and these general principles makes the general law. Neither eternal law nor natural law is positive law because these are not man made laws. Divine law consists of the commands of God communicated to man by revealation as through *Vedas* to Hindus, *Bible* to Christians & *Koran* to Muslims.

Positive laws are divine and human laws are manmade Divine law consists of direct revelation of divine purpose through the Bible or through the saints. Human law is derived from natural law and is valid if it is not against the natural law to whom it is subordinate. Human law is concrete then man made law but natural law is created in the conscience of man by God. He believed that there can be no clash or conflict between natural and divine law because God can never command unreasonable things. Revelation supplements reason. According to Sabine, "*Revelation does not destroy reason; it only supplements it.*" According to Sabine the structure of Thomas' system is built on reason and faith, but he never doubted that it was one structure. Human law is necessary to supplement natural law. For example, natural law may state that stealing is bad but how this bad act should be punished and who should punish? And in what manner? Comes within the purview of human law.

He is of the opinion that if human law is inconsistent with the natural law it loses his binding force. He states a law made by the ruler against the dictates of reason does not bind a citizen. In short he holds that in order to have binding force on citizen, Law should be just and virtuous and in conformity with the natural law, otherwise it can be disobeyed. It must aim at common good and must have backing of the community. It should also be in accordance with human-conscience and natural law. Thus, he links up political obedience with the moral obligation. Tilak and Gandhi etc. also refused to follow unjust laws.

St. Thomas Acquinas wanted to improve mankind by bringing about a combination between divine and human knowledge. He tried to compromise divine will and revelation and human reason and knowledge. He interpreted teachings of Plato, Aristotle and Cicero in accordance with Christian teachings. He was individualist and believed that the social and political order existed for the sake of individual. True end of human life is total salvation and in this direction only church can be of help so church is greater than the state. As such he gave powers of supervision and control to church or the Pope over secular rulers. As such he reconciled Christian ideas with Aristotelian ideas.

Evaluation

Thomas Acquinas was not an original writer but he possessed astonishing power of synthesis and blended book *Divinity and Humanity* into one compact whole and he was able to blend book *Faith and Reason* in simple manner. According to Dr. Jazi *"In this new world the Roman Catholic Church urgently needed a comprehensive of Christianity in harmony with the world diplomacy of the Pope's power."* The task was admirably accomplished by St. Thomas, not much by the originality of his ideas or the brilliancy of his analysis as by his extraordinary gift for combining and unifying different elements of thought in an apparently logical and convincing system...his work was an attempt to graft the cological idea of the church, and the lightness of the Pope as a noble thing on the wild system of Aristotelian theory of state.

He stated, "Law is an ordinance of reason for the common good promulgated by him who has care of its community." He supported conception of welfare state. He stated, "It is the function of earthly ruler to lay the foundation of human happiness by maintaining peace and order...by seeing that all needful services of public administration, of judicature and defence are performed and to correct it by removing all possible hindrances to good life." According to Dunning, *"His theory of law and justice is the channel through which the doctorines of Aristotle, the Stoics, Cicero, the Roman jurists and of St. Acquinas are blended."*

He paved the way for popular sovereignty, general will and of welfare state etc. As such he is regarded as a great thinker of medieval age.

Briefly it can he stated, supporters of Papal supremacy argued that origin of Church is divine, so head of church *i.e.,* Pope may wield supreme power and is supreme. They supported supremacy of Pope through lot of arguments as stated above.

Chapter 10

Supporters of Secularist Supremacy

(John of Paris, Marsiglio of Padua and Dante)

John of Paris, Marsiglio of Padua[1] and Dante were main personalities who argued for secular supremacy and refuted the arguments of Pope's supremacy and triumphed, so their views need careful study.

JOHN OF PARIS

Early Life

John of Paris (1269-1306) represented the spirit of his age. He says that the faith is necessary for the salvation everywhere and spiritual interests are similar in whole Christendom. As such a universal church and unity in religion is desirable. But in secular matter language, customs and manners differ from province to province and country to country. The political requirement of England is different from French and those of Germany from Italy, therefore, on secular side natural units are kingdoms or national states. There can be as many kingdoms as the diversities of political interest may demand. There is no need of unifying power or centralized state administration. This term is based on Aristotelian conception of diversities and the doctrine of self-sufficing communities which according to him are kingdoms.

His Views about States

He refutes the theory that the state is being rooted in human sin. He propounded Aristotelian theory that state is necessary for good life and without its independence social and personal virtues cannot develop. In this he uses the natural necessity to support its independence from the control of the Pope or the church.

He opposes Aristotle that higher controls the lower or lower is subordinate to higher. He agrees that the spiritual authority of the church is superior in dignity to the secular power of the prince but holds that times did not means that the former is superior to the latter in each and every respect. Superior dignity does not mean superior power. A teacher or preacher possesses greater dignity but less temporal power. As such though secular power is lower sovereignty but superior intemporal power. Both derive their authority from God. It is wrong to say that the secular power derives authority from the church. Aristotle's theory that the higher controls the lower does not bring us to conclusion that spiritual power should control the secular power.

He attacked the legal validity of donation of Constantine and stated that the Emperor had no right to alienate any part of the Empire. Suppose he possesses such a right it did not apply to France as France was never under the control of the Empire. Moreover, when France became free the Pope had no right to exercise any control over the independent kingdom of France through his henchman Emperor.

Defence of Property

He States that *every individual has full right of ownership and use over his property and these rights belong to him who acquires property by dint of his labour and industry.* The only right that ruler possesses is to regulate the use of property in public interest and tax it. So far church property is concerned it belongs to church as an organization and the Pope is only steward or manager of that property to administer it for public good. He says prince does not possess power to the ownership of property or to administer it, but he possesses the power of regulating its use for public good. The Pope possesses only right to administer the church property and to use the layman's property for the protection of common faith.

Limited Authority of Church

He states that the right of the church is limited to the duty of preaching, teaching and administering the church property. He stated communication amounts to protest and not to deposition and right of deposition if at all valid belongs to elector and not to the Pope. He says that the Pope possesses power over spiritual matters and did not possess any control over secular matters.

According to Sabine, "coming from a church man...limiting of church's authority is very strange."

About the ecclesiastical powers of church, he states that he is the administrative head of church, organization and not the supreme authority. He states that final authority resides in the general council of the church which can depose a Pope for corrupt practices. John of Paris justifies resistance to Pope who abuses his authority. Thus he supported secular state and popular sovereignty against the Pope.

According to Sabine, "*Without presenting a systematic political theory, the work of John of Paris was highly magnificent both for its own time and for the future. As Frenchman as well as clergy, he made a strong case on both his historic and legal grounds for the independence of the French monarchy.*" He adds "*substantially his argument is a protest against the invasion of religion by law and against investing the Pope with a sovereign power modeled on the legal position of the Emperor.*" He supported conception of national states against the universal state of Dante. His ideas have more national application of Aristolian theory of self sufficiency community than of Thomas or Dante, as such his theory is known Anerroist Aristotalism.

MARSIGLIO OF PADUA (1270-1340)

Marsiglio of Padua argued "It is not the priest that forgives sin, God alone judges in these matters." As such according to Sabine, Marsiglio wrote not only to defend the empire, but to destroy whole system of papal Imperialism. He further states Marsiglio's political philosophy was essentially a recrudescence of theory of city state, competent to regulate every branch of civilization. His theory was anti-Pope theory. As such he played a very important part in building up medieval secularism, therefore, study of his life and ideas is essential.

Life and Ideas

Marsiglio of Padua was born in or about 1278 and died near about 1343. John of Paris supported the cause of Philip of France against the Pope Poniface VII and Marsiglio of Padua supported the cause of lanis of Bavaria. He was a marvellous person, a medical man an ecclesiast (at one time he was appointed archbishop of Milan) lawyer, soldier and a politician by turn. He emancipated himself from the theories of middle ages that the other thinkers of the age. His books Defensor Paris was regarded as the epoch making political book in 14th & 15th centuries. According to Murray, *"he was the most original thinker of fourteenth century."* His political theory, says Sabine, is *"one of the most remarkable creations of medieval political thought. He was engaged by German Emperor to defend his cause against the Pope."* He referred neither Germany nor the empire but directly attacked the absolute authority of Pope because like Dante before and Machiavelli after wards he became against the Pope due to worldly anti Papel turn at Arignon. Moreover he belonged to the power of Franscisan order who were condemned by the Pope for keeping large property. The declaration of Pope that Fransciscan rulers should not possess property beyond certain limit annoyed him and William of occam who wrote against the Pope. He is considered as one of the greatest secular thinkers of medieval age. His philosophy prepared the intellectual background of Wycliff of England and John Hus of Bohemia for reformation of the 16th century.

During 14th century the power of the Pope declined. Dante describes the Pope as reigning wolf in the garb of shepherds. The Pope offended monarchs due to his undue interference and so in 1338 the imperial electors defied the authority of Popacy by stating in letters that no Popal information is necessary. Ideas of Marsiglio of Padua further weakened the authority of the Pope. He opposed Pope's superiority.

The first part of 'Defensor Paris,' which appeared in 1324, is a restatement of Aristotelian principles. It deals with origin of the state, its end, the nature and functions of law and legislature it was written by John of Paris and adopted by him. In second part Marsiglio draws state conclusions on the priest, church and their relations to secular authorities. According to Doyle "He wanted to show that the divine appointment of Popacy on which the entire authority of its claim rested was wrong and Church was an unnecessary encumbrance to the state. He desired to give theoretical supremacy to the state and to make church simply a department of the state. As such his work was banned, its authors communicated and Marsiglio was described by Pope Element VI as the "worst heretic" he has ever read.

On State

Following the footsteps of Aristotle, Marsiglio supposes the state as living organism, having its origin in the family. He agrees with

Aristotle that the state is a self sufficiency and good community for life on the earth and also for eternal life. The efficiency of the state consists in ordinary working of its organs and if parts collide, efficiency or peace of the state cannot be maintained. As such state should be independent of any control to promote general welfare and preserving peace and allowing free development of its members. All interests in the state should discharge its functions for the common welfare.

Following Aristotle he enumerates the classes which co-operate to form a society. The artisans and farmers supply the material wants and in strict sense, soldiers, officials and priests make up the state. He states that the function of priests is to know and teach these things which according to Scriptures, is necessary to believe, to do or to avoid in order to attain eternal salvation and escape. As such, he comes to conclusion that the secular questions are to be decided on their own rational merits without the help of faith or religion, secondly priest is only class of the society whose function is to preach salvation and state possesses the right to control priests as other classes such as farmers and traders etc. Finally, separation of faith and reason is scepticism.

He believes that the preservation of peace is the most important function of the state and duty of priest's to supplement the work of police and judge by the fear of hell. He holds that the work of the priest is to attain salvation for the next world and they have to do nothing about in this function of world. Ideas of Masiglio strike a deadly blow on the basic foundation of the church and at the theory of two swords and reduces the Church to the level of the department of the state.

Law

Thomas Acquinas regarded four kinds of law *i.e.*, eternal, divine, natural and human laws but Marsiglio regards four kinds of law as one at different levels of cosmic reality and thinks human law is derived from natural law. According to him, Divine law is meant for the salvation in next world and on the other hand human law is the command of whole body of citizens or its prevailing part to perform or to avoid certain acts to achieve the best in the world. Human law is enforced by a penalty or punishment by the government. Divine law may be enforced by God in life to come. Thus human law is enforced by the state in this life and Divine law may be enforced by God in life to come. Both are wholly independent and distinct. Human law is not derived from God or divine law. For Acquinas, *law meant right reason* but to *Marsiglio it meant expression of divine or human will.* Acquinas places emphasis on rightness of law but Marsiglio places emphasis on its coercive authority and he refuses to accept any rule as law whose violation is not punishable by the coercive authority of the persons in power. According to Allen *"Law is essentially a judgement as to what is just and advantageous to the community. It is imperative expression of the common need formulated by reason and promulgated by recognized authority sanctioned by force."* This definition means any rule which is punishable by persons in power is law and spiritual authority has no force except when delegated by secular power or to say in other words Law is command or will of sovereign body which obliges a person or persons to a course of conduct as stated by Austin and is accepted even now to some extent.

Marsiglio by saying that human law is based on the common of whole body of citizens did not support democracy. He by whole community meant only as ultimate repository of authority or possibility of delegating authority to Assembly, prince or commission. Behind this Assembly or commission or prince to whom law making powers may be delegated there, according to Dunning *"always stands the people as a whole, in whose collective will consists of the essence of law in the broadest sense and in whose aggregate life is the essence of the state."* He states by prevailing part I mean both their number and quality in the community being taking into account. He stated "Divine law is command of God for a man...Human law is command of those empowered to make law...enforced by penalty of punishment."

The Organs of Government

He holds that executive and judiciary be setup or elected by the body of citizens. He agrees that there are various way of election but all other authority comes from the legislative act of whole body. It must be powerful and supreme to supervise the functions of the state. The executive organ is to carry out the laws in force made by the legislators. He prefers monarchy because its unity is safe guarded against internal disorders and peace is secured. He supports elective monarchy than hereditary monarchy. He puts emphasis on unity of the executive and opposes separate jurisdiction of Church.

Popular Sovereignty

Some writers holds that the germs of the theory of the separation of powers are available in his writings because he distinguishes the executive from the legislature and subordinates the former to the later. Supporters of that view hold that by prevailing part, theory of majority rule may be conceived. But according to Prof. Mcllwain there is nothing of modern democracy in him. However his most notable contribution is that he gives power to the people and makes the ruler the servant of the people and supports their right to punish the ruler for his misdeeds or cruelty or for exceeding its limits thus he supports limited or constitutional monarchy. In this way he makes King only administrator and whole community as legislator. He emphasizes that the law should be acceptable to people and undesirable laws should not be enforced by the King. Perhaps he is the first medieval political philosopher who supports constitutional monarchy. For the best form of government, he desires a representative Assembly elected by the people, executive chosen by the people responsible to elected assembly directly and indirectly to the people and elected monarch to administer and interpret laws. Thus he supports popular sovereignty.

Church

The Church also, he extends principles of representative government which took shape of councillar movement. According to him Church includes all the Christians and not only clergymen whose ultimate authority lies in the whole body which is superior to Pope. The Pope should be elected by the general council and should be responsible to it. In general council of the Church, there should be both ecclesiastical and secular delegates. He gives even power of disposing Pope to the general Assembly because the Pope derives his authority from the general council. Which meant that the power of the Pope is not of divine origin. He regards the Church as a Christian commonwealth and the Pope as its head. He holds that only duty of clergy is that of preaching for the salvation of the soul and nothing else even the judgement of ex-communication is to be enforced by secular authority if it thinks proper to enforce. As such he makes Church and Clergy as not entity.

He was an Erastian and wanted to subordinate the Clergy and the Church of the state. He even gives power to the state to make law for regulating the organization of the Church in state on the ground that it will help the state in maintaining peace and order. He regarded the Pope as bishop of Rome, having no claim or superiority over other bishops. Thus he completely subordinated the Church under the state and for the state and to the state.

Other Views

Like Plato and Aristotle, he placed emphasis on education for the realization of representative government. He opposed the excessive disparity of wealth which may breed jealousy and discord and supported the cause of the state for regulating the economic life of the society. According to Sabine, *"By vesting the power of interpretation and settling dispute within the church in the representative general council, denouncing the Pope's supremacy and making the Pope subordinate to general council, he became the initiator councillor movement developed in the 15th century and of 16th century rebels Luther and Calvin etc."* Perhaps no other medieval thinker subordinated the church to the state as he does. His place for popular sovereignty gives him a high place as a modern thinker.

DANTE (1265-1321)

Dante's *De Monarchia*

Dante is considered as one of the greatest poets but he was also a great political Italian thinker. He wrote *De Monarchia* and argued for a universal secular empire against Thomas Acquinas who pleaded for spiritual empire based on supremacy of Church and Pope. Dante refuted the claim of Church to exercise central control over secular authority.

Dante was a very great poet and also a political thinker who supported the cause of empire. He is more logical in his exposition of Imperial theory than Marsiglio of Padua. Dante was born in Florentine in 1265 and dies as an exile in 1321 at Anerona. He was a great literary genius and perhaps the greatest poet of medieval age. He was drawn into the conflict against the Papacy because he thought that the wars amongst the secular rulers are created due to Papal interference. He became aggressive when Papacy was transferred to Aninguonn and supported French

Policy. He felt that disputes of the states can be wiped out under an all embracing authority of the Emperor and by excluding Pope from any secular authority. He possessed the experience of Italian politics and was a party man and believer in Roman supremacy to rule a vast empire.

De Monarchia – His Book

His great work *De Monarchia,* is a sincere and strong plea for the restoration of a world empire as the prerequisite of lasting peace and of depriving the Pope from all secular power. According to Dunning *"De Monarchia* contains the most complete and perfect system that we have of imperialistic philosophy."

The central theme of *De Monarchia,* is monarchy. By monarchy he means the universal dominion over all things temporal state is the state in which all the petty states and principalities would be united as semi-autonomous members. In this ideal empire whole Europe was to be organized. He holds that the peace is necessary for realization of rational life and only universal empire can maintain peace. His arguments may be summarized in the words of Doyle, *that all men have the same end which is the realization of potentialities of human reason.* This end can be realized only through a co-operative social process, no individual or small group of individuals could achieve it themselves. The whole of mankind must move forward in a harmonious effect of sustained co-operation towards the complete realization of the whole potentiality of the human intellect. Defection is honour of few of the members prevented the fulfilment of the ideal *i.e.,* believed that only a universal emperor can have power and strength to keep under control and check the forces of disruption. He supported the common and universal law as a bond of cohesion and unity among the mankind and desired for a universal monarch to enforce universal law. His ideal for universal empire was based on the Roman Empire which maintained peace in Europe for many centuries. He believed in a universal empire to maintain peace all over the world.

Peace would ensue. Civilization would press on to complete realization of whole potentiality of human intellect.

Empire based on Service and law. Dante desired world empire for the welfare of mankind and not for the sake of ruler. To Dante, the Empire was "Law personified, law throned and crowned and invested with majority and honour. Dante thought of a supreme law rather than of a super state. Supreme law may be called justice administered by emperor, not swayed by passion." According to Pollock, Dante's monarch is not a universal despot, but governor of higher order, set over the princes and rulers of particular states and keeping peace between them. He is to have the jurisdiction, in modern language of an international tribunal. In the second book he tried to prove the claim of Romans for world empire. Thus, he defended superiority of Roman ruling class.

Church and the Empire

In the third book he tried to prove that secular authority is derived, not from the Pope but from God directly. Man according to Dante is warmly and possess spiritual leanings, so he needs both spiritual and secular authorities to guide him. The Pope represents spiritual and the emperor temporal authorities and both derive their power from God directly. The two have their different sphere of work and must not encroach upon each other's jurisdiction Christ said, "my *kingdom is not of this world"* so the Pope must not interfere in secular affairs. The Emperor is divinely as the Pope. He held that the two powers Imperium and Sacredatium are combined only in God and none else.

He held that the spiritual power dealt with the eternal matter which he called the celestial paradise and earthly paradise has no place for it. Only the universal monarch should preside there with no rival claimant to supremacy exercising a subversive influence. Dante had made an effective breach in the theology of the schoolmen by denying their basic assumption that man had one end in life.

Defence of Empire

It this way Dante proved the complete independence of the empire and repudiate the claim of the church to exercise central control over secular authority. He first proved that the office of monarch was necessary for maintaining peace and well being of the world and then stated that he derives power from God and not from ecclesiastical authority. As such Church or the Pope have no place in a secular state and cannot control it because its sphere is heavenly life and celestial paradise.

Comparison with Acquina and Salisbury

In spite of the fact that Dante is ranged against Thomas Acquina and John of Salisbury in the controversy between the papacy and the empire, he was at one with them in his fundamental convictions. Firstly like them he believed in a single universal society containing all mankind and governed by the divinely ordained authorities the emperor for secular things and the Pope for spiritual things. In the days of Dante Christendom was divided into fragments of various kingdom but Dante overlooked this fact of contemporary life and looked back to Roman Empire as his ideal and preached for the world empire on its basis. As such saying that the ghost of Roman Empire haunted the middle age is fully applicable to Dante's ideas as he dreamt of the world empire on the basis of Roman quite contrary to the realities of contemporary would because he was poet.

Secondly, Dante accepted the dual nature of man and accepted the medieval tradition of the dual government in the single universal society because man possess both spirit and body is of dual nature. He further held that no one should interfere in the sphere of the other. Thus, he desired to rise the theory of two swords and the maxim that give unto Caesar the things that Caesar's and unto God the things that are God's. He differed very much in general background of his thought from other supporters of secular cause like John of Paris, William Occam and Marsiglio of Padua. His ideas belong to 13th Century rather than to 14th century.

Both St. Thomas Acquinas and Dante were influenced by the ideas of Aristotle. Dante attempted to prove his conclusion syllogistically, starting from generally accepted principles such saying of Aristotle that nature makes nothing in vain and deducting conclusions from them. Thus he tried to prove the universal desirability of peace and that it could be realized only in a universal empire of universal monarch. As such in fundamental assumptions Dante resembles to St. Thomas Acquinas who also built assumptions on the bases of Aristotelian philosophy and unified power and the ideas of Roman Empire, so saying of Sabine that they are one in their fundamental convictions is true but St. Thomas Acquinas supported the cause of the Church and Dante of a universal Empire through philosophy and here in lies their difference in spite of their similar fundamental convictions. He is minor thinker but a great Poet.

William of Occam

The last medieval thinker to support the cause of secular independence against papal claim was William of Occam or Ockham. He was born near about 1290 and died near about 1349. He was an English Franci can and a colleague of Marsiglio of Padua in the University of Paris. He was ex-communicated along with Marsiglio of Padua by Pope John XXII for his attack on papal authorities. Like Marsiglio he took refuse in the court of Emperor Lewis and championed his cause against the Pope. He was a scholastic theologian on whom Aristotelian philosophy had a great influence. He was more conservative and moderate than Marsiglio in his attack against papacy. Following true scholastic fashion, he always presented both sides of the case and made his own suggestions instead of making dogmatic statements. Unlike Marsiglio, he did not oppose reason and faith. Contrary to Marsiglio he wielded a great influence over his own generation which later on declined

His political ideas resemble with the ideas of Marsiglio. He was a dialectician rather than a philosopher. He held that church and state are useful institutions in their respective spheres. State to him was like a body and church like a soul and so he gave church a little higher position. Main theme of his thought is that every kind of authority whether it is secular or spiritual must be limited to the purpose for which it has been created and should-act for common welfare based on reason. If anyone who wields the authority crosses its limits should be deposed. Marsiglio placed authority of deposition in the hands of citizens in case of the Emperor and to general council in the case of general body of Christians in the church. Ockhom knew that neither the general people had the ability to control the Emperor nor general body of Christians to control the Pope. As such he suggested that the Emperor and the Pope should be bound by law of nature. He was of the opinion that a universal empire in spiritual and temporal side was an impossibility.

Arguments against Supremacy of Pope

Being annoyed by undue interference of Pope John XXII in secular matters he declared that the Pope had no right to interfere in temporal matters as his authority was limited to spiritual matters only. He stated that the Pope could have only those powers which would safely and prudently be committed to one man, for the sake of common utility in regard to all things morals and the spiritual need of believers. He refuted that the Pope is infallible and did not give any power to the Pope or priests. He deemed it unreasonable to give universal supremacy to Pope. He believed that the whole body of Christians is superior to Pope and as such he could not exceed to what was necessary for the common welfare of citizens. He disbelieved that Peter gave absolute powers to the people both in spiritual and temporal matters. Christ himself did not give the powers to Pope and did not authorize the Pope to deprive Princes and men of their property, rights and liberties. Moreover, the Pope could not go against gospel and so his resistance is justifiable, if he exceeds his limits.

He did not allow even Pope right to interpret gospel which was to be exercised by the wisest persons famous for their piety and integrity in the service of the church. He gave to the Pope position of the head of the church whose function was to secure eternal salvation of soul. He stated that the papal jurisdiction is of service and not of powers. He desired to vest whole power in the general council organized on the federal basis. He proposed that all Christians should choose their representatives of both the clergy and laity and even the women. He held that body to be the true representative of Christians. This body would have the power of interpreting scripture, settling matters of disputes and of ex-communication and of disposing the Pope. The Pope should neither possess the power of convening the council or of presiding over it.

He hated the clerical love for wealth and property and believed that possession of wealth made it secular minded. He desired that the church property should be treated on equal terms with that of other property and should not be exempted from taxation or appropriation. In the same manner he supported the punishment of clergy by secular power for violation of laws. He desired that both church and state should respect the rights of one another.

Conclusion

He did not give despotic powers either to the Emperor or the Pope. He stated that the emperor should make his rule just and useful to the people and conform to the will of God, natural reasons and equity and to international law. Emperor's authority is to be exercised within the framework of law. He desired checks on the despotic powers of both the Emperor and the Pope and supported ultimate powers of the public like Marsiglio.

Later on controversy between the Pope and the Emperor ended and problem of constitutional or despotic rule came on forefront. The conciliar movement which too got inspiration from the ideas of Marsiglio and Occam was an attempt to solve the problem but it failed on sharp rocks of realities but his ideas against despotism of both possess still some value as Islamic states lead by persons like Ayatullah Khomeni are again emerging-claiming supremacy of religious leaders and Islamic fanatic ideals. With the emergence of Islamic states of Pakistan, Bangladesh, Saudi Arabia and Shia state of Iran and Jews state of Israel etc., religion is again gaining importance. Consequently Roman Catholic religion in Poland and in Eastern European states is again becoming popular. In India also many religious parties are gaining popularity. As such controversy between secularism and religion has again gained importance and need of the hour is reconcilement between the two as propounded by Christian thinkers *i.e.,* give to God, spiritual supremacy and to caesar *i.e.,* to ruler in secular matters and to have democratic setup. Thus, medieval ideas and attempt of reconcilement has some philosophical value even now.

Chapter 11

The Conciliar Movement and Some Medieval Conceptions

Controversy between Church and secular powers for supremacy gave rise to Conciliar movements and brought into existence many medieval concepts. Conciliar movement pleaded for final authority to church's general council and refuted the idea of Papal supremacy. Thus, movement stated that ultimate power belongs to masses and supported ideas of liberty, equality and of fraternity. It recognized spirit of naturality and opposed despotism both in church and secular Govt. As such this movement made valuable contributions to medieval Political thought.

With the publication of Defensor Paus controversy between the church and the Empire subsided and after it Churchman and political philosophers began to discuss about the proper form of the Church government as the cause of the independence of secular powers settled in the favour of secular rulers.

The attempt to settle the form of Church government was at the councils of Constance (1414-1418) and Basle (1431-1449) and is known as the Conciliar movement in history. It is by itself insignificant in the history of political thought but the offshoots and repercussions that came out of it are important. From 11th up to 14th century medieval thinkers debated about the controversy between the Empire and the church but in first half of 15th century emerged Conciliar movement which represent the last important phase of modern period.

Environment

In general, church organization was corrupt from top to bottom. It was bitterly attacked by John of Paris, Marsiglio of Padua,

William Occam, Wycliff and John Huss etc. during the 14th century. Despotic and absolute papal rule meant much more than the rigid control of the Pope. The Pope heard appeals relating to religious matters from the different parts of the continent and so large sums of money use to go to the papal authority. As such problem of papacy was the concern of the Christian people of the whole Europe. The creation of two rival popes using all theological powers and political chicanery made papal authority notorious and the popes lost prestige and splendour in the eyes of the public Great schism of (1378-1417) made matters worse.

The Babylonish captivity under which the Popes lived at Avignon from 1309-1376 lived under the influence of the French monarchy made matters worse because all Christians believed Rome as the headquarters of the Pope. In 1377, Pope Gregory XI returned to Rome and Babylonish captivity came to end. However due to creation of two Popes, on at Auignon and one at Rome each claiming themselves as rightful Pope great schism took place. Italy, Germany and England favoured the Pope at Rome while France, Scotland, Castile and Naples followed the Pope of Augnon. The schism showed the degeneration of the Pope. As such a general demand of purification of the Church through the general council instead of the old despotic Papacy came to forefront. This movement is known as Conciliar movement.

There were two stages in the growth of this movement. In the first stage John of Paris, Marsiglio of Padua and William of Occam in 14th century put forth the demand of the general council of the church as the final authority and as the sole repository of power. In the second age the dream materialized and three councils were held to deal with the problem. Nicholas of Cusa, Gerson, Preire P. Ally were the prominent leaders who took part in the movement in its second phase. The protests of Padua, John of Paris and Occam against the absolute authority of the Pope coupled with the scandalism of schism gave birth to the Conciliar movement and turned it into a popular demands and tried to bring change.

Purpose

According to Mcllwan, "*The essential point in contention of the reformers was the assertion of the competence of universal council of the church to adjudicate a disputed claim to papal authority with so important corollary that the jurisdiction of this council is higher than that of the Pope."* As proper system of the accounts of the church was to be maintained in order to ensure legitimate expenditure of money for the Church purpose and to curtail the luxury and extravagance of the papul court. The schism was to be healed by the appointment of one Pope instead of two rival claimants to prevent discord and to achieve harmony. Wycliff of England and Huss of Bohemia desired churches and restraints on absolutism of Pope through popular discussion. The reform of the head of the church, moral reform of the clergymen and suppression of here say were the objects of Conciliar movement.

In order to reform the church and to remove above mentioned defects, many meetings of the general church council took place. The meetings were held as the council of Pisa 1409, the council of Constance (1414-1418) the council of Pauia 1423 and the council of Basle (1431-1448). Of these council of Constance and Balse was very important. The council of Constance and Gerson demanded another council and won the supports of calling the meeting of the council at Constance, which was the most representative council. But since no resoluteness was shown in reforming the church in head and members, so no success was achieved. The views of Huss and Wycliff were condemned as heretic, and Huss was burnt alive though he had been invited under the guarantee of protection. John Gerson who was the Chancellor of Paris University was leading theorist of the council and through his efforts schism was healed. It was agreed that plenitude of power belonged not to the Pope but to the General Council as representative on all Christians. Discussions ended in the famous decree of 1415, which has been described by Dr. Figgi's as *"probably the most revolutionary official document in the history of the world."* According to Jesus Christ, *"Where two or three are gathered together in my name, then I am in the midst of them* "and these words were taken to imply the superiority of Council over the Pope. The Pope as the executive head of the church was only an authorized agent of the community and responsible to the general council which derived its authority directly from Christ. Thus, he opposed infallibility of Pope.

According to Sabine, *"The church, being a complete and self-sufficing society, must possess all the powers needed to ensure its continuance, its orderly government and the removal of the abuses as they occur. Consequently, the spiritual powers with which it is endowed is vested in the church itself in the whole body of the faithful as a corporate body, and clergy including the Pope are merely the ministers or agents by which society acts."*

In 1417, another decree was passed by the general council by which meeting of church council after every ten years was proposed and its independence was guaranteed from the control of the Pope. These decrees were ratified in 1439. After healing of schism and with the appointment of one Pope, zeal of reforms took wings and nothing material was achieved for the reformation of the church and the Pope continued his work as in the past; and abuses remained unchecked as before.

The council of Basile failed to achieve the constitutional rule in the church or anything substantial so the movement failed. According to Sabine, *"A council which itself was to prey to every form of national jealousy was ill qualified to attack the stupendous mass of vested interests that made up ecclesiastical patronage."* However, main points of John Gerson, Cardinal Nicholas of Cuso and Aenaes Sylbius may be given here briefly.

Arguments for General Council

The sovereign power lies in the general council and not in Pope. Mixed form of Govt. consisting of the Pope Cardinals and prelates is better than the supremacy of the Pope. His is simply an administrator and not maker of law so not above the law. The Church as a whole makes law and the Pope is responsible to the General Council of the Church which is the true representative of the Christians. The community has inherent power to make their own laws, setup its own ruler. The difference between lawful government and tyranny is that the former rests on the will of the people and that other on force or compulsion. The natural rights of the people are inherent in the community and does not depend on the whims of the rulers. Papal decrees should depend on the popular acceptance and notions of natural rights and should be in conformity with the basic functions of the Pope.

The council represents the people and only its consent gives the binding force. The Church is a perfect society so it can reform itself and can even depose the Pope. Nicholas of Gusa stated, *"Since by nature all men are free, any authority by which subjects are perfected from evil and their freedom is restricted to doing good through fear of penalties comes from harmony and from the consent of the subjects, whether the authority resides in written law or the living law, which is in the ruler. Kings are therefore to be regulated by the general part of the society."*

This paragraph of Nicholas of Gusa shows verbal similarity with the later revolutionary thought. The main point of the Conciliar theory is that whole body of the church is the source of law and the Pope with its hierarchy are merely its administrators. According to Nicholas, Government is properly a co-operative enterprise, concordantial or harmony and not delegation of power from supreme head.

Causes of its Failure

The Conciliar movement represented spirit of Constitution against the absolute power of the Pope. But the movement failed because there were mutual suspicion, jealousy and little harmony in Europe and little Zeal for constitutionalism and zeal for reform.

As such it failed to draw up federal constitution for the whole Europe and consequently autocratic forms of Govt. came into existence both in ecclesiastical and secular fields. Secondly, the growing national sentiment gave a death blow to the ideas of Conciliar movement. With the growth of national states, all person became interested in their own national interests and problems and showed little Zeal for the reformation of the church. Thirdly, it lacked popular support of the masses. It was too academic and remained confined to universities. Fourthly, there was no strong leader whose influence may be helpful in setting aside the differences for the general cause. Leaders like Luther and Calvin could have overcome national jealousies but it lacked such leaders. Fifthly, according to Cooke the caution and moderate approach was also responsible for its failure. It led them to conservatism. Sixthly, the old tradition of papal authority proved too strong as soon as conservatism took its hold upon the general council. Seventhly, the Pope was able to play one faction against the other and thereby not only saved his position but made it strong. Eighthly, the organization and the bureaucracy was more clever than its leaders who were merely academicians. Ninthly, leaders of the movement failed to show originality and borrowed ideas from Marsiglio and Occam failed to get popular application. Finally, national Kings disfavoured the centralization and dreaded the rival of the power of the Pope which always kept them check, so they tried for its failure by hook or crook. Moreover, time was not yet ripe for constitutionalism as autocratic governments existed everywhere in Europe.

Significance of the Conciliar Movement

In spite of the fact that the movement failed in its objective of the establishment of the supremacy of the church council yet it can be said that it failed ignominiously. It did accomplish following things:

(1) It stated that the church was superior to the Pope and that general council possesses the final authority.

(2) It demanded a representative government for the Church.

(3) It made careful as not to exercise authority against the safety of the church.

(4) Failure was a blessing in disguise as potestanism emerged through Luther and Calvin etc. which reformed Christianity.

(5) The Church became better organized and efficient.

(6) The Papacy was re-organized and re-established on the national basis.

(7) It resulted in the establishment of national church which recognised the rights of layman.

(8) It was democratic, federal and national in tendencies and these tendencies later on affected church as well as the states.

(9) It sponsored the idea of that power was the trust and now it must not be misused and the current of the governed is the essence of the government and representatives should be consulted in important matters.

(10) It put emphasis on the constitution in preference to the absolute or despotic rule.

(11) The movement recognized the growing spirit of nationality.

(12) The germs of the revolution of 1688 and 1789 are traceable to the Conciliar movement.

(13) It gave notions of liberty, equality and fraternity.

(14) It stated that the ultimate power belongs to masses.

(15) It made democratic notions popular even in the church which was believed to be of divine origin.

(16) He propounded the idea of national rights.

As such its failure is the failure of a movement which was against his times but was one with the future as it triumphed later on.

John Gerson

John Gerson was the Chancellor of the Paris University. Being influenced by the writings of Marsiglio of Padua, he developed the idea of communal sovereignty. He pleaded for the mixed form of government, having non archaic, aristocratic and democratic elements both for the church and the state. He was opposed both to absolutism of the Pope as well as extreme democracy of Marsiglio of whole body of believers. He was in favour of giving supreme authority to general council in the church. According to him the Pope was merely in administrative head of the Church whose authority may be defied in the interest of the Church. He even favoured the authority of King to depose ecclesiastical head if act-contrary to natural or divine laws. According to Gettle, *Gerson aimed to preserve the rights Pope and King, within definite limits and at the sometime secure the liberties of the people.* Gerson held that as body was superior to the Pope and could depose him, if he abused his office. He framed his principle so skillfully that while giving supremacy to the general council of the church, he did as little violence as possible to the traditional theory of Pope. The substantial extinction of papay is disguised, indeed by Gerson though frequent suggestion that the assertion of Conciliar supremacy is mainly to be justified by the scandal of the schism and the mortal peril of the Church. Yet the trend of the system which is set forth is clearly manifest and the consciousness that doctorines subversive of the appellant ecclesiastical orders are unmistakable. He was one of the greatest leaders of Conciliar movement.

Nicholas of Gusa

Nicholas of Gusa, a cardinal who was born in 1400 and died on 1446 took more democratic view than Gerson. His book *The De Concordantia Catholica* gives the best exposition of the Conciliar movement. It has been described by Dr. G.N. Figgis as almost the last book which treats Christiandom as a single organic system in which a complete theory of politics in whole and parts in set forth. It gives philosophic expression to the constitutionalism. He embodied the main principles which under line theory of constitutional government and educated them with a university that increased their significance. It is original and profound and deals with the deepest movements of the age.

He believed that peace and unity in the church is the crying need of the day. He reconciles divine with human authority and unit's secular to the spiritual. He stated power ultimately comes from God but immediately from people. His own words as quoted by Sabine state, *"Since by nature all men are free, any authority by which subjects are prevented from evil and their freedom is restrained doing good through fear of penalties, come solely from harmony and from the consent of subjects... power could be setup only by the choice and consent of others just as law also is setup by consent."* Briefly it means by nature all men are free and equal so authority and superior power emerges from the consent of the governed and law is also found in the consent of the people and neither the Pope nor the ruler derives power from God. Sovereignty resides neither in Pope nor in the General council but in the people of whole Christendom. He wanted representative Government in every form of society, secular or spiritual. Thus, he was a great champion of democracy, liberty, equality and sovereignty of the people. In his idea there were the germs of cry of liberty equality, fraternity and sovereignty of the people for future revolution.

Medieval Political thought contributed a lot and gave idea of representation of Natural law, of corporations and of popular sovereignty as such medieval age cannot be considered unpolitical.

The middle ages did not produce giants like Plato or Aristotle and there was little originality in political thought as Prof. Hearnshaw remarks that Medieval thinkers seem like the students writing essays on political theory from text books, mainly three in number — the *Bible,* the *Roman Law* and the *Politics* of Aristotle, is true to a large extent.

Their main themes were universalism, supremacy of church, the monarchical government in the church and state, Aristotle checks absolutism of the Pope and the Emperor and controversy between the Pope and the secular rulers which have been already dealt. But their ideas of popular sovereignty, representative government and of kingship and natural law corporations need a little clarification. Medieval thought differed on these topics as given below:

Medieval Idea of Kingship

First supposition about the king was that the king was representative of God on earth. Secondly, it was said that the king is under the God and the law. Thirdly, kings were believed to be made for the peoples and not peoples for the kings. It was his bounden duty to further maintain, peace and justice. Thus, king inherited his throne, he was elected by the people and ruled by the grace of God.

Law

According to Teutons law was the common possession by which the group was held together. Thomas Acquinas and Marsiglio's conception of laws have been already stated. Here it can be said that "the modern democrat is prepared to respect law in so far as he can regard himself as its author, medieval obedience was founded on the opposite sentiment that laws were respectable so far as they were not made by man. As such divine law was respected more than human or manmade law."

Idea of Representation

In modern age representatives are elected but in medieval age, office holders were considered as trustee of the people and were charged with the mission of their peoples. Representative ideas reached to perfection during Conciliar movement through the ideas of Gerson and Nicholas of Cusa which gave us notions of popular sovereignty, liberty equality and justice etc. which later on brought revolutions of 1688 of England and 1789 of France and in 1776 in U.S.A.

Natural Law

Conception of Natural law began with the Stoics and Cicero stated that the law of nature springs from God and it is the basis of all morality and it ought to prescribe the provisions of positive law. Romans believed that law common to all nations is the law of nature and this concept became highly influential in the growth of Roman legal system and jurisprudence. It was supposed as the ultimate source of law and it as a touch stone limited the validity of positive laws themselves. Their ideas gave rise to theory of Natural law.

Corporations

During Conciliar movement, the concept of Roman law about universe as if corpus were pressed into services to define the character and significance of corporate entitles, like the church, the church council, the state, the universities, free cities and communes. These are partial wholes had an aim and an end of their own and therefore had a will and personality of truth of their own. The church was conceived of as a corporation consisting of all believers and endowed with ultimate and residuary powers and general council of the church as the corporate representative of the church of which the Pope was presiding officer. Later on these rights were conceded to the representative assembles or groups by recognising them as a great corporate and juristic person which passed the way for popular sovereignty and modern ideas of pluralism.

Popular Sovereignty

Leaders of Conciliar movement supported popular sovereignty, liberty, equality and fraternity and representative guides both in church and the state. These ideas developed into modern representative democracies which are main gifts of modern age. Thus, Conciliar movement supported democratic ideals against the supremacy of Pope and rulers and favoured ideas of popular sovereignty, so it proved useful for further progress and brought medieval controversy and ideas to an end. Democratic ideas and attempt of reconcilement between spiritualism, secularism and democratic ideals still possess some philosophical value and can help in solving conflict between secularism, religious ideals of newly emerging genis, Islamic states and democratic ideas with necessary changes and modification to suit modern environment and setup.

Struggle for Supremacy between church powers led by Pope and his supporters and secular powers led by emperor, kings and feudal lords ended with the ideas of Renaissance and reformation and growth of natural states. Growth of powerful national states enhanced the power of secular rulers and new thinking replaced medieval thinking. In spite of all drawbacks medieval thinking also contributed a lot to modern political thinking.

Chapter 12

Renaissance and Machiavelli (1469-1527)

In Western countries political ideas took its roots in Greece which produced political giants like Plato and Aristotle. Roman mind was legal than political and Polybius, Cicero or Saneaca were its main political thinkers. Romans thinking was based on the political philosophy of Stoic thinkers who gave us ideas of equality, natural law and of universal Empire. With the decline and fall of the Roman Empire and with the increase of the power of church, medieval age came into existence. Main theme of the medieval age was the idea of universal society under the Pope and the Emperor and the general acceptance of the Christian church as the ultimate authority to define man's place in the universe and his moral duties. In this age not only faith or revelation was considered superior to man, reason but earthly interests were subordinated to spiritual ends. As such ecclesiastical thinking remained supreme during middle ages.

Medieval thought concentrated itself to the conflict of the church and the secular authorities for supremacy, Division of two Popes and conciliar movement ended in the triumph of representative ideas and national states and in individualistic outlook. The new national state which was secular in outlook emerged with absolute monarch based on the policy of blood and iron emerged. With the emergence of national secular states medievalism came to an end.

With the discovery of America by Columbus in 1492 and India by Vasco Degama in 1498, new ideas came into existence. According to Doyle, new world opened with the end of fifteenth century before the staggered gaze of man already eager to explore already intoxicated with the intellectual stimulants they had received from their antiquity.

THE RENAISSANCE

The term usually is taken to mean knowledge or learning. The first took place in 8th century when something of old Roman Empire was revived, second took place in 13th century when study of Aristotle was revived. The third with which we are concerned here is called Italian Renaissance came into existence in 14th century to 16th century. In it humanistic ideas and scientific outlook came on forefront. It gave new values to life and new conception to liberty and democracy and equality. The other worldliness of medieval age supernatural ideas gave place to secular ideas. *Worldly success came to the regarded as more important than salvation.* Man became the measure of all things. According to Mayers, *"March of a new spirit which finally shattered medieval order laid the foundation of a new world of the 17th century world which in essentials put an end to the middle ages."*

In spite of the fact that conciliar movement died but its spirit emerged in the shape of Protastant reformation which shattered the authority of the Pope and hold of the Roman Catholic Church and consequently religion lost its hold and secular ideas triumphed. New ideal stood for individual success in this life and in this world. The success demanded self assertion, ruthlessness and disregard of conventional morality. Power became the new deity and power became good in itself and an end in itself. In recent age humanitarian ideas and universal outlook again emerged but each and everything is still in turmoil and no one can tell about the shape of the things to come and about future ideas.

MACHIAVELLI 1469-1527

Machiavelli was born in Florence in Italy in a well to do family in 1469. His father was a lawyer. In 1494, he began his career as a clerk and in 1498, he became second Chancellor and Secretary and held this August office up to 1512. During his service tenure he became diplomat and was sent on diplomatic mission to several courts. He visited the courts of Louis XII of France, of Emperor Maxmillan I and of Pope Julius II and Cesare Borgia, the Duke of Valentino.

In 1512 due to change of Government, his career came to an end and the Medici government which came into power threw him into prison. After one year, he was released on the condition to retire from public life, so he had to pass his nine years as a farmer. In 1521, he was again employed as a diplomat and in 1527, he died.

His Books

Although "the Prince" is his most famous book but he produced a number of popular novels, songs, poems and comedies. According to the Maxey, *"Prince" purpose to be practical handbook explaining the technique of successful rulership,"* let us seek rather to understand him and profit by the counsels he has to offer.

Environment

A man of very sensitive nature and known observation, he was very much influenced by political and intellectual tendencies of his age, up to 16th century the conciliar movement favouring constitutional government in the church and the state had disappeared beneath the wave of a monarchist reaction. In Spiritual sphere the Pope succeeded in establishing supremacy over church council and in secular sphere national monarchs crushed feudal aristocracies and feudal assemblies. In Italy no strong man appeared on the scene and it was divided in many states such as Venice, Florence, Naples, Milan and the papal states etc. Italy thus became the battleground of intriguing and ambitious potenties local as well as foreign. In such an atmosphere, public morality was extremely low and leaders were guided by selfish motives. This situation pained Machiavelli and restoring prosperity to Italy became a master passion with him. Machiavelli wrote like a patient to whom end justifies the means as power is an end itself. Machiavelli propounded idea of national state and secular thought.

Machiavelli was greatly influenced by the environments and growing spirit of renaissance. He gave a new outlook by unfettering the shells of scholastic dogma and domination of religion and morality over politics. As such Machiavelli was the creature of the Renaissance and a child of his times and environment. In the middle ages church or religious dogma dominated the political thought but renaissance impelled men to examine ideas free from religious domination. As such now it was possible to formulate political theories on a purely secular basic. He stood on a borderline between the middle and the modern ages and gave birth to a new era in the modern age by freeing politics of the vassalage of religion.

During middle ages political thought gave importance to the salvation of sol and God in the light of Christian theology. With the Renaissance, man instead of God, earthly enjoyment instead of salvation of soul, gained prominence. A new tendency to concentrate on this world, on the enrichment of personality and beauty in all forms development. Rationalism brought into existence a new outlook based on reason, individualism laid stress on the dignity of man and nationalism replaced the universalism of the middle ages. The new ideal put emphasis for individual success in this life and in this world. It demanded self assertion, ruthlessness and disregard of conventional morality. Idealistic approach gave place to realistic approach and power became an end in itself. With the decline of religion, end justified the means became the motto of life, Machiavelli was a true representative of his times as is depicted by his mental processes, the subject matter of his study his aims and ideals, his empiricism, his rationalism, his realism, his pragmation, his individualism, his nationalism and his hedonistic morality. Machiavelli gave prominence to secular thought.

Influence

Machiavelli was profoundly influenced by Aristotle. Machiavelli believed that human nature, and therefore human problems were almost the same at all times and places and therefore he interpreted the present with the help of past. He studied contemporary problems and politics, analysed it, formed conclusions and then summoned history to substantiate them. In this way his method was historical.

His Importance

Machiavelli believed that in the realm of state craft and in the affairs of government there is but one criteria by which to judge the character of an action and that is by the results. As such *"Niccolo Machiavelli is perhaps the most universally reprobated figure in the history of political literature"*, says Maxey, *"the man whose percepts are universally, disavowed in principle but regularly followed in practice."* He influenced Frederick Catherine etc.

Machiavelli has been described as first realist in politics. In his political theory, he is representative of Renaissance. He separated politics from morals and stated end justifies the means. It has been remarked Machiavelli more than any other Political thinker created the meaning that has been attached to the state in modern political usage.

With Machiavelli ends the period of Medieval political thought and begins period of modern political thought. As such he has been considered as first modern writer on politics. Machiavelli like Chanakya of India is considered as one of the greatest shrewd political thinkers known to history. He discarded religious and idealist thinking and gave new ideas to acquire and preserve power on the basis that end justifies the means, so Machiavelli's ideas are full of shrewdness and deserves to be studied with caution.

No political thinker can think in Vacuum but in no system of political philosophy, the influence of environment was more manifest than in that of Machiavelli. According to Dunning, *"The brilliant Florentine was in the fullest sense the child of his time."* He discarded religious thinking and stated, *"end justifies the means."*

Environment

The end of middle ages and the beginning of modern period took with two movements known as Renaissance and reformation. Renaissance came forth in Italy by the revival of ancient thought and learning which had been buried deep by Christianity in medieval age. Roman thought and Greek philosophy had been really burdened with the medieval thought. In the medieval ages people pondered about the spirit salvation and God. Renaissance made the study of man as centre of political thought instead of God. It inspired scholars to study the things from rational rather than clerical point of view. It revolutionized the attitude of man towards religion and morality. In reality, Renaissance was something more than mere revival or recovery of ancient learning, and what the medievalists have forgotten. It was rebirth of emotions and of faculties which have remained dormant for long. It awakened in man a new consciousness and new values of life. Instead of religion now secular study dominated the academic sphere. This world came to have more importance than the next world. It set aside conventional morality. Development of personality and the spirit of individualism emphasized the dignity of man natural and human. Machiavelli was the creature of this renaissance because it dominated Italy in general and Florence in particular. He stood on the border line between the middle and the modern age. He freed the political thought from shackles of religion. With the renaissance, new conditions and new individual success in this life and in this world. The success demanded self assertion, ruthlessness, disregard of conventional morality. It needed power which became the new deity. Power was good in itself and an end in itself. Machiavelli was true representative of his times who preached that the end justified the means and power is good in itself. He preached ideal of grasping and preserving power.

The significance of Machiavelli's thought lies in the fact that he was at the parting of ways of political philosophy. In him meet both the old and new. Due to this his political thought is important.

Age of Machiavelli has been called the age of bastards and adventures. It was a society intellectually brilliant and artistically creative. But at the time it was a victim to worst political corruption and degeneration, cruelty and murder were normal methods of government. Force and craft were keys to success. Society was leaderless and according so Sabine, *"Machiavelli was a thought of the masterless man. In Italy there was internecine wars and disorder due to wars and Italy became a Cockpit of Europe. Church according to Machiavelli has kept and still keeps our country (Italy) divided."*

In such atmosphere Machiavelli lived and wrote books. This degenerating and depressing state of Italy could not leave a sensitive patriot and keen observer like Machiavelli uninfluenced and unmoved. The challenge of the day was solution for this chaos of depravity by strongman. So Dunning remarked, *"The era was of the strong man and Machiavelli's writings give copious evidence that he realised this fact."* Unity prosperity and independence of Italy became a master passion with him. His works "The Prince" and "The Discourse" show that he was fully conscious of the fact that the contemporary politics was based on violence fraud and not on good Christian ethics. The book reveals him as a practical statesman concerned about the mechanism of govt. and how it can be made strong.

His Spiritual Ancestry and Method

Machiavelli was largely influenced by Aristotle but brushed aside the teaching of scriptures and of the church father. He did not pay attention to the controversy of church and the state and he separated the politics from the church. He believed that human nature, and therefore human problems, were almost the same at all times and places and, therefore, he thought of enlighting the present with the help of past. His method was that of generalisation from particulars. He studied contemporary politics, analysed it, formed conclusion and took help of history to support his conclusions. He choose selected examples from ancient history to substantiate his conclusions and to propagate his ideas.

Historical Method

Machiavelli claimed to have followed historical method thought strictly his method was not historical because he did not take pains to draw conclusions from historical facts but utilized carefully selected instances of history to support his arguments already arrived. He was pre-eminently a student of practical and not of speculative politics. As realist in politics, he cared little for political philosophy. His writings tell us about the art of government rather than the theory of the state. He was more concerned with the actual working of the government machinery than with the abstract principles of constitution. His main theme was preservation and continuation of the state. He believed that public morality was different from private morality. He believes that man's virtue is measurable by his power and fame and lies in a combination of force and intellect. For such a "virtue there is little place for any restraints imposed by general principles which natural law implies."

His Conception of Human Nature

He believed that man was a strange mixture of weakness, folly and knavery fit only to be hoodwinked and bearded over. He has very low idea of human nature. Like Hobbes he held that all men were wicked and essentially selfish. Selfishness and egoism were the chief motive forces of human conduct. Men were ungrateful, fickle, deceitful, and ambitious. They were only good when it paid him to be good. Fear is one of dominating element in life and is mightier than love. A Prince therefore ought to personify fear. A prince who is feared knows, how he stands in relation to his subjects. He is to excite fear in their minds but not hatred or contempt.

Machiavelli had a very poor idea of human nature and he did not believe in the moral progress of man and only on this conception he builds the whole structure of his political science. As such he builds his theory of state or rather preservation of state in an environment of fear or prohibition.

Separation of Politics and Ethics

Machiavelli had little place for religion and even for ethic in his political philosophy, Aristotle had already distinguished ethics from politics but did not go to the extent of separating the two and it was the achievement of Machiavelli that he brought about a complete divorce between them. He subordinated the morality of politics therefore he is not immoral but unmoral in his politics. Machiavelli may be called the founder of *"utilitarian ethics"*, *i.e.*, the ethics of gain.

He believed that state is the highest form of association and had a superior claim to man's obligation. Reasons of state and its welfare must overweigh any ethical consideration. For political action public interests should be given the highest priority. Public standards of morality are quite different from private standards of morality. Murder is crime for a private individual for which he may be hanged but for to hang a murderer for his crimes as punishment is not wrong because public safety demands it and public interests are more important than the private interests of an individual. Private interests or ethics have to do nothing with public action. Public action is to be judged not on the basis of ethics but on the basis of results because in public actions, "end justifies the means."

His Erastianism

Machiavelli and not believe in supernatural ends of man. He puts emphasis on worldly achievements of men such as material prosperity, power and fame etc. He not only separated morality from politics but gave to religion very subordinate position in his political system, and as such it is behind that the modern study of politics began with Machiavelli. Formerly Politics was the hand of religion, but to Machiavelli it has no place in his scheme of things.

He looked upon devotion to religion as a useful weapon in the hands of a statesman to be skillfully used in the furtherance of the ends of state. To Machiavelli church was the department of the state, not above or beside it but within the state. Property used it could reinforce a citizen's sense of duty to the state. As such Machiavelli was not irreligious but non-religious.

The Doctorine of Aggrandisement

He preferred the expansion of state's territory. It is immaterial what is the form of the state but whatever may be its form, a state must either expand or perish. Force of arms was necessary for political aggrandisment as well as for preservation of a state but force must be judiciously combined with craft. The doctorine of aggrandisment is the most characteristic feature of Machiavelli's political philosophy and brings out vividly his moral indifferentism. The government is ultimately based on force and fear, so as prince must have a well-trained army of his own subjects. A prince should draw more on spoils of war than on taxes. He must fulfil the imagination of his subjects by grand schemes and enterprise. His ideal prince is an enlightened despot of non-moral type. His approach was realistic and he believed in aggrandisment. To him a state was an end in itself a prince should save the state even at the expense of his soul. As such his teachings are related to the preservation of the state rather than to any theory of political philosophy. He was pragmatic thinker.

Machiavelli worshipped the deity of strength as the only deity worth consideration and homage. To him history was a mere illustration of strength based on force and fraud. Blessed were the strong and cunning. He believed that end justifies the means so the persons who capture the power and conquer other states should be honoured.

He demanded sacrifice of personal interests for the sake of country but he was not prepared to sacrifice the interest of a state for the sake of peace, solidarity and welfare of the whole mankind. He kept the welfare of the national state above the welfare of whole humanity and as such he was none of the pioneers who gave birth to the idea of national state and nationalism. Perhaps he is the first national writer to conceive of as sovereign, a unitary, a secular, a national and an isolated state.

According to Foster, Machiavelli's Political theory was the representative of Renaissance, while others think that Machiavelli stands on the border line between the medieval and modern political thought. As such Machiavelli, the brilliant Florantine, is an enigma. Some of his preachings have an element of medievalism and some preachings are quite modern and as such to categorise him either as a medieval or modern political thinker is a difficult tasks. He is an impassioned patriot, utter cynic and ardent democrat and a staunch nationalist. These inconsistent elements are due to the fact that he stands in no man's lands. He is a weather cock or more of a mariner's compass than a pioneer or precurseor or of new philosophy. This enigmas is due to the fact that he is more concerned with political statecraft than political philosophy. He is not a systematic thinkers or a political philosopher but his writings like Chanakya are full of maxims for a statesman. According to Sabine his writings are flooded with the maxims of a diplomatic nature and he cares for the preservation of the state rather than for political theory. As such according to Dunning, Machiavelli is sometimes called as the first modern political philosopher.

He gave insignificant place to morals, ethics and religion and in this way he departed from medieval political thinkers who gave a pride place to religion and ethics. He is wholly indifferent to religion, moral or ethics. According to Dunning, *Machiavelli was more unreligious than irreligious and more unmoral than immoral.* He had not the capacity to probe into the depths of political philosophy to search out these conceptions from a strictly rational and logical point of view. In short he relegated the ancient conceptions and he was only fortunate enough to stumble on a new ground. He was unable to find out the new lines of approach to politics. His main contributions is that he gave a secular approach to politics. He was like Hobbes who gave a new approach to political philosophy and secular basis in a systematic manner. According to Sabine, *Hobbes completed the unsystematic attempt of Machiavelli to give it a secular outlook in a systematic manner.*

In spite of these short comings two contributions may be attributed to Machiavelli. He himself said that he was the path breaker in bringing the historical method though his historical method is neither complete nor scientific. According to Sabine, his historical method is historical only in appearance and not in reality. He only uses history for the purpose of illustration and took examples from ancient history avoiding medieval illustration. Sabine goes a step further and says he is unhistorical as his whole thought hangs on the conception that human nature is egoistic and he uses history only to support his conclusions already arrived.

His conception about nationalism is not quite clear and it seems he groves in dark. He stumbled on certain characteristics of nationalism without consciously and convincingly grasping them. His belief in free thinking advocacy of national army aggressive belief in the extension of state, his idealization of prince are only poineers to new idea of nationalism. The dynamic force of nationalism and patriotism which was destined to re-map the Europe and to spread throughout the whole world is only discernable in a faint glimpse in his writing, he said, "I have opened a new route, which has yet not been followed."

Some of the characteristics of Machiavelli's thinking are definitely medieval and he is only layman in sensing the strings of new philosophy and a new age. He is mainly responsible to popularize the secular state and for making politics a common subject to be discussed by common persons. He brought the new conception of a state which is accepted now a days of having a definite territory, population, government and a sovereignty of it own. His emphasis on state is significant because it played an important role in the times to come. In short, he touched the new grounds but he could not stabilise them. It was left to Rousseau to bring political philosophy from the esoteric circles of mysterious of academies and here also we see the consummation of his achievement. To conclude, we may see that Machiavelli was the precursor of new outlook and new age and modern political thinking begins with him though in his political philosophy there are many medieval features and as such he stands on the border line between the medieval and modern political thought. He denied divine law and separated religion from politics, so he is called modern thinker.

The Classification of Govt. as stated by Machiavelli and his views about Monarchy and Republic are very important but Machiavelli's classification of Govt. is rather unsystematic for a thinker of his calibre. He accepts the Aristotelian classification of governments into monarchy, aristocracy and constitutional democracy with its corrupt forms of tyranny, oligarchy and democracy. He follows Polybius and Cicero that the mixed form of government with proper checks and balances is the best and most suitable constitution for the state. He believed in economic determinism and observed a close connection between wealth and political power. Behind all power for political liberty, there was always an economic interests. He shared his preference to a republican form of Government. He believed that the republican form of government is not only the most suitable but only form of govt. for a political community where there was a general economic equality. As republic can maintain its institutions and adopt itself to changing environments better than a sentimental prince. As republican government leads to a more uniform and universal material prosperity and ensured greater equality of opportunity than any other form of government. As republican system is more ending and provides more liberty to its citizens than monarchical forms of the government. He opposed aristocracy particularly based on land because in his opinion it leads to factions' quarrels and civil disorder which are harmful for the state.

Machiavelli showed his preference for republican form of state and he put more emphasis on the stability and efficiency of the state rather than its form. He was of the opinion that the different type of government suited to different places and times and that government is best which suits to particular environments and gives stability, efficiency and prosperity to general administration and people. Italy during his days was torn into many pieces and emergence of a strong person who may unite it and may bring deliverance from foreign yoke was the crying need of the hour, so he was of the opinion that elective monarchy is best suited to Italy. Perhaps he described the qualities of prince and stated maxims keeping in view the conditions of Italy, otherwise he favoured a republican form of government.

A prince being compelled knowingly to adopt the beast ought to choose fox and the lion, Machiavelli says so. Machiavelli's view on Politics and state are pragmatic and practical, scholars think his book, *The Prince* was great work which marked a break from medieval way of thinking as such Machiavelli's Prince is a very important book. *"The Prince purports to be a practical handbook"* writes Maxey, *"explaining the technique of successful rulership."* Machiavelli himself states in his dedicatory preface, "I have not embellished with smelling or magnified words, nor stuffed with rounded periods, nor with any extrinsic allurements or adornments whatever...for I have wished either that no honour should be given to it, or else that the truth of the matter and weightiness of them shall make it acceptable." In this way he told frank truth about his book. He stated, *"A Prince...who desires to maintain himself should not be always good."*

He stated in his *Prince* everything frankly, directly and stated naked truth in the simplest possible language so that even the most uneducated person or dumbest head that ever sat on throne may readily understand and grasp every grasp every word of it. He did not state fine spun theories speculations or doctorine but only stated practical rules of experiences, amply tested in the laboratory of everyday affairs. Like Aristotle, he overwhelms the reader with his knowledge and astonishing memory of facts.

The Prince of Machiavelli contains 26 chapters which can be divided in three divisions. Division I represents a general introduction and discusses various forms of despotic government. Second part opposes the use of mercenary troops and pleads for the establishment of national army. Third part contains the substance of Machiavelli's, philosophy. It states number of rules for the guidance of the princes especially the new Prime or leader of men who had seized a state with force or craft. Prince of Machiavelli is real politic and deals with the mechanics of government. It is pragmatic in character and gives the technique of successful rulership. He stated *"A wise Prince should take advice when it suits."*

The whole argument of *The Prince* is based mainly on two things borrowed from Aristotle. One of his main conception is that the state is the highest form of human associations and the most indispensable instrument for the promotion of human welfare and it is, by merging himself in the state that an individual maintains the state and thereby finds his full his best self-satisfaction. Consideration of the welfare of the state must, therefore, overweigh any consideration of individual or group welfare. Secondly, he believes that the material self-interestt is the most potent motive force in individual and public action. The art of government lies in the intelligent and unflinching pursuit by rulers of his self-interests regardless of ethical considerations.

Machiavelli identifies the state with the ruler and desires that state should be worshipped like God because it contains power of the God on earth. The Caesar must make himself worthy of the worship by a ruthless and successful seizure of power. Things which brought power were the virtues that mattered. Things like cunning deceit and ruthlessness are virtues because these qualities bring success and can be utilized to gain success.

The XVIII chapter of *The Prince* gives Machiavelli's idea of virtues which a successful prince must possess. Theoretically integrity is better than collusion but cunning and subtlety are often very useful. A Prince should be combination of the elements of rational as well as of mental force. He should be judicious combination of lion and fox. A wise prince will not keep his parole when by doing so he would ensure his own interests and when the reasons which bind himself no longer exist. A prince must play the fox and act as the hypocrite to disguise his real motives and inclinations. According to Machiavelli preservation of the state was the raisondietere of monarchy. A prince must regard his neighbours as likely enemies and keep on guard. A clever prince will strike his enemy before he is ready. Prince will realise his powers not by, internal unity of the state but by surrendering his powers to the people and establishing through going despotism. Economic motive being the mainspring of the human conduct, a prince should do, all he can to keep is subjects materially contented. A prince might execute his conspirators but should not confiscate his property, for confiscation would be more seriously noted by the affected family than the execution. He even remarks that a man is apt to forget the murder of his father but he cannot forget the confiscation of his patrimony.

According to Machiavelli, a prince should be free from emotional disturbances but must be ready and capable of taking advantages of the emotions of the other people. He must be cool and calculating opportunist. He must oppose for the force and evil by evil and must be ready to sin boldly for the interest of the state. A Prince should be unshakeable in his purpose and should not allow himself to be weighed down by good or bad, justice or injustice, right or wrong, mercy or cruelty, however, on dishonour in the matters of the state. It is often useful in public affairs. He considered himself on the physician of the state and cure the evils of the state, he even stated that dishonesty is the best policy. He believed that public necessity knows no law, end justifies the means. Public morals are quite different from private morals and rightness or wrongness of a state action should not be judged on ethical grounds but on the basis of result. If result is success all means are honourable because nothing succeeds like success.

He recommended that the two means of success for the ruler are law and force. The ruler should be rational as well as brutal in order to represent a judicious combination of lion and fox. Playing the fox was very useful for the prince to be hypocrite and disguise real motives. He should regard his neighbours as real enemies and keep on guard and attack before the other is ready. Machiavelli would like an prince to be cool and calculating opportunist always ready to sin boldly for the sake of stability of state. He must not be emotionally disturbed but take the advantage of the emotions of other people. He must fire the imagination of his subjects by grand schemes and enterprises. He must not bother about justice or injustice good or bad but oppose evil by evil or by dishonest means. He stated state must either expand or perish and expansion of dominion was easier in one's own country. He regarded expansion of Roman state as ideal. Force of arms was necessary for political aggrandizement as well as for the preservation of the state, but force must be judiciously combined with craft.

Attitude towards Religion and Morality

Machiavelli's attitude towards morality and religion was based on his belief regarding human nature and motive which force him for action. He regarded men as essentially selfish and force him for action. He regarded men as essentially selfish and bad. To him, a man was a strange mixture of weakness, folly and bravery fit only to be hoodwinked and lorded over. He believed that men are ungrateful, fickle, deceitful, cowardly and nefarious. He considered selfishness, egoisms, vanity and lust for power as the motives of human conduct. None would do good unless obliged to do so or unless it paid him to be good. To be called social virtues are nothing but expression of self interest in disguise. Besides human nature is aggressive and acquisitive. There is perpetual competition between them to have more and best. This state of affair is bound to result in anarchy unless restrained by Prince *i.e.,* by the government. Fear is dominating element in life. The ruler must, therefore, be feared than loved. But he must not be hated. Force breeds fear and fear is more disciplinary than love. He stated *"a Prince must esteem his nobles but not make himself hated by people."*

Men agree to restraints of law only because of selfish interest of security of their life and property. As such government is founded on the weakness, selfishness and insufficiency of the individual, who is unable to protect himself without the aid of the state. The effective motives on which a statesman must rely are egoistic. There is no limit to human desires of wealth and power. Hence there is always threat to anarchy unless restrained by force behind the law.

He frequently remarked that men are in general bad. In particular, government must aim at the security of life and property before anything else, since these are the most universal desires in human nature. He even remarked that *"Men forget more easily the death of their father than the loss of their patrimony."* His second remark was that a prudent ruler may kill but must not plunder. He particularly insisted that a prudent ruler shall abstain from property and women of his subjects because these matters offend men more easily. The prince should exploit the faith of the masses in religion and their credulity. In order to enhance safety and stability of the state, he advised the prince to respect the established customs and institutions of the people to patronize talent in art and to encourage trade and agriculture and to surround all his actions with an air of grandeur. He should do all to keep his subjects materially contented. According to Cook Machiavelli's Prince was meant to be a benevolent despot.

Machiavelli believed that man would never behave well towards others unless forced to do so and that human nature remains unchanged at all times and places. Man is incorrigible animal and he cannot be reformed. According to him, force and not will is the basis of state. To him, history was a mere illustration of strength based on force and fraud. Blessed were the strong and cunning. Thus, according to Machiavelli the Prince who would succeed must know 'how to do wrong and make use of it or not according to necessity. As Prince should strive ceaselessly by all manner of means to win glory and gains. In realms of states craft there is only one criteria of judgement and that is success. Thus, he believes nothing succeeds like success.

Machiavelli's "Prince" according to Maxey is a *"Practical handbook explaining the technique of successful rulership."* Maxey quotes examples of President Washington of breaking treaty with France in 1778 and of President Lincoln of assuming emancipation proclamation quite contrary to his solemn and explicit promise made in his first inaugural address to the effect that he would not interfere with slavery directly or indirectly. Similarly action of Mr. Theodore Roosevelt to double cross Columbias in the Panama's affair was how far right or wrong is debatable.

Impact

In the European world whether the actions of Napoleon the great and Napoleon III of championing the cause of democratic principles but of possessing dictatorial power were perhaps Machiavellian. Mussolini and Hitler too utilized the religious and egoistic feeling for gaining power and these were certainly Machiavellian. Breaking of treaty by Hitler with Russian in 1941, and attack of Russia on Japan in 1945, in spite of the fact that Japan did not attack it in direct violation of treaty may also be termed as Machiavellian. Recent rape of Tibet by China is another example of Machiavellian policy. It is true that Gandhi emphasized on morals and ethical side but it is doubtful if any of his followers, who wielded state power followed his ethical teachings; and those who followed Gandhian teachings like Vinoba Bhava etc; and others were treated as non-entity so far wielding of state power is concerned. Thus we see, politician even today resort to immoral means for the achievements of political power although they condemn them in principle. Even Lord Grey remarked that the policies of great states cannot always be governed by rules of morality. Lenin, Shivaji and Palmerston followed this policy.

Conclusion

But history bears witness that dictators like Napoleon I and III, Hitler or Mussolini may achieve glory of a short period but it is not everlasting. In India too congress declined as soon as it left Gandhian policy and followed Machiavellian policy. According to Maxey, *"he was the first, if not the noblest, of the great pragmatist but it may be added that he was clear sighted and not far sighted.* Thus, his *Prince* is a book for an opportunist but not for the far sighted statesman though it teaches how to gain power and keep it.

Machiavelli was a nationalist and also a patriot and he propagated these ideas so with Machiavelli ends one epoch and begins another in history of European Political thought and some writers think that Machiavelli is the founder of modern state, while some writers are of the opinion that Machiavelli stands on the border line between the medieval and modern political thought, therefore, his ideas require deep study. In 16th century in Italy, where Machiavelli lived and wrote his famous political works, the medieval order had collapsed. The feudal lords had vanished but, unlike other European lands such as U.K., Spain and France, no strong central authority unified the country. In Italy, there were many small states who used to fight. Political life was chaotic, laden with treachery and intrigue. Morals had decayed and men tended to live by their units, serving their own selfish interests without consideration of others, or of society as a whole. The pope, nominally supreme spiritual authority in Christiandom had become no more than a prince among the many, who divided the country between themselves, and the standard of world that he sat for others were not praiseworthy. He noticed the game for power and so he concerned himself with political state craft, but not with political science. He more is of a mariner's compass or the whether cock than a pioneer for new philosophy. He preaches opportunist philosophy.

However, it can be said of him that he broke totally from ancient moorings, when he gave almost an insignificant place for morals, ethics and religion. When he neglected them, he did not state only and how? As such according to Dunning, *he was more unreligious than irreligious and more unmoral than immoral.*

He was critical of Pope because he was responsible for the division of Italy into a number of princely states and was not strong enough to unite Italy under himself or to permit anyone else to unite it.

He was critical of religion because Christian principles seemed to him to make men feeble and more disposed to endure injuries than to avenge them. Machiavelli desired to make religion as hand maid of politics to be served as a device to use it to make it easier to rule over a body of people.

In ethical sphere also he did not ask whether power was good or evil but he wanted to know how to preserve it and also to increase it. In moral sphere, he stated that state knows no morals and end justifies the means and public morality is quite different than private morality. Thus he discarded the medieval conceptions of religion, morality and ethics.

He used historical method to support his contentions though in a defective manner. His belief in free thinking, advocacy of a national army, the criterion of state as extension, his idealisation of Prince point out his new thinking.

National State

His greatest contribution is nationalistic outlook. He popularised the name 'state' in the way in which it is used today, that is something having a definite territory, population, government and sovereignty of its own. He made politics a common subject to be discussed by common men. These are his contribution which make him a modern thinker.

Keynote of Medievalism was universalism but Machiavelli was the herald of the modern state and supported national monarchical states. Machiavelli wrote, *"the only way to establish any kind of order is to establish a monarchical government to curl the excessive ambitions, feudal lords and corruption of powerful individuals."*

Patriotism

He was a first patriot. He wanted glorification of Italy and desired it without any mental reservation of being either a confirmed monarchist or republican. He subordinated all consideration for the sake of his motherland. Machiavelli himself stated that after putting all other considerations aside, the only question should be what cause will save the life and liberty of country. He passionately desired to find some means by which Italy could be united and he made sufficiently strong plan to maintain internal peace and resist aggression by foreign states and expel the foreigner from her soil. This is the reason that his books tell the methods by which states can be made strong, the policy by which it can expand its power and the errors which it must avoid if it is to prosper and flourish. He came to conclusion that main purpose of politics is to preserve and increase political power; that is the criterion by which he measures the success or failure of Govt.

He also gives us glimpse of certain liberal and democratic principles. His statement that property and women should not be confiscated and fraud must be used in war shows him as a person interested in welfare of his countrymen.

Machiavelli was one of the founder father of nationalism. During his lifetime he was much impressed by the French and Swiss national army so he condemned the keeping of mercenary troops. If may be true that Machiavelli does not use the term nationality in the modern sense but he was aware of the forces which make a state united against other states *i.e.,* common tradition, a common language, a common history and a common system of law. Thus it appears that he understood the factors that produce the sentiment of nationalism in modern age. His advocacy of expansion of state up to the limits of ethical homogeneity clearly pointed to the fact that Machiavelli was the forerunner of the theory of national states and of wise and strong ruler.

He advocated for strong and wise ruler to keep order and promote the interest of the state. In this sphere he was the first political psychologist. Machiavelli proposed a strong absolute monarchy, again anticipating later political developments and theory of sovereignty. As such he is considered as first modern thinker.

In conclusion he must he given his due for having stumbled on those principles which smelled into mighty steams in the later centuries. His particular emphasis on the part played by the state is of great significance as it was through this instrument that the national states came into existence. He was a herald of nationalism. All these make him an important initiator of contemporary political philosophy. He united political theory with political practice, separated religion from politics and preached for strong national states and patriotism. As such Machiavelli was the first modern thinker.

According to Machiavelli, "A Prince should not always be good but to be so or not as necessity may require." He states, therefore, it is well to see to it that you are feared rather than loved, to provide first for fear and then if possible for love. He states let the prince look to the maintenance of state, the means will be deemed honourable. As such it has been remarked Machiavelli's doctrine is a theory of preservation of state rather than a theory of the state.

Machiavelli was shrewd so he stated "Let the prince look to the maintenance of the state, the means will be deemed honourable", as he was of the opinion that end justifies the means, he was cunning so Machiavelli had one theory for revolutions and another for government. Thus, he was most clever writer. Machiavelli based his ideas on the basis of conditions prevailing in his time. During his period Italy was divided into small princely kingdoms which were perpetually intriguing against one another. There was chaos and everyone was guided by selfish motives of monetary gain and lust for power. As such he came to the conclusion that man is selfish and egoistic.

Human Nature

According to Machiavelli human nature is selfish and each individual wants to promote his own ends. What man desires is security and power, they can be induced to do anything if they are offered an advantage such as money or position. Men are greedy and even if they possess much wealth or power, they desire for more. He believed that a body of men can be kept in peace and order only by a strong ruler. Men did not keep order of their own will because each person desires what the other possesses. Order had to be acceptable to the subjects when the ruler is wise and clever, and uses the weakness of the subjects to keep them satisfied but in check.

He is the forerunner of modern political psychology because to keep people under control by making use of material incentives is a political technique signifying a vast improvement on keeping them subdued by brute force or by evoking in them the fear of hell. Even now we say the same thing, in a refined language that a good government satisfies the needs and aspirations of the people and if fails to do so, the government would collapse.

Thus, Machiavelli is of firm conviction that goal of the ruler is to maintain power and to extend it if possible. He emphasized that any means used for the consolidation of power by the ruler are justified if it serves their purpose. He suggests that a new ruler should ruthlessly suppress those who are not likely to make submission to him, show generosity to those who may reconcile themselves to the new rule.

Machiavelli suggested that measures of repression should be carried out ruthlessly but speedily during a short span of time but not to be stretched out over a long period so that resistance may be organized.

In the same way he described that the ruler should follow showingly the religious belief of his subjects, because religion makes a people divide and easy to govern. In fact, not being religious minded himself but following a show or pretence of being religious minded, a prince could exploit the religious belief of his subjects in the better manner.

He considers that man is essentially selfish and acts in order to promote their private interests of security, power, wealth and prestige. Love means a person sacrifices his own personal interest for the sake of another, so love of his subjects by the ruler is likely to provide only an insecure basis for the political power of the prince. The game of politics is not a love affair; it is an unwedding struggle for power. In such a state of affairs, the sentiments of mutual affection are likely to hinder the ruler rather than to help him. Thus Machiavelli gave a psychological advice that it is well to see that you are feared than loved.

Fear is a threat held out to a person that his interests would suffer if he did not act as he was ordered to do. Practically all government rest on fear, for the persons are kept aware that if they break the law, they will be punished. The threat is the basis of the power. Ruler had to ensure that no one is more powerful or stronger than himself as such he should destroy his rivals to safeguard his power.

He is of firm opinion that king is to be judged by survival or the failure of the kingdom that he has founded. He supported king as law giver and absolute and above law. Thus, he propounded the modern belief that state stands as a higher authority above and beyond the people and other Associations.

He is well versed in human psychology and as such he knows that man is guided mainly by economic interests. As such he shows a strong sense of property rights. He is of the opinion that a son may forget the murder of his father but not of his patrimony. He believed that there are areas of self-interests where even the most despotic ruler should not interfere because to save honour of women folk and private property even the most decile and servile of the subjects would rise to defend.

States may be overthrown if they fail to govern with strength and cleverness. If bad blood is created between the ruler and the ruled or he encroaches upon the property right of subjects or disputes their family life or religious feelings or he allows his people to become more powerful than himself then his rule is doomed. Thus, in one way his writings are also guide to revolution. He might even say that a revolutionary leader should be first ruthless and then generous if he is to consolidate his power.

Machiavelli's philosophy is like a two edged sword which can be used by a ruler to consolidate his power and by a revolutionary to outwit the ruler. However, his philosophy increased people's knowledge of the methods of practical politics about the motives of rulers and the ruled about the practice of diplomacy and informed people about the causes of rise and fall of kingdoms. Thus he made politics a common subject of discussion which resulted in gain for popular democracy.

Evaluation

Machiavelli was not systematic philosopher and he mainly deals with the preservation of the state in face of disruptive forces and tendencies but to say that Machiavelli was not a philosopher at all as Sabine says is to go a long way. Machiavelli was a realistic thinker, who dealt with actual problems and enunciated a modern doctorine of state. To sum up we can say he was the first, if not the noblest of the great pragmatist though he was more clear sighted than a far sighted thinker. In spite of all this according to Dunning, *"He was the first modern Political Philosopher."* He based his ideas on realistic outlook.

Machiavelli is the first political thinker who separated politics from morality. He pleaded for strong, united national state based on patriotism. He supported that aim of gaining and preserving power ought to be achieved by hook or crook or by fair and foul means as end justifies the means. As such he has been considered as a great realist and shrewd thinkers, who gave pragmatic ideas without caring for morals.

Chapter 13

Reformation — Luther Martin and Calvin

Reformation contributed a lot for the growth of modern political thought, so modern political thought is based on Reformation and its influence was great for growth of political thought. The great intellectual upheaval popularly called Renaissance, of which Machiavelli was the forerunner brought the middle ages to an end in all spheres of life. In the beginning of 16th century new forces were working in the economic, political and intellectual fields and new methods were initiated but Roman church remained uninfluenced by it. According to Adams, *"In Government, in doctrine, and in life, it still placed the greatest emphasis upon those traditions with the peculiar conditions of the middle ages had built upon the foundations of the primitive Christianity, and it was determined to remain unchanged."* It was reformation which brought about the change in church and indirectly destroyed the conception that the church was the ultimate master of human affairs. It created the concept of national state and brought modern Europe into existence.

Reformation marks the beginning of new phase in the history of European political thought. It represented to a certain extent the result of Teutonic people from the religious domination of races, who chose the era of supremacy of Papacy which regulated the relations between the rulers and the ruled. Politically, the reformation represents the inspiration of young nations with distinct national interests and ideals of their own against their universal domination of papacy. These national states brought about the national temporal policies of their own. Economically the princes and people wanted to take possession of the enormous riches and landed estates of the church.

Influence

In the 16th century political theory was naturally influenced by the reformation movement. The movement thought primarily clerical could not fail to have ethical and political significance. The opposition of reformers to sole indulgences signified a reunion of morality and theology. In their opposition of papal authority, the reformations found princes anxious to save their subjects from papal exploitation, ready to help them. In turn, reformers helped the princes in seizing property and disruption of the jurisdiction of the church which increased the power of the rulers. In this way, they not only helped their rulers against the catholic church and papacy but they also helped them against the disorderly elements within the state by preaching the doctrine of passive obedience and helped them crushing feudal elements in knight's war and the common people in peasant's war and brought absolute monarchy into existence. The union between religion and politics which was heralded by Machiavelli was restored once again by the reformation movement. It also marked the reunion of religion and ethics.

The reformation movement of 16th century replaced the religious prescription of the church by the notion of justification by faith. They denied the right of Pope to grant pardons and weakened the church by Lutherian doctrine of justification of faith supported national states.

The fundamental doctrine of justification of faith bad to the growth of a marked individualism and after temporary culmination of rulers power it ultimately lead to take growth of individual liberty and democratic government as also the establishment of a strong united national state. According to J.M. Figgs, *"to the form of Government it was a reversion to the ideas of earlier middle ages which were largely disappearing under the combined influence of Aristotle and the Renaissance."*

In the initial stage of reformation between 1517-30, Martin Luther was the prominent figures. It gave rise to absolute state territorial and national in character with power to demand the allegiance of all of its citizens lay and ecclesiastical.

During second stage of 1530-1564, Calvin's theories became predominant which demanded a rigorous organisation and disciplining of human nature. During the period of 1564-1618 democratic nations and ideas of rights of man began to take its shape.

General Political Influence

The political teachings of the great reformers did much to counteract the rationalising non-moral and non-religious spirit of Machiavelli. Reformation rejected the idea of universal empire and a universal church and allied itself with the idea of nationalism and strong rulers.

According to Dunning, *"in monarchic lands the tendency of the reform was to enhance the hold of monarchical principle and in aristocratic government to confirm the principle of aristocracy. In both, the effect was to strengthen absolutism in the political sovereign."* Luther preached the doctrine of passive obedience and Calvin of secure secular right of rulers and strengthened the power of rulers of national states.

The importance of Martin Luther and Calvin cannot be ignored for bringing reformation so it is necessary to state the life of Martin Luther and his political ideas because he protested against Pope and championed the cause of reformation and brought Protestant religion.

Life

Martin Luther, the originator of reformation movement was born at Thuringia in 1483 and died in 1546. He joined an Augustinian monastery and became a professor of theology. His visit to Rome made him anti Pope and convinced him for the need of the reformation of the church. He cannot be regarded fully as the child of renaissance as Adams states. He was not by nature the heir of its spirit, nor all its tendencies. He accepted its principles and its methods because they were necessary to him.

Ideas

He opposed the indulgences for the forgiveness of sins which meant sins of an individual can be forgiven and entry into heaven can be assured on payment of certain sums of money to the church. Due to the opposition, he was ex-communicated by the church and this act forced him to break with the church and to take help of the princes against the church and the emperor who supported the church. Princes helped him because they saw that they could increase the wealth of the state by taking over possession of the church property themselves or vesting it in an ecclesiastical body under their control and subject to its authority.

Luther created a definite distinction between spiritual and secular authority. He exalted the national state against the universal notion of church. He preached for the Christian duty of passive obedience to the established social and political order. He preached that the secular authority is divine in origin of church and ruler is responsible only to God and thus led to royal absolutism. Luther was not a systematic thinker on any subject as he did possess the requisite degree of coolness and patience on the contrary he was hot and impatient. According to the Sabine, *Luther felt more than he considered and on the whole knew better what he did not believe than what he believed.* All his books are...items in an excited controversy. He brought Protestant religion.

He started as the champion of the right of individual judgement and freedom of conscience and supported the princes in killing peasant mercilessly during peasant's war. He declared that I would suffer a prince doing wrong than a people doing right. He preached to peasants the doctrine of passive obedience and sided with the prince because he depended on the support of princes. He preached that clergyman are ordinary citizens and therefore the subject of laws and courts of state and in this way he strengthened the monarchy. As such Calvinist, John Knox had to preach the duty of obedience to the state authority and resistance to the authority of the state in the interest of religion.

Luther did not believe in the essential equality of men. He stood for civil inequality. His doctorine of personal conscience freed the individual from the domination of the church but doctrine of passive obedience enhanced the power of the state. The state gained at the expense of the church as also of Holy Roman Empire. According to J.M. Figgs, "*The unity and universality and essential rightness of the sovereign territorial state, and the denial of every extraterritorial of independent communal form of life are Luther's lasting contribution to politics.*" Luther and Calvin brought Protestant Religion.

Calvin

While Luther tended to subordinate church to state but Calvin drew a clear boundary line between church and state and would not surrender the peculiar function of church to civil authority. As such study of John Calvin and his political ideas is necessary.

Life

John Calvin was a French and he was the first reformer who created a detailed system of doctrine for the reformed church. According to Dunning While Luther was the theologian, Malevetrethon the philosopher, and Zuingli the politician, Calvin was distinctly the law giver of reformations. In his Institutes of the Christian Religion, he tried to give a guidance as to what was necessary to do in order to live a good Christian life according to the injunctions of the Bible.

Ideas

He thought that the church must have a system of Government and discipline suited to itself and distinct from the secular one. It must have a body or somebody of elders to lay down the rules of proper conduct with power to punish the unbeliever and to exclude the state from clerical affairs and to exclude secular affairs from its organization.

Calvin based his conception of state on sovereignty of God and the Fall of Man. According to Dunning, *"he believed the authority of Magistrate is the most sacred and honourable of all things pertaining to mere moral life."* He believed that the state should maintain peace and order and protect life, liberty and property and its should guard truth, exclude, idolatry and blasphemy from society. Every Christian had a moral duty to help the state in these functions. He preached obedience to establish authority but showed preference to aristocracy. His ideas were theocratic in principle and aristocratic in operation. He supported the right of resistance to ruler if ruler contravened the orders of God. He believed in natural rights of law, liberty and freedom of worship. Those doctorines helped resistance in Holland, Scotland and France. According to Bowle Calvin, *"doctrine is hostile to Empire and Papacy."* Calvin and Luther ushered a new era of reformation and brough. It protestant religion and indirectly national states with strong monarchs. Thus, Martin Luther and John Calvin brought Protestant religion into existence and gave a death blow to omni potency and supremacy of Pope.

With the growth of Protestant religion, idea of one Christian state with Emperor and Pope got death blow and national states came into existence. With the growth of national states, Patriotism grew and new political ideas came into existence. Thus, Martin

Luther, John Calvin and their fallowers are pioneers to modern political ideas.

With Martin Luther and Calvin, Protestant Christian thinking gained ground and new powerful nations discarded papal supremacy as well as theoretical supremacy of emperor.

Chapter 14

"The Theory of Sovereignty" Bodin and Grotius

Bodin's statement of sovereignty is generally agreed to be the most important part of his political philosophy. Bodin states that "first mark of sovereignty is the power of giving laws to all people in general or to each one in particular without consent of any besides himself. He defines sovereignty as the supreme power unrestrained by law." His *De Republica* was the first comprehensive work on sovereignty. As such Bodin may he regarded as one of the great thinkers of the West.

He followed the methods of historical research and of contemporary observation and paved the way for research on historical basis and on contemporary observation.

Bodin's statement of the principle of sovereignty is generally agreed to be the most important part of his political philosophy and the contribution of Bodin and Hugo Grotius to the development of the theory of the sovereignty of the states very important.

John Bodin was a French thinker who is considered as one of the greatest thinkers of the 16th century. He was man of vast intellectual sympathetic and his reading was prodigious. He knew many languages, read Greek and Roman writers and had knowledge of Old Testament and physical sciences of the day. According to Hearnshaw, the chief of the influences in his intellectual life seem to have been the old testament and the new Platonic philosophy as interpreted by two Italian Platonists. his writings ware conservative in quality, yet glowing with the inspiration of renaissance.

His books, *The Response, A Treatise on Political Economy, Demonomanie, Heptapiometerss, Universal Nature Theraum* but *De Republica* are six books concerning the state. In the *Republica,* Bodin gives his main ideas in the form of well-defined definitions. He defines states as "an aggregation of families and their common possession ruled by a sovereign power, and by reason." He had been influenced by Plato and perhaps by the politics of Aristotle also. Like Plato, he states that the end of state is neither happiness nor well-being but the good life of citizens.

Law of Nature

Bodin believes that the law of nature regulates the human relations. The law of nature is merely the rules that distinguish right from wrong. He assumes that a ruler not in accordance with the law of nature is no better than a head of ruffians. Thus he supported rule of law.

Family and the State

Family, he conceives of as a group of individuals under the supreme powers of Pater families. To Bodin society was based on social instinct which made the individual energy out of state. Civil associations were formed out of natural associations and family because of social instinct, and these civil associations served the purpose of the promotion of trade, public worship etc. before the political society came into existence. The state unlike the society was based on force.

In primitive stage vanquished were reduced to slavery and even the victors submitted to the authority of the military chiefs. Thus slavery and political subjection appeared on the ruin of natural liberty. To him power is originated from and depended upon physical force.

According to Bodin, perpetual and absolute sovereign power is the outstanding characteristic of the state. Bodin believed that state is the ultimate form of association, "*holding together by supreme power a mass of lesser association and individuals*" like the family, corporation, commerce etc. The state is different to these associations because it alone possesses sovereignty *i.e.,* power to hold all other associations in their places. The state is substantially an aggregation of smaller groups and holds over them and possesses sovereignty.

He holds that political power actually belongs to God. it is exercised by the king as a representative of the almighty which may be interpreted that political power does not require the consent of the subjects and sovereign is independent of the will of the people.

He believed that unit of society is not the individual but family. According to him, family is the natural society, which served model for artificial society, the state. Each family has a head who holds it together, who defends it and ensure its survival. In the same way sovereign is head of the State and as the family does not elect its head so sovereign is also independent for his office and did not depend on the will and consent of his subjects. The power of sovereign in relation to his subjects is absolute and unrestrained and unrestricted.

Citizenship

According to him, "a citizen is a free man who is subject to sovereign power of another." The citizens enjoy rights and privileges among themselves but are all subject to sovereign. He condemns both slavery and communism. Different citizens enjoy different rights and privileges under the sovereign. The recognition of a common sovereign is the sole criteria of a state and subjection to him is the sole test of citizenship. His conception of citizenship is different than the conception of Aristotle.

Sovereignty

It is generally agreed that Bodin's doctrine of sovereignty is the most important part of political philosophy. Sovereignty originally says Bodin's sovereignty is vested in the people in their collective capacity but it is customary for the people to delegate it to princes or other functionaries of government. Sovereignty represents the highest and most potent will that can develop in human society. Sovereignty is the legal competence of the state which empowers the state to manage the affairs of the individual associations. Because of its sovereignty, a state is free from all legal limitations and compulsions and cannot be made subject to any legal process except through its own consent.

Bodin shares with Hobbes the glory of having formulated the modern secular theory of state, but to him, perhaps more than Hobbes the world is indebted for the first definite exposition of the doctrine of political sovereignty. In every independent community governed by law, there must be some authority whether residing in one person or several, by which laws themselves are established and from where they proceed. And this power being the source of law must itself be above the law *i.e.,* positive laws. The person or persons holding the power are the political sovereign. In his *De República,* he defines "*sovereignty as the supreme power under strained by law.*" Sovereignty can suffer no limitation in time, in function or in law for sovereignty belongs rather to state itself than to actual sovereign. An actual person who may be holder of sovereign power may die but sovereignty is continued as it is said in English "king is dead: Long live the King!" Bodin gave prominence to continuity of sovereignty.

According to Sabine, "*The primary attribute of sovereignty is the power to give laws to citizens collectively and severely without the consent of a superior or an equal or an inferior.*"

Following points from Bodin's definition of sovereignty may be stated:

(1) Sovereign's power over all the citizens and association within territorial limits is absolute.
(2) It is perpetual and is not limited by time.
(3) It is not alienable.
(4) It is undelighted or delighted without limit or condition.
(5) The sovereignty is the only source of law by which the community is governed and its affairs regulated.
(6) The sovereign is not bound by law.
(7) Sovereignty is legally superior but is limited by the law of God and nature.

As head of state sovereign has following powers:

(1) To declare war and make peace.
(2) To coin money.
(3) To have power of magistracy.
(4) To impose taxes.
(5) To grant pardon.
(6) To impose punishment.

According to Sabine, "*In general sovereignty meant for Bodin a perpetual, humanity, unlimited and unconditional right to make interpret and execute laws.*"

Limitation of Absolute Sovereignty

Conception of sovereignty of Bodin seems to be absolute but it is limited in following respects according to Bodin:

(1) All rulers are bound by divine law.

(2) It is limited by law of nature.

(3) He should not act against the constitutional law of the realm.

(4) The sovereign owes moral duty to observe treaty with other sovereigns.

(5) The sovereign owes moral duty to observe the compact with his subjects.

(6) The sovereign must exercise his authority with reason.

(7) The sovereign should not interfere with the private property of individuals without their consent.

In short, he believed that sovereign is subject to the laws of God and the law of nature and if he ignores them, he becomes tyrant. Thus, he believes that sovereign should act rightly.

Criticism

Bodin is the first modern thinker to propound the concept of sovereignty of state. He has analysed his theory but his analysis of supreme power contains serious confusions. According to Sabine, the preceding account of Bodin's theory of sovereign authority takes account of only the parts of his arguments which are clear and out of difficulties. It is entirely however, the argument is by no means so simple, but contains serious confusions. In general, to Bodin, sovereignty means a perpetual humanity unlimited by and unconditional right to make, interpret and execute laws. The existence of such a right, he believes to be necessary to any well-ordered state. But the exercise of sovereign's power which he regulates as justifiable is by no means so unlimited as his definition imply and the result is series of restrictions that introduce a great amount of confusion into the finished theory. He is not quite clear in his ideas.

On the one hand, sovereign is supreme and on the other hand, sovereign is bound by law of God *i.e.,* by law of nature. To quote Sabine, "*Bodin never doubts that sovereign is bound by the law of God and that of nature. Though he defines law a short act of the sovereign's will, he never supports that the sovereign can make right by mere fiat.*" For him law of nature stand above human law and sets certain unchangeable standards of right, it is the observance of the law that differentiates the true state from mere effective violence. "There is, of course, no sense to make the sovereign legally liable for violating the law of nature still natural law does not impose some real difficulties on him. In particular, it requires the keeping of agreement and respect for private property. The sovereign argument may involve political obligations towards his subjects or towards other sovereigns and in each case Bodin had no doubt he was bound. It was difficult for him to keep these obligations of the exclusively on a moral plane and separate from legal and political obligations, what, for instance would be the duty of the magistrates of the sovereign were to command something contrary to natural laws. He had no doubt that there might be cases so flagrant that the sovereign ought to be disobeyed. He did all, he could reduce such cases to the narrowest limits but the confusion was none the less there. Law is at once the will of the sovereign and an expression of external justice yet the two may be in conflict.

Another confusion is caused due to his emphasis on constitutional law. To him, king of France cannot modify the rules of succession. He admits that certain laws, king of France cannot change but still he regards him as an example par excellence of sovereign Sabine states, *"the confusion here is manifest; the sovereign is at once the source of the law and the subject of certain conditional law, which he has made and cannot change."*

Third confusion about the inviolability of private property is still more serious. The right is granted by law of nature but it constituted for Bodin more than a mere limitation on the power of the sovereign. To Bodin property is so sacred that the sovereign even cannot touch it without the consent of the owner. Accordingly he asserted that the taxation requires the assent of state. But there is nothing whatever about taxation to justify him in this setting apart from other legislation, and he holds that estates can only act as advisory bodies in this respect. Indeed the very existence of the estates depended upon the delegation by the sovereign of a qualified authority to a subordinate corporation. His defence of property guided modern thinkers.

Bodin's Importance

Bodin may be regarded as one of the greatest political thinkers of the west. His *De Republica* was the first comprehensive work on sovereignty. To quote Dunning *"Bodin brought back political theory to the form and form which it had gone far astray since Aristotle and gave it again the externals, at least, of a science.* He adds *his real work, admirably accomplished is to set the theory of the state and the science of government once more where Aristotle had placed it, on a foundation of history and observation, and by the side of, not dependent from, the sciences of ethics and theology."* He rejected medieval institutions and political dogmas. Like Machiavelli, he followed the methods of historical research and contemporary observation, but, whereas Machiavelli concentrated on political practice; and he wrote both on political practice and political science. Unlike Machiavelli, he stood against the total severance of relation between politics and ethics or theology, for he believed that justice and God controlled political life. But, still, he saw the necessity of a "clear separation of the legal from the ethical sphere of thought within political science itself." This is the reason that some consider him and not Machiavelli as first modern thinker. According to Me Govern, *"Bodin was most vigorous and logical."*

Bodin clearly distinguishes between the state and government. *"The possession of supreme power determines the form of state; but the system and method through which this power is exercised determine the form of government."*

Bodin defined state as a rightly ordained govt. Unlike Hobbes, he did not regard state as established by the contract because he regarded man social by nature. But he agrees with Hobbes that an absolute power was necessary for the existence of the state.

Machiavelli and Hobbes hold that sovereign power is an entirely secular matter but Bodin held that power of sovereign stemmed from God and unlike Hobbes holds that right and wrong, justice and injustice were ideas derived from God himself and king made only laws and the laws should correspond to right and justice. Although the sovereign was absolute over the people, he was an instrument of divine law.

An organised government will possess a senate, to act as a council having the constitutional right to advise the sovereign on political matters. Secondly, there will be a body of magistrates possessing jurisdiction to carry out the sovereign's commands, settle disputes and adjudicate cases. Thirdly, he holds that a well organized Govt. will possess a parliament of Estates or representatives of the various classes *i.e.,* clergy, the nobility and the commons to communicate the wishes of their fellow citizens to the sovereign and to communicate the command to his citizens. The senate, the magistracy, and the estates provide respectively council, execution and current. According to Bodin, "a *state cannot fail to prosper where the sovereign retains those rights prosper to his majesty, the senate preserves its authority, the justice runs its proper course. In short according to him sovereignty means power to make laws and this in turn imply, all other rights and prerogatives such as declaring war or conducting peace, or confirming appointments to public offices or hearing appeals etc.*"

According to Bodin, there are only three forms of states *i.e.,* monarchy, aristocracy and democracy, according to number of those holding supreme power. He did not believe in a mixed form of state and states, "a *society in which supreme power is claimed in part by various elements is not a state at all but anarchy.*" The seeming division is sovereignty in a mixed stage is really division for actual functioning of sovereignty. The principle of government is different from the form of the state which is sovereign. A state may be monarchic while its government may be aristocratic or democratic. Thus, a monarchic state is a democratic government when the monarch who alone is sovereign confers honours and offices alike. Joint participation of different elements in the state is possible in government but not in sovereignty.

All forms of Govt. many include many species. A monarchy may include following:

1. Despotism. In which monarch rules his subjects as the pater families rules his slaves.

2. Royal monarchy. In this monarch respects the laws of God and nature and rights and property of the subjects remains secure and enjoy peace and order.

3. Tyranny. In this ruler abuses his authority and rules according to his whim and treats subjects as slaves and treats the property of his subjects as his own.

He regards royal monarchy as the best form and states fourteen qualities of monarchy as given below:

(1) Monarch himself obeys the laws of nature as he desires to be obeyed by his subjects.

(2) Monarch fears God above all.

(3) He is kind to poor and afflicted persons.

(4) He is brave in exploits.
(5) He is prudent in business.
(6) He is modest in property.
(7) He is constant in adversity.
(8) He keeps his promise.
(9) He is wise in council.
(10) He is helpful to friends.
(11) He is terror to his enemies.
(12) He is charitable to men of good will.
(13) He is dreadful to evil doers.
(14) He is just to all.

Bodin has made a distinction between a good king and tyrant which may be given as below:

(1) A good king respects laws of nature but a bad king did not care for them.
(2) A good king respects piety, justice and faith but a tyrant neither follows God nor faith nor law.
(3) A good king cares for the well-being of his subjects but a bad king cares for private profits, for vengeance and for his own pleasure.
(4) A good king punishes for private wrongs while tyrant he who injures him.
(5) A good king protects honour of women but a bad king seeks pleasure in them.
(6) A good king maintains peace and unity while tyrant sows seeds of disunity by following policy of divide and rule.
(7) A good king tries to enrich his subject but a tyrant enriches himself and imposes cruel and unpopular rule.

To quote him, in a royal monarchy the subjects are secure in their property rights and personal rights, and monarch respects the laws of God and nature and acts according to laws which he himself establishes. On the other hand tyranny is worst form of state.

According to Bodin, democracy is in many respects more in conformity with nature than monarchy or aristocracy, yet a democracy is subject to fickleness, vanity or administrative inefficiency. Aristocracy too has many virtues but Bodin favours monarchy based on heredity, prerogative and the state law because it avoids factional rivalries of aristocracy and democracy.

Bodin on Revolution

Bodin defines revolution as a "displacement of sovereignty." Accepting Aristotelian conception, he also believes in the transformation of states as inevitable and the efforts should be directed not to prevent them but to the determination of the manner in which it shall take place. He states one change effects law or institutions but supreme power remains unaffected but the other effects in the location of sovereignty.

However, state may be established...when by the violent act of some strong man or by the consent of all subjecting themselves freely to a sovereign...and however, long they endure, none lasts forever, so changeable and uncertain are human affairs. Some states rise slowly to great heights and then fall at once of their own weight, they think themselves safest, still others by inferior maladies...by a change of state, I mean a change of seat of sovereignty whether voluntary and involuntary, changes may be either natural or violent...change of state may be either slow and gradual the one scarcely notices it...of it may happen all at once, as a consequence of sudden, violent blow. He favours the last type of change, because it is more natural and happier.

Causes of Revolution

He believes that the causes that render revolution are inevitable and beyond human control and these may be grouped as under:

(a) Divine causes,

(b) Natural causes and

(c) Human causes.

Divine causes are hidden from man's view and cannot be marked. Regarding natural causes he states, "the event which immediately precede the effects but rather the more remote celestial causes of their accuracies." To Bodin inequality of wealth is potent cause of sedition but to him Plato or More's Utopias has no fascination. To him not the change in laws and religion but change in location of sovereignty is real revolution. He believes that democracy is more liable to revolution than monarchy.

According to Sabine, "*His discussion of the prevention of revolutions was a curious excisions of into the use of astrology for this purpose, while his analysis of the means for preventing them led him to cover every branches of administration and permitted him to display a really great feud of political occurrences and wisdom."* Bodin gives modern outlook but probably Machiavelli is pioneer.

There are similarities and differences in the political thought of Machiavelli and Bodin and some writers are of the opinion that "Bodin has ceased to be medieval without being modern." But other writers think that Bodin represents the beginning of modern political thought much better than Machiavelli and state that Bodin, not Machiavelli is the first modern thinker and further say that in political thought it is Bodin, and not Machiavelli who is the pioneer of modernity.

It is guessed that some writings of Machiavelli came to Bodin's attention. It fact Bodin refers them in his writings. There are similarities as well as differences between these two great thinkers of 16th century. Both derive their principles from study of actual happenings. Machiavelli studied the rise and fall of rulers and kingdom of the ancient and modern world and drew conclusions and to a great extent Bodin did the same and elaborated a method of observing a broader range of phenomena, including the influence of geographical factors on political developments. Both are concerned with the preservation and strengthening of government and attempt to draw lessons from the teachings of history. Both are philosophers of modern state.

Differences

In spite of their similarities, they differ in many respects, Machiavelli completely separates state craft or diplomacy from moral or religious principles. He preaches that a Prince may keep or break the treaty according to his self interest. Machiavelli is complety secular in outlook and is concerned only with the strengthening of the state without caring for moral or religious principles. But on the other hand Bodin holds power belongs to God and only derivately to king. Bodin stats a ruler must not break the treaty if it hurts the other party. Machiavelli says fear is more effective than love in running a government but Bodin believes that love is more effective than fear. According to Bodin, the prince is only creature of God. Bodin considers state, a means for safeguarding the family and carrying God's will. But Machiavelli thinks government as a game that is played for sake of Power.

Bodin and Machiavelli both were influenced by their times. During their time feudalism was on its last legs and both were antifeudal in their outlook. As such both supported for the establishment of an absolute power to curb feudalism and to bring national states into existence. Bodin supported absolutism that the power belongs to God and King gets power from him. Machiavelli believed that source of power lay in the ability of ruler to maintain himself against his rivals and by ensuring the obedience of his subjects. As such Machiavelli is more secular in his outlook than Bodin.

Difference in their outlook was as Bodin belonged to a stable and unified country ruled by a monarch whose authority had to be supported to save country from anarchy. As such Bodin dreaded that Machiavelli's advice to the ruler for preservation of sate may be used by a rebel to overthrow the ruler and so he discarded Machiavelli's views. On the other hand in Italy there were petty unstable states and so Machiavelli had to state the means by which the Prince could maintain his power where in so many were trying to overthrow him. As such he devoted his major part to an analysis of the art of maintaining political power. The prince had to be ever vigilant because one wrong step may lead to his downfall.

In the same way Bodin stated treaties are to be preserved because in a stable international order if a prince breaks a treaty, he is likely to suffer later on. But Machiavelli keeping in view the unstable conditions of Italy treats treaties as a part of diplomacy to maintain his power by deceiving others successfully.

According to Machiavelli fear is the main instrument of political power because fear means the threatened loss of self-interest. He believes that a man would do everything possible to preserve his life and possessions and for this reason he would be willing to do the bidding of the prince. Love, since it may mean the surrender of one's interests to those of another, is not as effective a motive force in human conduct. As such he did not believe much in love.

Thus, Machiavelli preaches for fear and Bodin for love. Cause of differences in outlook is that. Bodin is preaching for a state in which there is continuation of rule and ruler can depend on the affection of his subjects because time has changed, emotions in love to throne and loyalty of subjects. In Italy conditions were unstable and there was no certainty that prince would be allowed time to grow roots in the soil. To exact obedience and to curb opponents, fear is the only practicable weapon. To a great extent fear is more potent motive force than love.

Bodin holds that real bonds that integrate the state are bounds of morality and fear of God because people obey king because they think him as representative of God. He preaches toleration of religion so that people may not become disbeliever of God. Because he thought if people cease to believe in God, they will cease to believe in king and by throwing him they will become rebels and may undermine the state's stability and prosperity.

Opposite to it Machiavelli discounted religion because he thought religion and the Pope are preventing the unity of Italy. Machiavelli thought religion is merely a tool in the hands of prince to ensure the obedience of his subjects.

Machiavelli believes that power is an end in itself so his theory deals with the acquiring and preserving of power but to Bodin power is a means for ensuring the moral life of the people, to safeguard the sanctity of family and security and protection of property of the subjects as such his outlook is considered modern.

Bodin's place in the history of Political thought is very controversial as it is true that Machiavelli also preached that a prince should not violate the honour of women and should not touch the property of his subjects because man may forget the murder of his father but not the confiscation of property and these two cases are likely to offend people to make them rise against the prince. Thus Machiavelli preaches for sanctity in this respect with a view of strengthening political power while in Bodin protection of property is an ultimate object.

Machiavelli is a political pragmatist but Bodin is absolutist. But he is not fully absolutist as he conditions the sovereign obeying the commands of God and safeguarding family, property, and ensuring political and economic stability.

Both thinkers differ in their conceptions about human nature. To Machiavelli men are essentially selfish greedy to the extent that a man may not mind murder of his father if he is assured of his patrimony. According to Bodin man is product of many circumstances such as history, climate social customs, geography and rituals etc. he believes that man is creature of tradition and environment. The understanding of human nature show that Bodin is more historical than Machiavelli but the latter's conception is very simple and probably universal in space and time.

Both Bodin and Machiavelli believed in the cyclical theory of history due to different reasons. The later believed men reason the same so cyclical theory will be constant. But Bodin believed that political course of events were a result of complex historical geographical and cultural factors and constancy of political phenomena was due to order.

Bodin recognised the distinction between the sovereign and the government. Sovereign reserves certain functions to himself and delegates other function to his magistrates and other bodies. Machiavelli is unable to draw this distinction between sovereign prince and his government. Distinction between sovereign and his government played a notable part later on.

Evaluation

It is difficult to answer whether Machiavelli or Bodin is more modern. Machiavelli's method of deriving political conclusion from observance of actual phenomena is nearer the contemporary way of thinking. His secular outlook is now accepted universally among political scientists. To him political considerations are supreme, and anything that promotes is justified, but success cannot be achieved only by deceiving others and line is more complex than Machiavelli makes it out to be. According to McGovern, *"Bodin was most vigorous and logical of political theorist of the 16th century."* According to Jones, "Bodin is most frequently mentioned Political theorist."

But after close examination it seems Bodin is more realistic than Machiavelli as circumstances which Bodin reflects are more common than those obtained in Italy during Machiavelli's time. Political stability is needed for the purpose of social peace and economic progress and people are often willing to give up their political aims for sake of maintaining their beliefs or safeguarding their economic interests. Moreover, historical, cultural and geographical factors play a much more important role in political developments than Machiavelli thought. All these make Bodin relevant to our times. But in his thinking Bodin is not unique while Machiavelli's circumstances prevailing at the time of Machiavelli may not occur but these are applicable where there is anarchy and these are universally applicable. Thus Machiavelli's impact has been more dramatic than of Bodin.

Bodin's impact was not at all during the British rule in India either on Viceroys or on Gandhiji but in the India after Nehru's days Machiavellian policy is in full play due to unstable state and whosoever discards the faith in his old party is a gainer and perhaps his gain may last so long unstable conditions prevail in India. As such Machiavelli's impact is more profound and is applicable in all countries and at all times where unstable political confusion prevails. In weak and unstable rules Machiavellian policy succeeds, but fails in long run.

However, in modernity perhaps Bodin is more modern because his view of the state that it is a social and religious institution more suitable with political realties of modern age. Bodin is more important as founder of political science and his concept of Sovereignty, of power of making laws. Bodin is more modern because his thinking applies to modern states he preaches religious toleration. His concept of sovereignty is a great contribution to political science though he is neither unique nor a clever thinker than Machiavelli. To be brief perhaps Bodin is more modern than Machiavelli.

Bodin's place in the history of political thought is great as idea sovereignty is great contribution made by Bodin to modern political thought and power of sovereignty makes state supreme.

Bodin was a versatile genius. History, Politics and Jurisprudence were his fields in which he left his mark. He also wrote essays on money and public finance. Murray states, "*He was a scholar who strove to be a thinker, a lawyer, who was interested in the origin of legal rules as in themselves, a man of the world who brought all the resources of the solved common sense to the application of political problems, a sociologist who neither dealt in names nor played with words.*"

According to Maxey, "*Jean Bodin belongs to immortals. In an age of bigotry and fanatism he walked by the steady light of reason. In an age of distractions and dissensions, he created unity and order, in an age of irrational creeds he was believer in none, but an unrebutting foe of intolerance, in an age of intellectual sterility, he was an enlightened and independent thinker abbreviated by the true spirit of philosophy.*"

Bodin belonged to that class of philosophers, who desired the reconstructions of peace and order. Bodin believed that for the success of France and suppression of political fictions and controversies and the establishment of strong monarchy is necessary. He accordingly justified teachings of religion. His works on religion were broad and tolerant so as to draw fire from every quarter. Thus, Bodin is a great French thinker.

His contributions to political thought may be given as below:

(1) He stated that political theory must be based on historical observation. As per Gettle, he anticipated the analytical method of Hobbes and the historical method of Montesquieu both of whom he studied and profited by their works.

(2) According to Sabine, "*Bodin's statement of the principle of sovereignty is generally agreed to be the most important part of his political philosophy.*"

(3) He made distinction between legal and moral obligation and contributed to the separation of legal and ethical concepts.

(4) Bodin asserted the theory of human advancement against the contemporary dogma of human degeneration.

(5) He condemned slavery and preached religious toleration but opposed communistic theory of equality but recognized the close relation between the distribution of wealth within the source of real political power.

(6) As per Dunning, "Bodin's study of social and political bearings of climate and topography, which he conceived and exalted incentive scientific spirit justifies the claim to originality."

(7) He gave modern concept of citizenship of defining "a free man subject to sovereign power of another."

(8) Bodin was first to pronounce sovereignty. According to Murray, "*It was for Bodin to point out that the day of empires whether Roman or French had altogether passed a way.*" The day of ascent of nationalism had arrived, and with its arrival it was high time to devise a theory of sovereignty, to this talk Bodin addresses himself in Republica and it constitutes his most permanent achievement.

He established the foundation of national sovereignty which effects political thought even at present. Both Hobbes and Filmer were influenced by his idea of sovereignty. According to Dunning, Bodin made political philosophy stable. He popularized idea of sovereignty and protection of property and welfare of people as the main function of state.

HUGO GROTIUS (1583-1645)

Grotius is known as father of International law as he was the pioneer to bring ideals of International law. The life and works of Hugo Grotius reflect his ideal and he states that "The law of nature is dictate of right reason." Grotius was a genius so his ideals ought to be studied carefully.

Life

Hugo Grotius (1583-1645) was the son of an eminent lawyer in Holland. He showed himself as an intellectual giant from his early age and at the age of sixteen he got the degree of doctor of laws from London university and started practice of law. At the age of 30, he was appointed the magistrate in Rotterdom and took part in the controversy of Arminianism and Gomarism. Prince Maurice of Orange sided with Gomarism and charged Grotius for sedition and sentenced him to life imprisonment. From Jail, he made a dramatic escape, thanks to the courage and ingenuity of his wife and spent the remaining days of his life in exile and poverty. It was during his exile that he wrote a famous book "The Law of War and Peace"; about International law.

Though Grotius was a versatile genius and cultivated many fields of learning like history, classics, poetry, drama and theology but his fame rests in his achievement in the field of international jurisprudence and on his monumental work, *The Law of War and Peace.* It is unanimously regarded as the first comprehensive authoritative commentary on the practices that prevailed in the sphere of international relations during those days. It laid foundation of modern law of nations.

He was profoundly influenced by the unstable conditions of his times, he noticed gun powder plot of England of 1605, and in 1610 assassination of Henry IV of France, and thirty years war of Europe in which Catholic league and Protestant confederation mercilessly fought with one another, like Bodin. He believed in peace and religious toleration. He desired peace in the interest of Christianity and the comity of European nations and so he wrote his most important treatise "De Jure Beeliet Pacis."

His Percursors

Spanish Jurist Surcze wrote even before than Hugo Grotius, Protestant writer Winder reduced the law of nature into a well defined code of 21 articles. Melanchthom held that content of the law of nature were to be found in right reason. Grotius' credit to the formation of the International law is due to the fact that he co-ordinated and codified what existed before him. To quote Hearns Shaw *De Jure Belli Pacis* "summed up the accepted wisdom of the ancients and applied it to the unprecedent conditions of Renaissance and reformation world it epitomised all that had been written by Stoic philosophers, Roman lawyers, Scholastic theologians and Jesinlical Jusites concerning the law of nature and the law of Nations and combined it into a solid foundation for an incalculably valuable superstructure of international morality and customs.

His *De Jure Belli Pacis* represents the creation of liberal mind against the in humanities of 36 years war. He states, *"I saw prevailing throughout Christian world, a licence in making war, recourse bring heart to arm for slight reasons or for no reason and when human laws were lost; just as men more henceforth authorised to commit all crimes without restraint...He set out, to discover a philosophy that would provide a standard for the conduct of war in terms of social and earthly objectives."*

De Jure Belli Pacis contains a dedication to Louis XIII of France, a Prolegomena and three books. In book I Grotius treats war in general and maintains that war can be just. Book II deals with just grounds of war and book III most important of all the three, discusses the laws of war embodying moral and customary limits which the belligerents must not cross. His political philosophy, however, is to be found mainly in book I and is based on the law of nature, the law of nations and the doctrine of sovereignty.

If Bodin laid the foundation of national sovereignty Hugo Grotius no less severely laid the foundation of the international sovereignty. If Bodin, a French thinker propounded the sovereignty as the indispensable foundation of peace and progress in a well ordered state, Hugo Grotius, the Dutch thinker and jurist formulated the concept of international order of which all the independent nations are members. He held that vorries stoiles form a community with a common law force in regard to war and conduct of war. His great book, *The war and peace* was designed to prove his thesis. Therefore, he became the founder of international law and international jurisprudence. It is true that Grotius could not stop war but regulated the struggle between nations and laid foundation of international morality and of International law.

According to Dunning, Hugo Grotius promoted the course of absolute monarchy on the other side advocated limited Govt. due to his ideas on International Relations. He wrote book on International law and stated rules of International relations so he is considered father of modern science of International law.

Hugo Grotius is considered father of International law so views of Hugo Grotius on Jus Naturale, Jus gentium and sovereignty are very important and the contribution of Grotius to Political thought particularly regarding International law is great. Grotius thought, law as a necessary ingredient of social existence following the footsteps of Aristotle that man by nature is a social animal. He behaved that man and society are so interlinked that one cannot exist without the other. According to him, originals have need of some common regulatory measures as there should be some system of law and justice in their common relations. For a higher type of human society there is greater need of law and justices because human society is product of reason. He believes wherever there is social life there is reason and likewise natural law.

Natural Law

He classified all laws as being natural *i.e.,* based on reason and volitional *i.e.,* based on will. He called the law of nature as Jus Naturale and defined as "the dictate of right reason, indicating that any act, from its argument and disagreement with the national nature, has in its moral turpitude or moral necessity."

Grotius's law conceded that there is a body of universal law, the law of nature or right reason which equally applied to all people and is absolute as supreme reason itself. He believes that the law of nature again is unchangeable.

Grotius formulated his conception of the law of nature on the basis right and justice embodied in the essential, universal and unchangeable quality of human nature. He rejected the idea that all law, justice and rights have their basis in utility or expediency. Human nature and reason constitute the original fountain of all laws, utility is necessary. Civil law, to Grotius is rooted in the law of nature. He held that there were certain principles of universal recognition. If they represent the necessary deduction from the principles of nature, they fell under the category of law of nature, if they represent the deliberate choice of all men, they belong to the law of nations.

He defined natural law in these words, "*The law of nature is, a dictate of right reason which points out that an act according to it is or is not in conformity with rational nature, has in it a quality of moral baseness or moral necessity and that in consequence such an act is either forbidden or enjoyed by the author of nature, i.e., God.*" Regarding distinction with voluntary laws, he says "The distinction between these kinds of law is not to be drawn from testimonies themselves...but from the character of the nature. For whatever cannot be deducted from certain principles by a sure process of reasoning and yet it is clearly observed everywhere, must have its origin in the free will of man...The volitional law is not based upon absolute reason but upon universal consent rendered by unbroken custom and testimony of those who are skilled in it. Any institution of universal acceptance is national law if it satisfies reason, otherwise it represents Jus Gentium. He distinguished even Jus Naturale as (i) pure law of nature representing state of nature prior to the formation of society and (ii) law of nature after the formation of society but prior to civil law. He suggested that criterion for recognition of natural law is conscience of normal individual and general among best minds and practice of most civilised nations. In short his criteria was "common dictates of conscience." He based his theory of International law on this.

Following facts may be noted about Jus Naturale:

(1) The natural law is the dictate of right reason, agreeing with rational nature and as such with God.

(2) Natural law is permanent, eternal, universal, authoritative and absolute reason itself and is unchangeable.

(3) Its sanction is to be found in rational nature. It is based on ideal of peace & harmony all over the world.

Law of Nations or Jus Gentium

According to Grotius, as against law of nature which represents dictates of reason there is Jus Voluntarium, a body of positive commands which were dictates of will. He defined Jus Gentium as "law governing the intercourse between the nations. He took it as a human and national law." Its consent is what has been accepted as obligatory by the consent of all or many nations.

He stated all mankind or at least, the great part of it constitutes society of people for which the rule of general law is indispensable. According to Hearn Shaw, Just Gentium or law of nations was to Grotius, a code of percepts distinct from the Jus Naturale and of lower authority yet immensely valuable. It provided a body of international custom which in most serviceable way could supplement the universal morality of the law of nature.

Thus, Grotius was the first to produce a comprehensive and systematic treatise on international law, and therefore he is regarded as the father of international law. The central theme of Grotius was the totality of relations between the states. He distinguished just wars from unjust wars and rejected the idea that states have absolute right to make war. The will of states was not to be the only source of international law. The basis of international law according to him, is the nature of man which is endowed with goodness, altruism and morality and refuted the conception of reason of state. He propounded the theory of qualified neutrality by which nations carrying on a just war was to be bound.

The Jus Gentium included the practices which civilized nations follow in their dealings with one another. As per Dunning, "its *content is what has been accepted as obligatory by the consent of all or many nations.*" What is included under it is proved by constant usage and the testimony of the learned, the occasions for such a body of right is wolf are of that aggregate which included all or many nations just as the occasion of civil law is the welfare of the aggregate which consists of many individuals. According to him law of nations is based on the consent of nations.

The central theme of Grotius seems to lay down rules of justice which would be binding on man and as also to apply those rules, under the name of natural law, to the mutual relations of nations. He held that the rights common to all were derived from natural law which is the dictate of right reason, indicating that any act from its agreement and dis-agreement with its rational nature has in it a more turpitude or moral necessity.

According to Sabine, Grotius's importance in the history of jurisprudence rests not upon a theory of the state or upon anything that he had to say upon international law, but upon his conception of a law regulating the relations between sovereign states...Grotius's contribution to the special subject of international law is beyond the limits of a history of political theory. In respect to the latter his importance lay in the philosophical principles upon which he sought to find his special subjects and which he set out specially in the prolegomena to his great work. He brought International law into prominence.

Sovereignty

Political sovereignty to Grotius is human in origin and is vested in people who may delegate its conditionally or unconditionally but after delegating it, he agrees with Hobbes that they cannot take it back. To Grotius sovereignty means supreme political power and by political power he means that moral faculty of governing a state under which are included functions of general and of special character, of public or of primary interest and functions performed either by sovereign immediately or by persons commissioned by him. The sovereign must obey Natural law, divine law, constitutional law and the law of nations but no civil law or human law is binding upon him. As command of a sovereign against divine or natural law must not be obeyed, but the punishment for disobedience must be endured without resistance to a legitimate sovereign.

Sovereignty and International Law

He believed that a sovereign is completely independent of other sovereign and each sovereign state is on terms of complete equality with other sovereign states, legally and diplomatically. The natural relations between nations can be of three kinds, *i.e.,* of peace, of war and of neutrality. To Grotius, "*war is an armed conflict carried on under conditions, fixed by morality and custom between the public forces of respective states.*" He held that even among the combatant forces superfluous cruelty must be avoided.

He held that sovereignty of state is not incompatible with compliance of international law like an individual who submits to the sovereignty of his state and to its law for his own good so a sovereign state should submit to international law for his own good because it represents the will of community of nations.

The greatest positive contribution of Grotius to political science was of course, his foundation of a scheme of rights and duties applicable to the relations of nation and nation.

According to Brierly, *"Few books have won so great a reputation as the De Juri Deliac Pacis but to regard its author as founder of International law is to exaggerate its originality and to do less than justice to the writers who proceeded him, nor Grotius nor any other single writer can properly be said to have founded the system."*

As per Starkes, *"Grotius had an abiding influenced in the history of international law. He was continually relied upon as a work of reference and authority in the decisions of courts and in the textbooks of later writings of standing."*

According to Jackson, *"His work has remained a living force,... essence of his thought has passed into the conscience of civilised world."*

Grotius introduced an ideal or normative element in his conception of natural law and provided a scientific method as Sabine says, "the references which Grotius made to Mathematics are significant" and gave conception of equality of nations which laid the basis of certain provisions of League of Nations, League Assembly and of U.N. Charter and the procedure of U.N. Assembly etc. The contribution of Grotius in International law is great.

Chapter 15

Seventeenth Century thought Some Minor Thinkers

Sir Thomas More, Milton, Hooker, Spinoza Filmer and Harrington etc., are important to 17th century political thought so brief study of their ideas is necessary.

According to Maxey, *"few theories have served political society more usefully than much belaboured dogma of divine right of kings."* In *Bible,* Lord Jehovah himself states "By me kings reign and princes decree justice." St. Peter and St. Paul said "The powers that he ordained of God; Whosoever, therefore, resisth power, resisth the ordinance of God." This gave rise to "Divine Origin Theory" of kings.

Robert Filmer was according to Maxey the most artful and effective conversationalist on the royal side of the struggle. Thus, absolute monarchy was supported by King James I of England as well as by Sir Robert Filmer. Thomas Hobbes though based royal power on social contract but supported a absolute monarchy.

His Thesis gives rise to anti thesis, so theory of divine right of kings gave rise to the conceptions of the rights of man. In Greek, individual existed primarily as an ingredient of his family and his city, in Roman world individual existed for the advantage and use of state. Individual rights depended upon the social status of the person claiming them, but as a human being he had to rights whatever. As such Napoleon Bonaparte once remarked, Obedience is the destiny of men but dispute of parliament and king brought into existence the famous petition of rights in 1628 and the old poem that

The richman in his castle
The poor man at his gate
God made them high or lovely
And ordered their estate.

lost its glamour. War of American independence was logical corollary of petition of rights and Bill of rights which claimed, "no taxation without representation." Stuart Kings and Filmer lost ground as democratic ideas gained prominence.

Voices of freedom were raised by Milton in Aeropagitica and the Tenure of Kings and Magistrates and by John Locke. Thus, in 17th century for the first time according to Maxey, almost in twelve dismal centuries men began to explore the essence of things...to arrive at ultimate truth and reality.

In 17th century, England took lead in the sphere of political speculation. The development of political speculation in Rome and in England has been more or less on similar ancient lines. In both cases after political institutions has ripened and were functioning well that political speculation involving abstract principles of political philosophy entered into consciousness of political theorists about power of king and parliament.

Englishmen developed strong monarchy, a council for checking tyranny parliament for legislation and taxation and an organisation of fiscal and judicial administration. The controversy between the king and parliament resulted into armed conflict and brought into existence thinkers like Filmer, Hobbes, Locke and Milton etc. For our purpose we shall study only minor thinkers of 17th century in this chapter, who contributed to political thought and Hobbes and Lockes will be studied separately.

Sir Thomas More and his *Utopia*

Sir Thomas More was born in 1478, in judge's family. He was educated at the house of Arch of Cantebry and he studied law in London and became a member of parliament. He held the post of a member of Privy council, treasurer of the Exchequer, Speaker of House of Commons and finally he became Lord Chancellor, but in 1532, due to his difference with king Henry VIII, he was forced to resign and was beheaded in 1535 as he was charged of treason due to his stubbornness.

Utopia

He wrote a famous book *Utopia,* which means in Greek, nowhere or "knowing in trifles." In which a Portuguese wanderer tells about an island's administration. In this way, he has attacked criminal justice of England and other institutions and also on Government. More held that institution of private property is root cause of all evils. To get rid with the evils of society, he advocates communism. He states, "as long as there is any property...I cannot think, a nation can be governed either justly or happily..." His views were unrealistic.

Utopia is an island in which every man or woman is obliged to learn a trade and everyone had to labour six hours a day. The family is basic unit and each is trained in the arts of agriculture, youths who show aptitude for arts or sciences are excused from manual Labour. The condemnation of war and military glory and a remarkable theory of religious toleration are other important features of *Utopia.* Plato's ideal commonwealth is a military aristocracy ruled over by a philosopher king. More's commonwealth is a republic with ultrademocratic institutions. *Utopia* is more unrealistic and imaginary.

Richard Hooker

Richard Hooker was the most noteworthy philosopher of the puritan revolutionary period in England. He was primarily a theologian and aimed to refute the attacks of the priestly theoreticians on the policy of Angilcan church. Hooker applies some principles both to secular and ecclesiastical governments. He made examination of the origin, nature and obligation of law in general. His work carried an important influence on later political thought.

According to Hearnshaw, he insisted *"that the law of reason which governed the thought of men, and the law of conduct which bound them into political societies, was equally divine in origin and binding in character with the special laws of religion revealed in the Bible."*

He believed that men originally lived in a state of nature in which there was no organized authority. As the condition was full of violence and anarchy prevailed everywhere, so men being social animal, established and organized political authority by formal contract. His theory of government based on popular consent proved to be very useful to future theorists, who had leaning towards democracy. He also expressed his views on law of nations. He agreed if it is good for individual to avoid anarchy and adopt civil society, so it is good for nations to do so.

According to Gettel, *"his work contained either explicitly or secretly germ of most of the leading ideas of 18th century."*

Political Ideas of John Milton

He was mainly a poet next to Shakespeare, is the greatest literary giant of England. Shakespeare and Milton are the two immortal literary giants of England, as such literary fame of Milton eclipsed his fame as a political thinker. However, he can be said to be a political thinker also. He stood for liberty and opposed king's absolute power. Milton like Dante was very great poet and a thinker.

Life

John Milton was born in 1608 and got his early education at school and Cambridge. His youthful and effeminate appearance won him the sobriquet of "The lady of Christ's." He wrote famous poems even when he was a student. He was lover of freedom and he wrote Aeropagitica, a speech of Mr. John Milton for the liberty of unlicenced printing and wrote "The Tenure of kings and Magistrates" to defend execution of the king Charles I and so he was made Secretary during republican regime but restoration of kingship of Charles II forced him to retire from active politics and he passed his life in writing poems and died in 1674 at the age of 65. He wrote "Paradise lost" etc., famous all over the world.

In Aeropagitica, Milton pleaded that censorship and suppression discourage all scholarship, these are useless and intelligent and fair administration of laws is impossible and those who proceed due to ulterior motives. He stated, *"who kills a man kills a reasonable creature, God's image; but who destroys a good book, kills the reason itself, kills the image of God. Many man live a burden to the earth; but a good book is the precious life blood of a master spirit, imbalmined and treasured up and purpose to a life beyond," Aeropagitica.*

Milton published his *Endure of Kings and Magistrates* a few days after the execution of Charles I. He set out to prove "That it is lawful and hath been held so through all ages, for any who have the power, to call to account a tyrant, or wicked King and, after due conviction, to depose and put him to death..." He added "No man who knows ought" he wrote "can be so stupid today that all man were naturally born free, being the free, being the image and resemblance of God himself and were by privilege along all creature, born to command and not to obey...the power of king and magistrates is nothing else but what only is derivative, transferred and committed to them untrust from the people to the common good of all. He added to say King has as good a right to his crown and dignity, as any man to his inheritance, is to make subject no better than King's slave his chhattell, or his possession that may be bought or sold. He refuted divine origin theory by saying that to say kings are accountable to none but God, is overturning all lord and governments. For if they may refuse to give account, then all convents made with them at coronation, all oaths are in vain, and were mockeries; all laws which they swear to keep made to no purpose." Perhaps his arguments are still good against tyrants and dictators. He was against absolute power of Kings.

Milton stood for popular sovereignty and status "the right of choosing, and of changing their Govt., is by the grant of God himself to the people."

Liberty was the first and controlling passion of Milton's philosophy he wrote *"Give me liberty to know, to utter to argue freely according to consciousness above all liberty."*

Harrington and his book Oceana greatly contributed to the development of modern political thought so the importance of Harrington's Oceana in the history of political thought is great.

James Harrignton was born in England in 1611 and died in 1677. In the history of political philosophy, he has an important place. His book "The commonwealth of Oceana" is his greatest contribution to political philosophy. He may be considered as the first modern political philosopher who put forward a suggestive plan of Government to replace the monarchy. According to Gettle *"He prefaced his plan of model commonwealth by a sketch of seven principal republican constitution of history. 'The commonwealth of oceana' was written in the form of Utopia. It was dedicated to Cromwell because he hoped that Cromwell will put principles into effect."*

Views

He believed that basic principle of Govt. is balance of forces. He held that a government may be either the empire of laws or not of men or the empire of men and not of laws. The end of the state is public interest and secondly private interest. Governments may be either foreign or national based on wealth or intellectual distinction. Stability of government can be stable by delegating power to land owning class. Monarchy, aristocracy or democracy was natural as land may be in the hands of one, few of many, The relation between property and political power represents the balance of dominion. Thus, he stated that distribution of power must correspond to the distribution of property.

He desired that Govt. must consist of a senate of natural aristocracy, a council and a Magistracy. He advocated for a system of rotation in Govt., a system of ballot and also for limitation of land. Both Milton and Harrington maintained the doctrine of popular sovereignty but were aristocratic in their outlook.

His influence was propounded in America. As per G.P. Gooch, *"The constitutions of Carolina, New Jersy and Pennsylvania reflected his thought and a century later his authority was fully quoted in the discussion which followed the elaboration of American constitution."* His works formed the political Bible of Otis, John Adams and Jofferson's copy is preserved in the congress. Translated into French. The Harrington's name sieges with many of his ideas. The Harrington's name comes in three great revolutions of modern world.

ROBERT FILMER AND HIS POLITICAL THOUGHT

He was supporter of absolute sovereign power. His political philosophy was influenced by Hobbes and Bodin. he agreed with Bodin that there must be in every state, a single, absolute power. He stated, "Government originated in an enlargement of family, the king being father and people his children and by obeying king can preserve true religion. He opined that king was the source of law and parliament was just an advisory body.

Filmer's conception that state is natural and of organic growth is perhaps his only valuable thing in his theory.

Filmer wrote only one book *Patriarchs*. It is important because it was the best statement of theory of monarchy adopted by many torries after the restoration and secondly because it was answered by Sydney and Locke who discarded his views.

Benedict Spinoza

Spinoza was born in 1634, at Amsterdam. Highly educated and an accomplished linguist, he studied science and optics and was greatly influenced by Hobbes, Grotius and Machiavelli. He wrote *Tractatus Theolgio Politicus, Tractatus Politicus* and *Ethics* etc.

Views

Like Hobbes, Spinoza also held that the chief motive of human action is self-interest. To him, the state was not a necessary evil but a positive good. It was created to promote general happiness. It came into existence through a voluntary compact with which the powers of individual were combined and their natural right to do what seemed for their separate advantage were resigned in favour of a ruling power which employed the natural right of whole community. For the fullest employment of freedom men entered into a contract and bound by it. His compact was quite different from that of Hobbes and Locke.

According to Spinoza, it was foolish to expect a man to keep compact when the violation of it does him less harm than good. He suggested organic unity of state and conceived its sovereignty resting upon the common reason and on general mind of its members. He favoured republican form of Govt. He desired individual liberty and stated that power of state is limited by natural rights of men. He favoured federation of states to diminish war among states.

Rousseau borrowed from him theory of general will and Locke was greatly influenced by Spinoza. According to Maxey *"No cult of political pragmatism dears his name, but his utilitarian concept of the state gradually permeated the thought of the world and later thought of the genius of such theorist as Bentham and Mill was evolved into a dynamic system of political philosophy."*

Sir Thomas More, Richard Hooker, Harrington, Robert Filmer and Benedict Spinoza and Milton etc., were great thinkers of 17th century. Spinoza holds chief motive of human action is self-interest. Like Hobbes and his utilitarian concept of state was developed by Bentham and Milt.